Plant Based Cookbook 2022

600
Inspired, Flexible Recipes with 21-Day Meal Plan for Nourishing Your Body and Eating From the Earth

Trudy Goldsmith

CONTENTS

Chapter 3. Snacks, Appetizers & Side Dishes

Chapter 4. Legumes, Rice & Grains

Chapter 5. Soups, Stews & Salads...79

Chapter 6. Sauces & Condiments..102

Chapter 7. Desserts & Sweet Treats..111

Chapter 8. Other Favorites..132

Introduction

Losing weight and trying a new lifestyle is hard, but there is help. Adopting a new diet can be challenging, but this change is for the best because of the long-term health and sustainability benefits. On an individual level, this plant-based approach will greatly improve your overall well-being, health, and longevity. And for the earth, a plant-based diet is more sustainable because it requires fewer natural resources. In fact, according to an article in Environmental Research Letters, "shifting away from animal-based foods could add up to 49% to the global food supply without expanding croplands."

This book is packed with valuable advice, delicious recipes, and useful tips that will make the journey to a plant-based lifestyle smooth and easy. Follow these guidelines and enjoy feeling the mental and physical benefits while having fun learning new recipes.

Chapter 1. Easy Plant-Based Eating

Get Healthy by Eating Plants

Plant-based eating is the most effective way to lose weight and get healthy. On this diet, fewer calories are eaten, you feel full longer, and the health benefits are extensive. A plant-based eating plan is not simply another fad diet but rather a lifestyle change. Making changes is not easy, but understanding the benefits and feeling the positive effects will help. The benefits are vast and include:

1. Improved Digestion. Fiber from plants supports the growth of beneficial bacteria and the production of short-chain fatty acids that play an important role in maintaining a healthy gut.

2. Strengthened Immune System. There are many essential nutrients such as phytochemicals, vitamins, and minerals in plants that are beneficial for immunity. Plants typically contain these nutrients in higher amounts than other foods.

3. Heart Health. Lowering your intake of cholesterol and most saturated fats means healthier blood vessels and a lower risk of heart disease and stroke, which can contribute to longevity. Certain types of fiber (such as the viscous, gel-forming fiber found in oat products, barley, and legumes) are found to lower total cholesterol and are therefore beneficial in decreasing the risk for cardiovascular disease.

4. Lower Risk of Cancer. A plant-based meal plan is full of phytonutrients and antioxidants, which may help prevent or reduce cancer risk. In fact, the American Institute for Cancer Research published a recommendation stating that "scientific evidence shows that eating mostly plant-based foods—whole grains, vegetables, fruits, and beans—plays a big role in preventing cancer."

5. Increased Satiety. Diets based on vegetables, legumes, fruit, and grains are full of healthy fats, moderate in protein, and rich in carbohydrates, which are an essential source of energy and fiber. These foods are low calorie and energy dense and contribute to feeling full. This fiber also improves glycemic control by reducing nutrient absorption and delaying gastric emptying, making it beneficial for those with diabetes.

Diet and lifestyle change isn't easy, but this book is packed with valuable advice, delicious recipes, and useful tips that will make the journey smooth and rewarding.

Foods to Love and to Limit

Foods to Love

There are numerous foods to be enjoyed on a WFPB diet, including:

1. Whole Grains and Starchy Vegetables. A great source of carbohydrates that provides fiber, fullness, and reduced cholesterol while improving gut health. This includes brown rice, rolled or steel-cut oats, quinoa, farro, potatoes, sweet potatoes, corn, and peas.

2. Beans and Legumes. A great source of protein on a plant-based diet. Not only do they help keep you full and satiated so you don't feel the need to overeat, but studies have also shown that eating more legumes like black beans, chickpeas, and lentils can lower blood pressure and blood sugar and reduce the risk of heart disease.

3. Fruits and Berries. Full of fiber, phytonutrients, vitamins, and antioxidants. Choose from a variety of fruits like melons, bananas, plantains, apples, pears, mangos, pineapple, grapes, and others. For berries, consider raspberries, strawberries, blueberries, blackberries, and cranberries.

4. Cruciferous Vegetables. Low-calorie foods rich in folate; vitamins C, E, and K; and fiber and protect against certain types of cancer. These include broccoli, cauliflower, Brussels sprouts, cabbage, and arugula.

5. Leafy Greens. These are an excellent source of fiber and a good source of vitamins A and C. Dark, leafy greens contribute vitamin K to the diet. These are spinach, kale, lettuce spring mix, and so on.

6. Non-Starchy Vegetables. Great low-calorie and highly nutritious foods that provide vitamins, antioxidants, and phytochemicals. These include carrots, beets, tomatoes, cucumbers, zucchini, squash, and many more.

7. Aromatics and Herbs. These are edible plants or parts of plants used to add flavor to dishes. They will help you develop healthy eating habits with less salt, sugars, and fats. Incudes things such as onion, garlic, fenugreek, ginger, chives, dill, parsley, cilantro, thyme, oregano, marjoram, basil, lemongrass, tarragon, and so on.

8. Mushrooms. Mushrooms are great for the gut microbiome. Some mushrooms are a good source of vitamin D (which must be stated on the label). Varieties include portabella, shiitake, porcini, and oyster.

9. Spices. Some spices, such as turmeric and ginger, contribute anti-inflammatory properties to meals, and some are primarily used for enhancing flavor and aroma. Commonly used spices in this book are chilies, paprika, cayenne pepper, turmeric, red pepper flakes, black pepper, cloves, and coriander.

Foods to Limit

We suggest consuming the following foods in moderation because of their higher fat or salt content.

1. Nuts and Seeds. High-calorie and high-fat foods. These include pecans, walnuts, almonds, pine nuts, cashews, hazelnuts, chia seeds, sesame seeds, pepitas, and many others. It also includes nut and seed butters such as peanut butter, almond butter, sunflower butter, and tahini. Make sure you buy nut and seed butters that do not include salt, sugar, or vegetable oils. Also, drain the separated oil when you open the nut butter jar.

2. Minimally Processed Foods. Many processed foods have additives and undesirable ingredients such as preservatives, food dyes, and sweeteners. Choose whole-grain breads that are high in fiber and low in sodium with only a few ingredients, whole-grain tortillas, whole-grain pasta, and tofu.

3. Unsweetened Plant-Based Milks and Beverages. These foods fall under minimally processed foods and contain preservatives, flavoring ingredients, and sometimes emulsifiers. Use soy, almond, cashew, coconut, flax, and oat beverage alternatives. It is important to know that coconut milk in the carton has fewer calories than canned coconut milk and is usually called coconut milk alternative or coconut beverage. Canned coconut milk is also called full-fat coconut milk, as it is high in saturated fat and calories. Limit usage of canned coconut milk or buy coconut milk packaged in cartons. Choose plant-based milks and beverages that contain no added sugar and that contain at least 30 to 40 percent of your daily value of calcium.

4. Sweeteners. High in calories but low in nutritional value. Sweeteners include maple or agave syrup, and molasses.

5. Olives. High in fat and sodium. Choose from black, green, or Kalamata. There are no salt-free olives as natural olives are very bitter, so use low-sodium olives and only consume a few per day.

6. Broth. Store-bought broth is typically high in sodium, so use our recipe for Flavorful Vegetable Broth to make your own. If using store-bought broth, choose low-sodium or salt-free vegetable broth.

7. Vegan Processed. These foods include meat alternatives, packaged snacks, vegan ice cream, and vegan mayonnaise.

8. Animal Products. These are all the products that come from animals such as poultry, fish, seafood, eggs, milk, dairy products, cheese, honey, and gelatin.

Shopping Tricks

1. Take an inventory. It's helpful to run a quick inventory of your current stock in the kitchen and pantry. Doing so helps avoid food waste from items going stale or expiring and can help you keep track of which items you're running low on and need to resupply.
2. Make a list. Grocery shopping can be a highlight of the week for some and a chore for others. Either way, it pays to have a plan before making the trip. Research shows that you can save both time and money at the grocery store by having a plan in the form of a shopping list.
3. Don't shop on an empty stomach. After making a list and checking the current state of your pantry, try timing your shopping after a meal. Many people have experienced regret while unpacking groceries purchased on an empty stomach.
4. Buy in bulk. After you've been following a WFPB diet for a while, you'll more than likely have a few staple foods that you eat as the base of many of your meals, such as oats, potatoes, rice, or beans. Buying these foods in bulk saves you money and can also help save space in the shopping cart, as you may only need to purchase them once a month or so.

Quick Tips for Starting and Staying on a Plant-Based Diet

Whether you're just beginning to explore a plant-based diet or you're already an old pro, here are some of our tips for easing into plant-based eating and sticking with it.

1. Start by re-creating your favorite comfort foods with plant-based ingredients. As mentioned previously, the goal is to limit mock meats and cheese. However, when starting out they can be convenient and comforting replacements. While they're not as healthy as whole foods, they are very similar in texture and taste to the foods they're replacing. This will help satisfy your cravings as you slowly start to incorporate more unprocessed whole foods into your diet.
2. Plan out your meals and consider prepping them a few days or a week in advance. Meal planning and advance prepping can save you lots of time and money and prevent you from buying a lot of ingredients you won't end up needing. We like to prepare double the amount of dinner every night so we can eat the leftovers for lunch the next day.
3. Be open with your family and friends about your dietary needs. Chances are most, if not all, of your loved ones will be more than willing to accommodate your plant-based diet. But you have to tell them about it first! For holiday parties and other gatherings, offer to bring a plant-based dish to guarantee you have something to enjoy while also introducing others to plant-based eating. You never know—they may decide to give it a try themselves.
4. Do a little research before you dine out. Vegetarian and vegan restaurants and meal options are popping up everywhere as plant-based eating becomes more popular. Still, it's always a good idea to check a restaurant's menu ahead of time when possible. Indian, Mexican, Thai, Japanese, and Middle Eastern restaurants are typically very plant-based–friendly, with easily adaptable dishes.

Be kind to yourself. It's not uncommon for people to put a ton of pressure on themselves when they start eating plant-based. But you don't have to go from eating meat one day to eating only plant-based whole foods the next. Listen to your body and make the best decisions for you

Chapter 2. Breakfast & Smoothies

Crunch Cereal With Almonds

Servings: 8
Cooking Time: 35 Minutes
Ingredients:
- 1 cup spelt flakes
- 1 cup old-fashioned oats
- 1 ½ cups almonds, roughly chopped
- 1/4 cup date syrup
- 7 tablespoons coconut oil, melted

Directions:
1. Start by preheating your oven to 330 degrees F. Line a baking sheet with parchment paper or a Silpat mat.
2. In a mixing bowl, thoroughly combine all the ingredients until everything is well incorporated. Now, spread the cereal mixture onto the prepared baking sheet.
3. Bake for about 33 minutes or until crunchy. Allow it to cool fully before breaking up into clumps. Serve with a plant-based milk of choice. Bon appétit!

Frybread With Peanut Butter And Jam

Servings: 3
Cooking Time: 20 Minutes
Ingredients:
- 1 cup all-purpose flour
- 1/2 teaspoon baking powder
- 1/2 teaspoon sea salt
- 1 teaspoon coconut sugar
- 1/2 cup warm water
- 3 teaspoon olive oil
- 3 tablespoons peanut butter
- 3 tablespoons raspberry jam

Directions:
1. Thoroughly combine the flour, baking powder, salt and sugar. Gradually add in the water until the dough comes together.
2. Divide the dough into three balls; flatten each ball to create circles.
3. Heat 1 teaspoon of the olive oil in a frying pan over a moderate flame. Fry the first bread for about 9 minutes or until golden brown. Repeat with the remaining oil and dough.
4. Serve the frybread with the peanut butter and raspberry jam. Enjoy!

Mexican-style Omelet

Servings: 2
Cooking Time: 15 Minutes
Ingredients:
- 2 tablespoons olive oil
- 1 small onion, chopped
- 2 Spanish peppers, deseeded and chopped
- 1/2 cup chickpea flour
- 1/2 cup water
- 3 tablespoons rice milk, unsweetened
- 2 tablespoons nutritional yeast
- Kala namak salt and ground black pepper, to taste
- 1/2 teaspoon dried Mexican oregano
- 1/4 cup salsa

Directions:
1. Heat the olive oil in a frying pan over medium-high flame. Once hot, sauté the onion and peppers for about 3 minutes until tender and aromatic.
2. Meanwhile, whisk the chickpea flour with the water, milk, nutritional yeast, salt, black pepper and dried Mexican oregano.
3. Then, pour the mixture into the frying pan.
4. Cook for about 4 minutes. Turn it over and cook for an additional 3 to 4 minutes until set. Serve with salsa and enjoy!

Almond & Raisin Granola

Servings:8
Cooking Time:20 Minutes
Ingredients:
- 5 ½ cups old-fashioned oats
- 1 ½ cups chopped walnuts
- ½ cup shelled sunflower seeds
- 1 cup golden raisins
- 1 cup shaved almonds
- 1 cup pure maple syrup
- ½ tsp ground cinnamon
- ¼ tsp ground allspice
- A pinch of salt

Directions:
1. Preheat oven to 325 F. In a baking dish, place the oats, walnuts, and sunflower seeds. Bake for 10 minutes. Lower the heat from the oven to 300 F. Stir in the raisins, almonds, maple syrup, cinnamon, allspice, and salt. Bake for an additional 15 minutes. Allow cooling before serving.

Oatmeal With Banana And Figs

Servings: 2
Cooking Time: 15 Minutes
Ingredients:
- 1 ½ cups almond milk
- 1/2 cup rolled oats
- A pinch of sea salt
- A pinch of grated nutmeg
- 1/3 teaspoon cinnamon
- 3 dried figs, chopped
- 2 bananas, peeled and sliced
- 1 tablespoon maple syrup

Directions:
1. In a deep saucepan, bring the milk to a rapid boil. Add in the oats, cover the saucepan and turn the heat to medium.
2. Add in the salt, nutmeg and cinnamon. Continue to cook for about 12 minutes, stirring periodically.

3. Spoon the mixture into serving bowls; top with figs and bananas; add a few drizzles of the maple syrup to each serving and serve warm. Bon appétit!

Tropical Smoothie Bowl

Servings:4
Cooking Time:10 Minutes
Ingredients:
- 4 bananas, sliced
- 1 cup papaya
- 1 cup baked granola, crushed
- 2 cups fresh raspberries
- ½ cup slivered almonds
- 4 cups plant-based milk

Directions:
1. Put bananas, raspberries, and milk in a food processor and pulse until smooth. Transfer to a bowl and stir in granola. Top with almonds and serve.

Breakfast Banana Muffins With Pecans

Servings: 9
Cooking Time: 30 Minutes
Ingredients:
- 2 ripe bananas
- 4 tablespoons coconut oil, room temperature
- 2 tablespoons maple syrup
- 1/2 cup brown sugar
- 1 ½ cups all-purpose flour
- 1/2 teaspoon baking powder
- 1/2 teaspoon baking soda
- 1/2 teaspoon salt
- 1/4 teaspoon grated nutmeg
- 1/4 teaspoon ground cardamom
- 1/3 teaspoon ground cinnamon
- 1/2 cup pecans, chopped

Directions:
1. Begin by preheating your oven to 350 degrees F. Coat 9-cup muffin tin with muffin liners.
2. In a mixing bowl, mash the bananas; stir in the coconut oil, maple syrup and sugar. Gradually stir in the flour, followed by the baking powder, baking soda and spices.
3. Stir to combine well and fold in the pecans. Scrape the mixture into the prepared muffin tin.
4. Bake your muffins in the preheated oven for about 27 minutes, or until a tester comes out dry and clean. Bon appétit!

Cinnamon-banana French Toast

Servings: 3
Cooking Time: 25 Minutes
Ingredients:
- 1/3 cup coconut milk
- 1/2 cup banana, mashed
- 2 tablespoons besan (chickpea flour)
- 1/2 teaspoon baking powder
- 1/2 teaspoon vanilla paste
- A pinch of sea salt
- 1 tablespoon agave syrup
- 1/2 teaspoon ground allspice
- A pinch of grated nutmeg
- 6 slices day-old sourdough bread
- 2 bananas, sliced
- 2 tablespoons brown sugar
- 1 teaspoon ground cinnamon

Directions:
1. To make the batter, thoroughly combine the coconut milk, mashed banana, besan, baking powder, vanilla, salt, agave syrup, allspice and nutmeg.
2. Dredge each slice of bread into the batter until well coated on all sides.
3. Preheat an electric griddle to medium heat and lightly oil it with a nonstick cooking spray.
4. Cook each slice of bread on the preheated griddle for about 3 minutes per side until golden brown.
5. Garnish the French toast with the bananas, brown sugar and cinnamon. Bon appétit!

Mixed Seeds Bread

Servings:6
Cooking Time:55 Minutes
Ingredients:
- 3 tbsp ground flax seeds
- ¾ cup coconut flour
- 1 cup almond flour
- 3 tsp baking powder
- 5 tbsp sesame seeds
- ½ cup chia seeds
- 1 tsp ground caraway seeds
- 1 tsp hemp seeds
- ¼ cup psyllium husk powder
- 1 tsp salt
- 2/3 cup cashew cream cheese
- ½ cup melted coconut oil
- ¾ cup coconut cream
- 1 tbsp poppy seeds

Directions:
1. Preheat oven to 350 F and line a loaf pan with parchment paper.
2. For the vegan "flax egg," whisk flax seed powder with ½ cup of water and let the mixture sit to soak for 5 minutes. In a bowl, evenly combine the coconut flour, almond flour, baking powder, sesame seeds, chia seeds, ground caraway seeds, hemp seeds, psyllium husk powder, and salt.
3. In another bowl, use an electric hand mixer to whisk the cream cheese, coconut oil, coconut whipping cream, and vegan "flax egg." Pour the liquid ingredients into the dry ingredients, and continue whisking with the hand mixer until a dough forms. Transfer the dough to the loaf pan, sprinkle with poppy seeds, and bake in the oven for 45 minutes or until a knife inserted into the bread comes out clean. Remove the parchment paper with the bread, and allow cooling on a rack.

Almond & Coconut Granola With Cherries

Servings:6
Cooking Time:45 Minutes
Ingredients:

- ½ cup coconut oil, melted
- ½ cup maple syrup
- 1 tsp vanilla extract
- 3 tsp pumpkin pie spice
- 4 cups rolled oats
- ⅓ cup whole-wheat flour
- ¼ cup ground flaxseed
- ½ cup sunflower seeds
- ½ cup slivered almonds
- ½ cup shredded coconut
- ½ cup dried cherries
- ½ cup dried apricots, chopped

Directions:
1. Preheat oven to 350 F.
2. In a bowl, combine the coconut oil, maple syrup, and vanilla. Add in the pumpkin pie spice. Put oats, flour, flaxseed, sunflower seeds, almonds, and coconut in a baking sheet and toss to combine. Coat with the oil mixture. Spread the granola out evenly. Bake for 25 minutes. Once ready, break the granola into chunks and stir in the cherries and apricots. Bake another 5 minutes. Allow cooling and serve.

Old-fashioned Cornbread

Servings: 10
Cooking Time: 50 Minutes
Ingredients:

- 2 tablespoons chia seeds
- 1 ½ cups plain flour
- 1 cup cornmeal
- 1 teaspoon baking powder
- 1 teaspoon baking soda
- 1 teaspoon kosher salt
- ⅓ cup sugar
- 1 ½ cups oat milk
- ⅓ cup olive oil

Directions:
1. Start by preheating your oven to 420 degrees F. Now, spritz a baking pan with a nonstick cooking spray.
2. To make the chia "egg", mix 2 tablespoons of the chia seeds with 4 tablespoons of the water. Stir and let it sit for about 15 minutes.
3. In a mixing bowl, thoroughly combine the flour, cornmeal, baking powder, baking soda, salt and sugar.
4. Gradually add in the chia "egg", oat milk and olive oil, whisking constantly to avoid lumps. Scrape the batter into the prepared baking pan.
5. Bake your cornbread for about 25 minutes or until a tester inserted in the middle comes out dry and clean.
6. Let it stand for about 10 minutes before slicing and serving. Bon appétit!

Mushroom & Spinach Chickpea Omelet

Servings:4
Cooking Time:25 Minutes
Ingredients:

- 1 cup chickpea flour
- ½ tsp onion powder
- ½ tsp garlic powder
- ¼ tsp white pepper
- 1/3 cup nutritional yeast
- ½ tsp baking soda
- 1 green bell pepper, chopped
- 3 scallions, chopped
- 1 cup sautéed button mushrooms
- ½ cup chopped fresh spinach
- 1 cup halved cherry tomatoes
- 1 tbsp fresh parsley leaves

Directions:
1. In a medium bowl, mix the chickpea flour, onion powder, garlic powder, white pepper, nutritional yeast, and baking soda until well combined. Heat a medium skillet over medium heat and add a quarter of the batter. Swirl the pan to spread the batter across the pan. Scatter a quarter each of the bell pepper, scallions, mushrooms, and spinach on top and cook until the bottom part of the omelet sets, 1-2 minutes.
2. Carefully flip the omelet and cook the other side until set and golden brown. Transfer the omelet to a plate and make the remaining omelets. Serve the omelet with the tomatoes and garnish with the parsley leaves.

Tropical French Toasts

Servings:4
Cooking Time:55 Minutes
Ingredients:

- 2 tbsp flax seed powder
- 1 ½ cups unsweetened almond milk
- ½ cup almond flour
- 2 tbsp maple syrup + extra for drizzling
- 2 pinches of salt
- ½ tbsp cinnamon powder
- ½ tsp fresh lemon zest
- 1 tbsp fresh pineapple juice
- 8 whole-grain bread slices

Directions:
1. Preheat the oven to 400 F and lightly grease a roasting rack with olive oil. Set aside.
2. In a medium bowl, mix the flax seed powder with 6 tbsp water and allow thickening for 5 to 10 minutes. Whisk in the almond milk, almond flour, maple syrup, salt, cinnamon powder, lemon zest, and pineapple juice. Soak the bread on both sides in the almond milk mixture and allow sitting on a plate for 2 to 3 minutes.
3. Heat a large skillet over medium heat and place the bread in the pan. Cook until golden brown on the bottom side. Flip the bread and cook further until golden brown on the other side, 4 minutes in total. Transfer to a plate, drizzle some maple syrup on top and serve immediately.

Spring Onion Flat Bread

Servings: 3
Cooking Time: 30 Minutes
Ingredients:
- 1 cup all-purpose flour
- 1/2 teaspoon baking powder
- 1/4 teaspoon sea salt
- 1/2 cup warm water
- 1 cup spring onions, chopped
- Sea salt and ground black pepper, to taste
- 1/2 teaspoon garlic powder
- 1/2 teaspoon cayenne pepper
- 1/2 teaspoon dried thyme
- 3 teaspoons olive oil

Directions:
1. Thoroughly combine the flour, baking powder and salt in a mixing bowl. Gradually add in the water until the dough comes together.
2. Add in the spring onions and spices and knead the dough one more time.
3. Divide the dough into three balls; flatten each ball to create circles.
4. Heat 1 teaspoon of the olive oil in a frying pan over a moderately high flame. Fry the first bread, turning it over to promote even cooking; fry it for about 9 minutes or until golden brown.
5. Repeat with the remaining oil and dough. Bon appétit!

Scallion And Pepper Omelet

Servings: 2
Cooking Time: 15 Minutes
Ingredients:
- 2 tablespoons olive oil
- 3 scallions, chopped
- 2 bell peppers, chopped
- 6 tablespoons besan (chickpea flour)
- 10 tablespoons rice milk, unsweetened
- Kala namak salt and ground black pepper, to season
- 1/3 teaspoon red pepper flakes
- 2 tablespoons fresh Italian parsley, chopped

Directions:
1. Heat the olive oil in a frying pan over medium-high heat. Once hot, sauté the scallions and peppers for about 3 minutes until tender and aromatic.
2. Meanwhile, whisk the chickpea flour with the milk, salt, black pepper and red pepper flakes.
3. Then, pour the mixture into the frying pan.
4. Cook for about 4 minutes. Turn it over and cook for an additional 3 to 4 minutes until set. Serve with fresh parsley. Bon appétit!

Sweet Orange Crepes

Servings:4
Cooking Time:30 Minutes
Ingredients:
- 2 tbsp flax seed powder
- 1 tsp vanilla extract
- 1 tsp pure date sugar
- ¼ tsp salt
- 2 cups almond flour
- 1 ½ cups oat milk
- ½ cup melted plant butter
- 3 tbsp fresh orange juice
- 3 tbsp plant butter for frying

Directions:
1. In a medium bowl, mix the flax seed powder with 6 tbsp water and allow thickening for 5 minutes to make the vegan "flax egg." Whisk in the vanilla, date sugar, and salt.
2. Pour in a quarter cup of almond flour and whisk, then a quarter cup of oat milk, and mix until no lumps remain. Repeat the mixing process with the remaining almond flour and almond milk in the same quantities until exhausted.
3. Mix in the plant butter, orange juice, and half of the water until the mixture is runny like pancakes. Add the remaining water until the mixture is lighter. Brush a non-stick skillet with some butter and place over medium heat to melt.
4. Pour 1 tablespoon of the batter into the pan and swirl the skillet quickly and all around to coat the pan with the batter. Cook until the batter is dry and golden brown beneath, about 30 seconds.
5. Use a spatula to flip the crepe and cook the other side until golden brown too. Fold the crepe onto a plate and set aside. Repeat making more crepes with the remaining batter until exhausted. Drizzle some maple syrup on the crepes and serve.

Orange-carrot Muffins With Cherries

Servings:6
Cooking Time:45 Minutes
Ingredients:
- 1 tsp vegetable oil
- 2 tbsp almond butter
- ¼ cup non-dairy milk
- 1 orange, peeled
- 1 carrot, coarsely chopped
- 2 tbsp chopped dried cherries
- 3 tbsp molasses
- 2 tbsp ground flaxseed
- 1 tsp apple cider vinegar
- 1 tsp pure vanilla extract
- ½ tsp ground cinnamon
- ½ tsp ground ginger
- ¼ tsp ground nutmeg
- ¼ tsp allspice
- ¾ cup whole-wheat flour
- 1 tsp baking powder
- ½ tsp baking soda
- ½ cup rolled oats
- 2 tbsp raisins
- 2 tbsp sunflower seeds

Directions:
1. Preheat oven to 350 F. Grease 6 muffin cups with vegetable oil.
2. In a food processor, add the almond butter, milk, orange, carrot, cherries, molasses, flaxseed, vinegar, vanilla,

cinnamon, ginger, nutmeg, and allspice and blend until smooth.

3. In a bowl, combine the flour, baking powder, and baking soda. Fold in the wet mixture and gently stir to combine. Mix in the oats, raisins, and sunflower seeds. Divide the batter between muffin cups. Put in a baking tray and bake for 30 minutes.

Spicy Apple Pancakes

Servings:4
Cooking Time:30 Minutes
Ingredients:
- 2 cups almond milk
- 1 tsp apple cider vinegar
- 2 ½ cups whole-wheat flour
- 2 tbsp baking powder
- ½ tsp baking soda
- 1 tsp sea salt
- ½ tsp ground cinnamon
- ¼ tsp grated nutmeg
- ¼ tsp ground allspice
- ½ cup applesauce
- 1 cup water
- 1 tbsp coconut oil

Directions:
1. Whisk the almond milk and apple cider vinegar in a bowl and set aside. In another bowl, combine the flour, baking powder, baking soda, salt, cinnamon, nutmeg, and allspice. Transfer the almond mixture to another bowl and beat with the applesauce and water.
2. Pour in the dry ingredients and stir. Melt some coconut oil in a skillet over medium heat. Pour a ladle of the batter and cook for 5 minutes, flipping once until golden. Repeat the process until the batter is exhausted. Serve warm.

Almond Flour English Muffins

Servings:4
Cooking Time:20 Minutes
Ingredients:
- 2 tbsp flax seed powder
- 2 tbsp almond flour
- ½ tsp baking powder
- 1 pinch of salt
- 3 tbsp plant butter

Directions:
1. In a small bowl, mix the flax seed with 6 tbsp water until evenly combined and leave to soak for 5 minutes. In another bowl, evenly combine the almond flour, baking powder, and salt. Then, pour in the vegan "flax egg" and whisk again. Let the batter sit for 5 minutes to set.
2. Melt plant butter in a frying pan and add the mixture in four dollops. Fry until golden brown on one side, then flip the bread with a spatula and fry further until golden brown. Serve.

Delicious Matcha Smoothie

Servings:4
Cooking Time:5 Minutes
Ingredients:

- 1 cup chopped pineapple
- 1 cup chopped mango
- 1 cup chopped spinach
- ½ avocado
- ½ cup almond milk
- 1 tsp matcha green tea powder

Directions:
1. Purée everything in a blender until smooth, adding 1 cup water if needed. In a food processor, place the pineapple, mango, spinach, avocado, almond milk, water, and matcha powder. Blitz until smooth. Divide between 4 glasses and serve.

Raspberry Almond Smoothie

Servings:4
Cooking Time:5 Minutes
Ingredients:
- 1 ½ cups almond milk
- ½ cup raspberries
- Juice from half lemon
- ½ tsp almond extract

Directions:
1. In a blender or smoothie maker, pour the almond milk, raspberries, lemon juice, and almond extract. Puree the ingredients at high speed until the raspberries have blended almost entirely into the liquid. Pour the smoothie into serving glasses. Stick in some straws and serve immediately.

Fruit Salad With Lemon-ginger Syrup

Servings: 4
Cooking Time: 10 Minutes
Ingredients:
- 1/2 cup fresh lemon juice
- 1/4 cup agave syrup
- 1 teaspoon fresh ginger, grated
- 1/2 teaspoon vanilla extract
- 1 banana, sliced
- 2 cups mixed berries
- 1 cup seedless grapes
- 2 cups apples, cored and diced

Directions:
1. Bring the lemon juice, agave syrup and ginger to a boil over medium-high heat. Then, turn the heat to medium-low and let it simmer for about 6 minutes until it has slightly thickened.
2. Remove from the heat and stir in the vanilla extract. Allow it to cool.
3. Layer the fruits in serving bowls. Pour the cooled sauce over the fruit and serve well chilled. Bon appétit!

Gingerbread Belgian Waffles

Servings: 3
Cooking Time: 25 Minutes
Ingredients:
- 1 cup all-purpose flour
- 1 teaspoon baking powder
- 1 tablespoon brown sugar
- 1 teaspoon ground ginger

- 1 cup almond milk
- 1 teaspoon vanilla extract
- 2 olive oil

Directions:

1. Preheat a waffle iron according to the manufacturer's instructions.
2. In a mixing bowl, thoroughly combine the flour, baking powder, brown sugar, ground ginger, almond milk, vanilla extract and olive oil.
3. Beat until everything is well blended.
4. Ladle 1/3 of the batter into the preheated waffle iron and cook until the waffles are golden and crisp. Repeat with the remaining batter.
5. Serve your waffles with blackberry jam, if desired. Bon appétit!

Kid-friendly Cereal

Servings: 5
Cooking Time: 15 Minutes
Ingredients:

- 1 ½ cups spelt flour
- 1/2 teaspoon baking powder
- 1 teaspoon cinnamon
- 1/2 teaspoon cardamom
- 1/4 teaspoon ground cloves
- 1/2 cup brown sugar
- 1/3 cup almond milk
- 2 teaspoons coconut oil, melted

Directions:

1. Begin by preheating your oven to 350 degrees F.
2. In a mixing bowl, thoroughly combine all the dry ingredients. Gradually, pour in the milk and coconut oil and mix to combine well.
3. Fill the pastry bag with the batter. Now, pipe 1/4-inch balls onto parchment-lined cookie sheets.
4. Bake in the preheated oven for about 13 minutes. Serve with your favorite plant-based milk.
5. Store in an air-thigh container for about 1 month. Bon appétit!

Baked Apple Pie Oatmeal

Servings: 5
Cooking Time: 45 Minutes
Ingredients:

- 1 ½ cups old-fashioned oats
- 1/2 teaspoon cinnamon
- 1/4 teaspoon grated nutmeg
- 1/4 teaspoon ground cloves
- 1/4 teaspoon sea salt
- 1 cup oat milk
- 1/2 cup canned applesauce
- 1/4 cup agave syrup
- 1 tablespoon chia seeds
- 1 tablespoon coconut oil
- 1/2 teaspoon almond extract
- 1/3 cup walnuts, chopped

Directions:

1. Start by preheating your oven to 370 degrees F. Spritz a casserole dish with a nonstick cooking spray.
2. In a mixing bowl, thoroughly combine all ingredients until everything is well incorporated.
3. Next, spoon the oatmeal mixture into the prepared casserole dish.
4. Bake in the preheated oven for about 35 minutes, until the center is set. Allow it to cool for 10 minutes before cutting and serving. Bon appétit!

Tangerine Banana Toast

Servings: 4
Cooking Time: 25 Minutes
Ingredients:

- 3 bananas
- 1 cup almond milk
- Zest and juice of 1 tangerine
- 1 tsp ground cinnamon
- ¼ tsp grated nutmeg
- 4 slices bread
- 1 tbsp olive oil

Directions:

1. Blend the bananas, almond milk, tangerine juice, tangerine zest, cinnamon, and nutmeg until smooth in a food processor. Spread into a baking dish. Submerge the bread slices in the mixture for 3-4 minutes. Heat the oil in a skillet over medium heat. Fry the bread for 5 minutes until golden brown. Serve hot.

Traditional Ukrainian Blinis

Servings: 6
Cooking Time: 1 Hour
Ingredients:

- 1 teaspoon yeast
- 1 teaspoon brown sugar
- 3/4 cup oat milk
- 1 cup all-purpose flour
- A pinch of salt
- A pinch of grated nutmeg
- A pinch of ground cloves
- 2 tablespoons olive oil

Directions:

1. Place the yeast, sugar and 2 tablespoons of the lukewarm milk in a small mixing bowl; whisk to combine and let it dissolve and ferment for about 10 minutes.
2. In a mixing bowl, combine the flour with the salt, nutmeg and cloves; add in the yeast mixture and stir to combine well.
3. Gradually pour in the milk and stir until everything is well incorporated. Let the batter sit for about 30 minutes at a warm place.
4. Heat a small amount of the oil in a nonstick skillet over a moderate flame. Drop the batter, 1/4 cup at a time, onto the preheated skillet. Fry until bubbles form or about 2 minutes.
5. Flip your blini and continue frying until brown, about 2 minutes more. Repeat with the remaining oil and batter,
6. Serve with toppings of choice. Bon appétit!

Lemony Quinoa Muffins

Servings:5
Cooking Time:25 Minutes
Ingredients:
- 2 tbsp coconut oil melted, plus more for coating the muffin tin
- ¼ cup ground flaxseed
- 2 cups unsweetened lemon curd
- ½ cup pure date sugar
- 1 tsp apple cider vinegar
- 2 ½ cups whole-wheat flour
- 1 ½ cups cooked quinoa
- 2 tsp baking soda
- A pinch of salt
- ½ cup raisins

Directions:
1. Preheat oven to 400 F.
2. In a bowl, combine the flaxseed and ½ cup water. Stir in the lemon curd, sugar, coconut oil, and vinegar. Add in flour, quinoa, baking soda, and salt. Put in the raisins, be careful not too fluffy.
3. Divide the batter between greased with coconut oil cups of the tin and bake for 20 minutes until golden and set. Allow cooling slightly before removing it from the tin. Serve.

Vegan Banh Mi

Servings: 4
Cooking Time: 35 Minutes
Ingredients:
- 1/2 cup rice vinegar
- 1/4 cup water
- 1/4 cup white sugar
- 2 carrots, cut into 1/16-inch-thick matchsticks
- 1/2 cup white (daikon) radish, cut into 1/16-inch-thick matchsticks
- 1 white onion, thinly sliced
- 2 tablespoons olive oil
- 12 ounces firm tofu, cut into sticks
- 1/4 cup vegan mayonnaise
- 1 ½ tablespoons soy sauce
- 2 cloves garlic, minced
- 1/4 cup fresh parsley, chopped
- Kosher salt and ground black pepper, to taste
- 2 standard French baguettes, cut into four pieces
- 4 tablespoons fresh cilantro, chopped
- 4 lime wedges

Directions:
1. Bring the rice vinegar, water and sugar to a boil and stir until the sugar has dissolved, about 1 minute. Allow it to cool.
2. Pour the cooled vinegar mixture over the carrot, daikon radish and onion; allow the vegetables to marinate for at least 30 minutes.
3. While the vegetables are marinating, heat the olive oil in a frying pan over medium-high heat. Once hot, add the tofu and sauté for 8 minutes, stirring occasionally to promote even cooking.
4. Then, mix the mayo, soy sauce, garlic, parsley, salt and ground black pepper in a small bowl.
5. Slice each piece of the baguette in half the long way Then, toast the baguette halves under the preheated broiler for about 3 minutes.
6. To assemble the banh mi sandwiches, spread each half of the toasted baguette with the mayonnaise mixture; fill the cavity of the bottom half of the bread with the fried tofu sticks, marinated vegetables and cilantro leaves.
7. Lastly, squeeze the lime wedges over the filling and top with the other half of the baguette. Bon appétit!

Coconut Oat Bread

Servings:4
Cooking Time:50 Minutes
Ingredients:
- 4 cups whole-wheat flour
- ¼ tsp salt
- ½ cup rolled oats
- 1 tsp baking soda
- 1 ¾ cups coconut milk, thick
- 2 tbsp pure maple syrup

Directions:
1. Preheat the oven to 400 F.
2. In a bowl, mix flour, salt, oats, and baking soda. Add in coconut milk and maple syrup and whisk until dough forms. Dust your hands with some flour and knead the dough into a ball. Shape the dough into a circle and place on a baking sheet.
3. Cut a deep cross on the dough and bake in the oven for 15 minutes at 450 F. Reduce the temperature to 400 F and bake further for 20 to 25 minutes or until a hollow sound is made when the bottom of the bread is tapped. Slice and serve.

Nutty Granola With Dried Currants

Servings: 12
Cooking Time: 25 Minutes
Ingredients:
- 1/2 cup coconut oil
- 1/3 cup maple syrup
- 1 teaspoon vanilla paste
- 1/2 teaspoon ground cardamom
- 1 teaspoon ground cinnamon
- 1/3 teaspoon Himalayan salt
- 4 cups old-fashioned oats
- 1/2 cup pecans, chopped
- 1/2 cup walnuts, chopped
- 1/4 cup pepitas
- 1 cup dried currants

Directions:
1. Begin by preheating your oven to 290 degrees F; line a large baking sheet with a piece parchment paper.
2. Then, thoroughly combine the coconut oil, maple syrup, vanilla paste, cardamom, cinnamon and Himalayan salt.
3. Gradually add in the oats, nuts and seeds; toss to coat well.

4. Spread the mixture out onto the prepared baking sheet.

5. Bake in the middle of the oven, stirring halfway through the cooking time, for about 20 minutes or until golden brown.

6. Stir in the dried currants and let your granola cool completely before storing. Store in an airtight container.

7. Serve with your favorite plant-based milk or yogurt. Bon appétit!

Fluffy Banana Pancakes

Servings: 4
Cooking Time: 25 Minutes
Ingredients:

- 2 tablespoons ground flaxseeds
- 1/2 cup oat flour
- 1/2 cup coconut flour
- 1/2 cup instant oats
- 1 teaspoon baking powder
- 1/4 teaspoon kosher salt
- 1/4 teaspoon ground cardamom
- 1/4 teaspoon ground cinnamon
- 1/2 teaspoon coconut extract
- 1 cup banana
- 2 tablespoons coconut oil, at room temperature

Directions:

1. To make the "flax" egg, in a small mixing dish, whisk 2 tablespoons of the ground flaxseeds with 4 tablespoons of the water. Let it sit for at least 15 minutes.

2. In a mixing bowl, thoroughly combine the flour, oats, baking powder and spices. Add in the flax egg and mashed banana. Mix until everything is well incorporated.

3. Heat 1/2 tablespoon of the coconut oil in a frying pan over medium-low flame. Spoon about 1/4 cup of the batter into the frying pan; fry your pancake for approximately 3 minutes per side.

4. Repeat until you run out of batter. Serve with your favorite fixings and enjoy!

Omelet With Mushrooms And Peppers

Servings: 4
Cooking Time: 30 Minutes
Ingredients:

- 4 tablespoons olive oil
- 1 red onion, minced
- 1 red bell pepper, sliced
- 1 teaspoon garlic, finely chopped
- 1 pound button mushrooms, sliced
- Sea salt and ground black pepper, to taste
- 1/2 teaspoon dried oregano
- 1/2 teaspoon dried dill
- 16 ounces tofu, drained and crumbled
- 2 tablespoons nutritional yeast
- 1/2 teaspoon turmeric powder
- 4 tablespoons corn flour
- 1/3 cup oat milk, unsweetened

Directions:

1. Preheat 2 tablespoons of the olive oil in a nonstick skillet over medium-high heat. Then, cook the onion and pepper for about 4 minutes until tender and fragrant.

2. Add in the garlic and mushrooms and continue to sauté an additional 2 to 3 minutes or until aromatic. Season with salt, black pepper, oregano and dill. Reserve.

3. In your blender or food processor, mix the tofu, nutritional yeast, turmeric powder, corn flour and milk. Process until you have a smooth and uniform paste.

4. In the same skillet, heat 1 tablespoon of the olive oil until sizzling. Pour in 1/2 of the tofu mixture and spread it with a spatula.

5. Cook for about 6 minutes or until set; flip and cook it for another 3 minutes. Slide the omelet onto a serving plate.

6. Spoon 1/2 of the mushroom filling over half of the omelet. Fold the unfilled half of omelet over the filling.

7. Repeat with another omelet. Cut them into halves and serve warm. Bon appétit!

Blueberry Chia Pudding

Servings:2
Cooking Time:5 Minutes + Chilling Time
Ingredients:

- ¾ cup coconut milk
- ½ tsp vanilla extract
- ½ cup blueberries
- 2 tbsp chia seeds
- Chopped walnuts to garnish

Directions:

1. In a blender, pour the coconut milk, vanilla extract, and half of the blueberries. Process the ingredients at high speed until the blueberries have incorporated into the liquid. Open the blender and mix in the chia seeds. Share the mixture into two breakfast jars, cover, and refrigerate for 4 hours to allow the mixture to gel. Garnish the pudding with the remaining blueberries and walnuts. Serve immediately.

Carrot-strawberry Smoothie

Servings:2
Cooking Time:5 Minutes
Ingredients:

- 1 cup peeled and diced carrots
- 1 cup strawberries
- 1 apple, chopped
- 2 tbsp maple syrup
- 2 cups unsweetened almond milk

Directions:

1. Place in a food processor all the ingredients. Blitz until smooth. Pour in glasses and serve.

Coconut Granola With Prunes

Servings: 10
Cooking Time: 1 Hour
Ingredients:

- 1/3 cup coconut oil
- 1/2 cup maple syrup
- 1 teaspoon sea salt
- 1/4 teaspoon grated nutmeg
- 1/2 teaspoon cinnamon powder

- 1/2 teaspoon vanilla extract
- 4 cups old-fashioned oats
- 1/2 cup almonds, chopped
- 1/2 cup pecans, chopped
- 1/2 coconut, shredded
- 1 cup prunes, chopped

Directions:

1. Begin by preheating your oven to 260 degrees F; line two rimmed baking sheets with a piece of parchment paper.
2. Then, thoroughly combine the coconut oil, maple syrup, salt, nutmeg, cinnamon and vanilla.
3. Gradually add in the oats, almonds, pecans and coconut; toss to coat well.
4. Spread the mixture out onto the prepared baking sheets.
5. Bake in the middle of the oven, stirring halfway through the cooking time, for about 1 hour or until golden brown.
6. Stir in the prunes and let your granola cool completely before storing. Store in an airtight container.
7. Bon appétit!

Morning Naan Bread With Mango Jam

Servings:4
Cooking Time:40 Minutes
Ingredients:

- ¾ cup almond flour
- 1 tsp salt + extra for sprinkling
- 1 tsp baking powder
- 1/3 cup olive oil
- 2 cups boiling water
- 2 tbsp plant butter for frying
- 4 cups heaped chopped mangoes
- 1 cup pure maple syrup
- 1 lemon, juiced
- A pinch of saffron powder
- 1 tsp cardamom powder

Directions:

1. In a large bowl, mix the almond flour, salt, and baking powder. Mix in the olive oil and boiling water until smooth, thick batter forms. Allow the dough to rise for 5 minutes. Form balls out of the dough, place each on a baking paper, and use your hands to flatten the dough.
2. Working in batches, melt the plant butter in a large skillet and fry the dough on both sides until set and golden brown on each side, 4 minutes per bread. Transfer to a plate and set aside for serving.
3. Add mangoes, maple syrup, lemon juice, and 3 tbsp water in a pot and cook until boiling, 5 minutes. Mix in saffron and cardamom powders and cook further over low heat until the mangoes soften. Mash the mangoes with the back of the spoon until relatively smooth with little chunks of mangoes in a jam. Cool completely. Spoon the jam into sterilized jars and serve with the naan bread.

Raw Morning Pudding

Servings: 3
Cooking Time: 10 Minutes
Ingredients:

- 2 ½ cups almond milk
- 3 tablespoons agave syrup

- 1/2 teaspoon vanilla essence
- A pinch of flaky salt
- A pinch of grated nutmeg
- 1/4 teaspoon ground cardamom
- 1/4 teaspoon crystalized ginger
- 1/2 cup instant oats
- 1/2 cup chia seeds

Directions:

1. Add the milk, agave syrup and spices to a bowl and stir until everything is well incorporated.
2. Fold in the instant oats and chia seeds and stir again to combine well. Spoon the mixture into three jars, cover and place in your refrigerator overnight.
3. On the actual day, stir with a spoon and serve. Bon appétit!

Crispy Corn Cakes

Servings:4
Cooking Time:35 Minutes
Ingredients:

- 1 tbsp flaxseed powder
- 2 cups yellow cornmeal
- 1 tsp salt
- 2 tsp baking powder
- 4 tbsp olive oil
- 1 cup tofu mayonnaise for serving

Directions:

1. In a bowl, mix the flax seed powder with 3 tbsp water and allow thickening for 5 minutes to form the vegan "flax egg." Mix in 1 cup of water and then whisk in the cornmeal, salt, and baking powder until soup texture forms but not watery.
2. Heat a quarter of the olive oil in a griddle pan and pour in a quarter of the batter. Cook until set and golden brown beneath, 3 minutes. Flip the cake and cook the other side until set and golden brown too. Plate the cake and make three more with the remaining oil and batter. Top the cakes with some tofu mayonnaise before serving.

Classic Walnut Waffles With Maple Syrup

Servings:4
Cooking Time:15 Minutes
Ingredients:

- 1 ¾ cups whole-wheat flour
- ⅓ cup coarsely ground walnuts
- 1 tbsp baking powder
- 1 ½p cups soy milk
- 3 tbsp pure maple syrup
- 3 tbsp plant butter, melted

Directions:

1. Preheat the waffle iron and grease with oil. Combine the flour, walnuts, baking powder, and salt in a bowl. Set aside. In another bowl, mix the milk and butter. Pour into the walnut mixture and whisk until well combined. Spoon a ladleful of the batter onto the waffle iron. Cook for 3-5 minutes, until golden brown. Repeat the process until no batter is left. Top with maple syrup to serve.

Classic Breakfast Burrito

Servings: 4
Cooking Time: 15 Minutes
Ingredients:
- 1 tablespoon olive oil
- 16 ounces tofu, pressed
- 4 whole-wheat tortillas
- 1 ½ cups canned chickpeas, drained
- 1 medium-sized avocado, pitted and sliced
- 1 tablespoon lemon juice
- 1 teaspoon garlic, pressed
- 2 bell peppers, sliced
- Sea salt and ground black pepper, to taste
- 1/2 teaspoon red pepper flakes

Directions:
1. Heat the olive oil in a frying skillet over medium heat. When it's hot, add the tofu and sauté for about 10 minutes, stirring occasionally to promote even cooking.
2. Divide the fried tofu between warmed tortillas; place the remaining ingredients on your tortillas, roll them up and serve immediately.
3. Bon appétit!

Hearty Smoothie

Servings: 3
Cooking Time: 5 Minutes
Ingredients:
- 1 banana
- ½ cup coconut milk
- 1 cup water
- 1 cup broccoli sprouts
- 2 cherries, pitted
- 1 tbsp hemp hearts
- ¼ tsp ground cinnamon
- ¼ tsp ground cardamom
- 1 tbsp grated fresh ginger

Directions:
1. In a food processor, place banana, coconut milk, water, broccoli, cherries, hemp hearts, cinnamon, cardamom, and ginger. Blitz until smooth. Divide between glasses and serve.

Easy Breakfast Wafers

Servings: 8
Cooking Time: 30 Minutes
Ingredients:
- 1 ¼ cups rice flour
- 1/4 cup tapioca flour
- 1/2 cup potato starch
- 1/2 cup instant oats
- 1 teaspoon baking powder
- 1/2 teaspoon baking soda
- 1 pinch sea salt
- 1/2 teaspoon vanilla essence
- 1/2 teaspoon cinnamon
- 1 ½ cups oat milk
- 1 teaspoon apple cider vinegar
- 1/3 cup coconut oil, softened
- 1/3 cup maple syrup

Directions:
1. Preheat a waffle iron according to the manufacturer's instructions.
2. In a mixing bowl, thoroughly combine the flour, potato starch, instant oats, baking powder, baking soda, salt, vanilla and cinnamon.
3. Gradually add in the milk, whisking continuously to avoid lumps. Add in the apple cider vinegar, coconut oil and maple syrup. Whisk again to combine well.
4. Beat until everything is well blended.
5. Ladle 1/2 cup of the batter into the preheated iron and cook according to manufacturer instructions, until your wafers are golden. Repeat with the remaining batter.
6. Serve with toppings of choice. Bon appétit!

Chocolate & Carrot Bread With Raisins

Servings: 4
Cooking Time: 75 Minutes
Ingredients:
- 1 ½ cup whole-wheat flour
- ¼ cup almond flour
- ¼ tsp salt
- ¼ tsp cloves powder
- ¼ tsp cayenne pepper
- 1 tbsp cinnamon powder
- ½ tsp nutmeg powder
- 1 ½ tsp baking powder
- 2 tbsp flax seed powder
- ½ cup pure date sugar
- ¼ cup pure maple syrup
- ¾ tsp almond extract
- 1 tbsp grated lemon zest
- ½ cup unsweetened applesauce
- ¼ cup olive oil
- 4 carrots, shredded
- 3 tbsp unsweetened chocolate chips
- 2/3 cup black raisins

Directions:
1. Preheat oven to 375 F and line a loaf tin with baking paper. In a bowl, mix all the flour, salt, cloves powder, cayenne pepper, cinnamon powder, nutmeg powder, and baking powder.
2. In another bowl, mix the flax seed powder, 6 tbsp water, and allow thickening for 5 minutes. Mix in the date sugar, maple syrup, almond extract, lemon zest, applesauce, and olive oil. Combine both mixtures until smooth and fold in the carrots, chocolate chips, and raisins.
3. Pour the mixture into a loaf pan and bake in the oven until golden brown on top or a toothpick inserted into the bread comes out clean, 45-50 minutes. Remove from the oven, transfer the bread onto a wire rack to cool, slice, and serve.

Ciabatta Bread Pudding With Sultanas

Servings: 4
Cooking Time: 2 Hours 10 Minutes
Ingredients:
- 2 cups coconut milk, unsweetened
- 1/2 cup agave syrup
- 1 tablespoon coconut oil
- 1/2 teaspoon vanilla essence
- 1/2 teaspoon ground cardamom
- 1/4 teaspoon ground cloves
- 1/2 teaspoon ground cinnamon
- 1/4 teaspoon Himalayan salt
- 3/4 pound stale ciabatta bread, cubed
- 1/2 cup sultana raisins

Directions:
1. In a mixing bowl, combine the coconut milk, agave syrup, coconut oil, vanilla, cardamom, ground cloves, cinnamon and Himalayan salt.
2. Add the bread cubes to the custard mixture and stir to combine well. Fold in the sultana raisins and allow it to rest for about 1 hour on a counter.
3. Then, spoon the mixture into a lightly oiled casserole dish.
4. Bake in the preheated oven at 350 degrees F for about 1 hour or until the top is golden brown.
5. Place the bread pudding on a wire rack for 10 minutes before slicing and serving. Bon appétit!

Easy Morning Polenta

Servings: 2
Cooking Time: 20 Minutes
Ingredients:
- 2 cups vegetable broth
- 1/2 cup cornmeal
- 1/2 teaspoon sea salt
- 1/4 teaspoon ground black pepper, to taste
- 1/4 teaspoon red pepper flakes, crushed
- 2 tablespoons olive oil

Directions:
1. In a medium saucepan, bring the vegetable broth to boil over medium-high heat. Now, add in the cornmeal, whisking continuously to prevent lumps.
2. Season with salt, black pepper and red pepper.
3. Reduce the heat to a simmer. Continue to simmer, whisking periodically, for about 18 minutes, until the mixture has thickened.
4. Now, pour the olive oil into a saucepan and stir to combine well. Bon appétit!

Mango Rice Pudding

Servings:4
Cooking Time:30 Minutes
Ingredients:
- 1cup brown rice
- 1 ½ cups non-dairy milk
- 3 tbsp pure date sugar
- 2 tsp pumpkin pie spice
- 1 mango, chopped
- 2 tbsp chopped walnuts

Directions:
1. In a pot over medium heat, add the rice, 2 cups water, milk, sugar, and pumpkin pie spice. Bring to a boil, lower the heat and simmer for 18-20 minutes until the rice is soft and the liquid is absorbed. Put in the mango and stir to combine. Top with walnuts to serve.

Autumn Cinnamon And Apple Oatmeal Cups

Servings: 9
Cooking Time: 30 Minutes
Ingredients:
- 2 cups old-fashioned oats
- 1/2 teaspoon baking powder
- 1 teaspoon cinnamon
- 1/4 teaspoon grated nutmeg
- 1/4 teaspoon sea salt
- 1 cup almond milk
- 1/4 cup agave syrup
- 1/2 cup applesauce
- 2 tablespoons coconut oil
- 2 tablespoons peanut butter
- 1 tablespoon chia seeds
- 1 small apple, cored and diced

Directions:
1. Begin by preheating your oven to 360 degrees F. Spritz a muffin tin with a nonstick cooking oil.
2. In a mixing bowl, thoroughly combine all the ingredients, except for the apples.
3. Fold in the apples and scrape the batter into the prepared muffin tin.
4. Bake your muffins for about 25 minutes or until a toothpick comes out dry and clean. Bon appétit!

Morning Kasha With Mushrooms

Servings: 2
Cooking Time: 30 Minutes
Ingredients:
- 1 cup water
- 1/2 cup buckwheat groats, toasted
- Sea salt and ground black pepper, to taste
- 2 tablespoons olive oil
- 1 cup button mushrooms, sliced
- 2 tablespoons scallions, chopped
- 1 garlic clove, minced
- 1 small avocado, pitted, peeled and sliced
- 1 tablespoon fresh lemon juice

Directions:
1. In a saucepan, bring the water and buckwheat to a boil. Immediately turn the heat to a simmer and continue to cook for about 20 minutes. Season with sea salt and ground black pepper to taste.
2. Then, heat the olive oil in a nonstick skillet, over medium-high heat. Sauté the mushrooms, scallions and garlic for about 4 minutes or until they've softened.
3. Spoon the kasha into two serving bowls; top each serving with the sautéed mushroom mixture.

4. Garnish with avocado, add a few drizzles of fresh lemon juice and serve immediately. Bon appétit!

Spicy Vegetable And Chickpea Tofu Scramble

Servings: 2
Cooking Time: 15 Minutes
Ingredients:
- 2 tablespoons oil
- 1 bell pepper, seeded and sliced
- 2 tablespoons scallions, chopped
- 6 ounces cremini button mushrooms, sliced
- 1/2 teaspoon garlic, minced
- 1 jalapeno pepper, seeded and chopped
- 6 ounces firm tofu, pressed
- 1 tablespoon nutritional yeast
- 1/4 teaspoon turmeric powder
- Kala namak and ground black pepper, to taste
- 6 ounces chickpeas, drained

Directions:
1. Heat the olive oil in a nonstick skillet over a moderate flame. Once hot, sauté the pepper for about 2 minutes.
2. Now, add in the scallions, mushrooms and continue sautéing for a further 3 minutes or until the mushrooms release the liquid.
3. Then, add in the garlic, jalapeno and tofu and sauté for 5 minutes more, crumbling the tofu with a fork.
4. Add in the nutritional yeast, turmeric, salt, pepper and chickpeas; continue sautéing an additional 2 minutes or until cooked through. Bon appétit!

Simple Apple Muffins

Servings:4
Cooking Time:40 Minutes
Ingredients:
- For the muffins:
- 1 flax seed powder + 3 tbsp water
- 1 ½ cups whole-wheat flour
- ¾ cup pure date sugar
- 2 tsp baking powder
- ¼ tsp salt
- 1 tsp cinnamon powder
- 1/3 cup melted plant butter
- 1/3 cup flax milk
- 2 apples, chopped
- For topping:
- 1/3 cup whole-wheat flour
- ½ cup pure date sugar
- ½ cup cold plant butter, cubed
- 1 ½ tsp cinnamon powder

Directions:
1. Preheat oven to 400 F and grease 6 muffin cups with cooking spray. In a bowl, mix the flax seed powder with water and allow thickening for 5 minutes to make the vegan "flax egg."
2. In a bowl, mix flour, date sugar, baking powder, salt, and cinnamon powder. Whisk in the butter, vegan "flax

egg," flax milk, and fold in the apples. Fill the muffin cups two-thirds way up with the batter.
3. In a bowl, mix remaining flour, date sugar, cold butter, and cinnamon powder. Sprinkle the mixture on the muffin batter. Bake for 20 minutes. Remove the muffins onto a wire rack, allow cooling, and serve.

Blueberry Muesli Breakfast

Servings:5
Cooking Time:10 Minutes
Ingredients:
- 2 cups spelt flakes
- 2 cups puffed cereal
- ¼ cup sunflower seeds
- ¼ cup almonds
- ¼ cup raisins
- ¼ cup dried cranberries
- ¼ cup chopped dried figs
- ¼ cup shredded coconut
- ¼ cup non-dairy chocolate chips
- 3 tsp ground cinnamon
- ½ cup coconut milk
- ½ cup blueberries

Directions:
1. In a bowl, combine the spelt flakes, puffed cereal, sunflower seeds, almonds, raisins, cranberries, figs, coconut, chocolate chips, and cinnamon. Toss to mix well. Pour in the coconut milk. Let sit for 1 hour and serve topped with blueberries.

Coconut & Raspberry Pancakes

Servings:4
Cooking Time:25 Minutes
Ingredients:
- 2 tbsp flax seed powder
- ½ cup coconut milk
- ¼ cup fresh raspberries, mashed
- ½ cup oat flour
- 1 tsp baking soda
- A pinch salt
- 1 tbsp coconut sugar
- 2 tbsp pure date syrup
- ½ tsp cinnamon powder
- 2 tbsp unsweetened coconut flakes
- 2 tsp plant butter
- Fresh raspberries for garnishing

Directions:
1. In a medium bowl, mix the flax seed powder with the 6 tbsp water and thicken for 5 minutes. Mix in coconut milk and raspberries. Add the oat flour, baking soda, salt, coconut sugar, date syrup, and cinnamon powder. Fold in the coconut flakes until well combined.
2. Working in batches, melt a quarter of the butter in a non-stick skillet and add ¼ cup of the batter. Cook until set beneath and golden brown, 2 minutes. Flip the pancake and cook on the other side until set and golden brown, 2 minutes. Transfer to a plate and make the remaining pancakes using

the rest of the ingredients in the same proportions. Garnish the pancakes with some raspberries and serve warm!

Coconut Blueberry Muffins

Servings:12
Cooking Time:30 Minutes
Ingredients:
- 1 tbsp coconut oil melted
- 1 cup quick-cooking oats
- 1 cup boiling water
- ½ cup almond milk
- ¼ cup ground flaxseed
- 1 tsp almond extract
- 1 tsp apple cider vinegar
- 1 ½ cups whole-wheat flour
- ½ cup pure date sugar
- 2 tsp baking soda
- A pinch of salt
- 1 cup blueberries

Directions:
1. Preheat oven to 400 F.
2. In a bowl, stir in the oats with boiling water until they are softened. Pour in the coconut oil, milk, flaxseed, almond extract, and vinegar. Add in the flour, sugar, baking soda, and salt. Gently stir in blueberries.
3. Divide the batter between greased muffin tins. Bake for 20 minutes until lightly brown. Allow cooling for 10 minutes. Using a spatula, run the sides of the muffins to take out. Serve.

Morning Nutty Oatmeal Muffins

Servings: 9
Cooking Time: 30 Minutes
Ingredients:
- 1 ½ cups rolled oats
- 1/2 cup shredded coconut, unsweetened
- 3/4 teaspoon baking powder
- 1/4 teaspoon salt
- 1/4 teaspoon vanilla extract
- 1/4 teaspoon coconut extract
- 1/4 teaspoon grated nutmeg
- 1/2 teaspoon cardamom
- 3/4 cup coconut milk
- 1/3 cup canned pumpkin
- 1/4 cup agave syrup
- 1/4 cup golden raisins
- 1/4 cup pecans, chopped

Directions:
1. Begin by preheating your oven to 360 degrees F. Spritz a muffin tin with a nonstick cooking oil.
2. In a mixing bowl, thoroughly combine all the ingredients, except for the raisins and pecans.
3. Fold in the raisins and pecans and scrape the batter into the prepared muffin tin.
4. Bake your muffins for about 25 minutes or until the top is set. Bon appétit!

Grandma's Breakfast Gallete

Servings: 5
Cooking Time: 40 Minutes
Ingredients:
- 1 cup all-purpose flour
- 1/2 cup oat flour
- 1 teaspoon baking powder
- 1 teaspoon baking soda
- 1/2 teaspoon kosher salt
- 1 teaspoon brown sugar
- 1/4 teaspoon ground allspice
- 1 cup water
- 1/2 cup rice milk
- 2 tablespoons olive oil

Directions:
1. Mix the flour, baking powder, baking soda, salt, sugar and ground allspice using an electric mixer.
2. Gradually pour in the water, milk and oil and continue mixing until everything is well incorporated.
3. Heat a lightly greased griddle over medium-high heat.
4. Ladle 1/4 of the batter into the preheated griddle and cook until your galette is golden and crisp. Repeat with the remaining batter.
5. Serve your galette with a homemade jelly, if desired. Bon appétit!

Amazing Yellow Smoothie

Servings:4
Cooking Time:5 Minutes
Ingredients:
- 1 banana
- 1 cup chopped mango
- 1 cup chopped apricots
- 1 cup strawberries
- 1 carrot, peeled and chopped
- 1 cup water

Directions:
1. Put the banana, mango, apricots, strawberries, carrot, and water in a food processor. Pulse until smooth; add more water if needed. Divide between glasses and serve.

Chocolate Granola Bars

Servings: 12
Cooking Time: 40 Minutes
Ingredients:
- 1 1/3 cups old-fashioned oats
- 1/2 cup fresh dates, pitted and mashed
- 1/2 cup dried cherries
- 1/3 cup agave syrup
- 1/3 cup almond butter, room temperature
- 2 tablespoons coconut oil, melted
- 1/2 cup almonds
- 1/2 cup walnuts
- 1/4 cup pecans
- 1/2 teaspoon allspice
- A pinch of salt
- A pinch of grated nutmeg

- 1/2 cup dark chocolate chunks

Directions:

1. In a mixing bowl, thoroughly combine the oats, dates and dried cherries.
2. Add in the agave syrup, almond butter and coconut oil. Stir in the nuts, spices and chocolate.
3. Press the mixture into a lightly greased baking dish. Transfer it to your refrigerator for about 30 minutes.
4. Slice into 12 even bars and store in airtight containers. Enjoy!

Classic French Toast

Servings: 2
Cooking Time: 20 Minutes
Ingredients:

- 1 tablespoon ground flax seeds
- 1 cup coconut milk
- 1/2 teaspoon vanilla paste
- A pinch of sea salt
- A pinch of grated nutmeg
- 1/2 teaspoon ground cinnamon
- 1/4 teaspoon ground cloves
- 1 tablespoon agave syrup
- 4 slices bread

Directions:

1. In a mixing bowl, thoroughly combine the flax seeds, coconut milk, vanilla, salt, nutmeg, cinnamon, cloves and agave syrup.
2. Dredge each slice of bread into the milk mixture until well coated on all sides.
3. Preheat an electric griddle to medium heat and lightly oil it with a nonstick cooking spray.
4. Cook each slice of bread on the preheated griddle for about 3 minutes per side until golden brown.
5. Bon appétit!

Broccoli Hash Browns

Servings:4
Cooking Time:35 Minutes
Ingredients:

- 3 tbsp flax seed powder
- 1 head broccoli, cut into florets
- ½ white onion, grated
- 1 tsp salt
- 1 tbsp freshly ground black pepper
- 5 tbsp plant butter, for frying

Directions:

1. In a small bowl, mix the flax seed powder with 9 tbsp water, and allow soaking for 5 minutes. Pour the broccoli into a food processor and pulse a few times until smoothly grated.
2. Transfer the broccoli into a bowl, add the vegan "flax egg," white onion, salt, and black pepper. Use a spoon to mix the ingredients evenly and set aside 5 to 10 minutes to firm up a bit. Place a large non-stick skillet over medium heat and drop 1/3 of the plant butter to melt until no longer shimmering.
3. Ladle scoops of the broccoli mixture into the skillet. Flatten the pancakes to measure 3 to 4 inches in diameter,

and fry until golden brown on one side, 4 minutes. Turn the pancakes with a spatula and cook the other side to brown too, another 5 minutes.
4. Transfer the hash browns to a serving plate and repeat the frying process for the remaining broccoli mixture. Serve the hash browns warm with green salad.

Choco-berry Smoothie

Servings:2
Cooking Time:10 Minutes
Ingredients:

- 1 tbsp poppy seeds
- 2 cups unsweetened soy milk
- 2 cups blackberries
- 2 tbsp pure agave syrup
- 2 tbsp cocoa powder

Directions:

1. Submerge poppy seeds in soy milk and let sit for 5 minutes. Transfer to a food processor and add in the soy milk, blackberries, agave syrup, and cocoa powder. Blitz until smooth. Serve right away in glasses.

Grits With Fried Tofu And Avocado

Servings: 3
Cooking Time: 30 Minutes
Ingredients:

- 3 teaspoons sesame oil
- 12 ounces firm tofu, cubed
- 1 small white onion, chopped
- 1/2 teaspoon turmeric
- 1/2 teaspoon red pepper flakes
- 3 cups water
- 1 cup stone-ground corn grits
- 1 thyme sprig
- 1 rosemary sprig
- 1 bay leaf
- 1/4 cup nutritional yeast
- 1 medium tomato, sliced
- 1 medium avocado, pitted, peeled and sliced

Directions:

1. Heat the sesame oil in a wok over a moderately high heat. Now, fry your tofu for about 6 minutes.
2. Add in the onion, turmeric and red pepper and continue cooking until the tofu is crisp on all sides and the onion is tender and translucent.
3. In a saucepan, place the water, grits, thyme sprig, rosemary sprig and bay leaf and bring to a boil. Tun the heat to a simmer, cover and let it cook for approximately 20 minutes or until the most of the water is absorbed.
4. Add in the nutritional yeast and stir to combine well.
5. Divide the grits between serving bowls and top with the fried tofu/onion mixture. Top with tomato and avocado, salt to taste and serve immediately. Bon appétit!

Chocolate-mango Quinoa Bowl

Servings:2
Cooking Time:35 Minutes
Ingredients:
- 1 cup quinoa
- 1 tsp ground cinnamon
- 1 cup non-dairy milk
- 1 large mango, chopped
- 3 tbsp unsweetened cocoa powder
- 2 tbsp almond butter
- 1 tbsp hemp seeds
- 1 tbsp walnuts
- ¼ cup raspberries

Directions:
1. In a pot, combine the quinoa, cinnamon, milk, and 1 cup of water over medium heat. Bring to a boil, low heat, and simmer covered for 25-30 minutes. In a bowl, mash the mango and mix cocoa powder, almond butter, and hemp seeds. In a serving bowl, place cooked quinoa and mango mixture. Top with walnuts and raspberries. Serve immediately.

No-bread Avocado Sandwich

Servings:2
Cooking Time:10 Minutes
Ingredients:
- 1 avocado, sliced
- 1 large red tomato, sliced
- 2 oz gem lettuce leaves
- ½ oz plant butter
- 1 oz tofu, sliced
- Freshly chopped parsley to garnish

Directions:
1. Put the avocado on a plate and place the tomato slices by the avocado. Arrange the lettuce (with the inner side facing you) on a flat plate to serve as the base of the sandwich.
2. To assemble the sandwich, smear each leaf of the lettuce with plant butter, and arrange some tofu slices in the leaves. Then, share the avocado and tomato slices on each cheese. Garnish with parsley and serve.

Banana-strawberry Smoothie

Servings:4
Cooking Time:5 Minutes
Ingredients:
- 4 bananas, sliced
- 4 cups strawberries
- 4 cups kale
- 4 cups plant-based milk

Directions:
1. In a food processor, add bananas, strawberries, kale, and milk and blitz until smooth. Divide between glasses and serve.

Coconut Porridge With Strawberries

Servings:2
Cooking Time:12 Minutes

Ingredients:
- 1 tbsp flax seed powder
- 1 oz olive oil
- 1 tbsp coconut flour
- 1 pinch ground chia seeds
- 5 tbsp coconut cream
- Thawed frozen strawberries

Directions:
1. In a small bowl, mix the flax seed powder with the 3 tbsp water, and allow soaking for 5 minutes.
2. Place a non-stick saucepan over low heat and pour in the olive oil, vegan "flax egg," coconut flour, chia seeds, and coconut cream. Cook the mixture while stirring continuously until your desired consistency is achieved. Turn the heat off and spoon the porridge into serving bowls. Top with 4 to 6 strawberries and serve immediately.

The Best Chocolate Granola Ever

Servings: 10
Cooking Time: 1 Hour
Ingredients:
- 1/2 cup coconut oil
- 1/2 cup agave syrup
- 1 teaspoon vanilla paste
- 3 cups rolled oats
- 1/2 cup hazelnuts, chopped
- 1/2 cup pumpkin seeds
- 1/2 teaspoon ground cardamom
- 1 teaspoon ground cinnamon
- 1/4 teaspoon ground cloves
- 1 teaspoon Himalayan salt
- 1/2 cup dark chocolate, cut into chunks

Directions:
1. Begin by preheating your oven to 260 degrees F; line two rimmed baking sheets with a piece parchment paper.
2. Then, thoroughly combine the coconut oil, agave syrup and vanilla in a mixing bowl.
3. Gradually add in the oats, hazelnuts, pumpkin seeds and spices; toss to coat well. Spread the mixture out onto the prepared baking sheets.
4. Bake in the middle of the oven, stirring halfway through the cooking time, for about 1 hour or until golden brown.
5. Stir in the dark chocolate and let your granola cool completely before storing. Store in an airtight container.
6. Bon appétit!

Everyday Oats With Coconut And Strawberries

Servings: 2
Cooking Time: 15 Minutes
Ingredients:
- 1/2 tablespoon coconut oil
- 1 cup rolled oats
- A pinch of flaky sea salt
- 1/8 teaspoon grated nutmeg
- 1/4 teaspoon cardamom
- 1 tablespoon coconut sugar
- 1 cup coconut milk, sweetened

- 1 cup water
- 2 tablespoons coconut flakes
- 4 tablespoons fresh strawberries

Directions:
1. In a saucepan, melt the coconut oil over a moderate flame. Then, toast the oats for about 3 minutes, stirring continuously.
2. Add in the salt, nutmeg, cardamom, coconut sugar, milk and water; continue to cook for 12 minutes more or until cooked through.
3. Spoon the mixture into serving bowls; top with coconut flakes and fresh strawberries. Bon appétit!

Homemade Chocolate Crunch

Servings: 9
Cooking Time: 35 Minutes
Ingredients:
- 1/2 cup rye flakes
- 1/2 cup buckwheat flakes
- 1 cup rolled oats
- 1/2 cup pecans, chopped
- 1/2 cup hazelnuts, chopped
- 1 cup coconut, shredded
- 1/2 cup date syrup
- 1 teaspoon vanilla paste
- 1/2 teaspoon pumpkin spice mix
- 1/4 cup coconut oil, softened
- 1/2 cup chocolate chunks

Directions:
1. Start by preheating your oven to 330 degrees F. Line a baking sheet with parchment paper or a Silpat mat.
2. In a mixing bowl, thoroughly combine all the ingredients, except for the chocolate chunks. Then, spread the cereal mixture onto the prepared baking sheet.
3. Bake for about 33 minutes or until crunchy. Fold the chocolate chunks into the warm cereal mixture.
4. Allow it to cool fully before breaking up into clumps. Serve with a plant-based milk of choice. Bon appétit!

Classic Applesauce Pancakes With Coconut

Servings: 8
Cooking Time: 50 Minutes
Ingredients:
- 1 ¼ cups whole-wheat flour
- 1 teaspoon baking powder
- 1/4 teaspoon sea salt
- 1/2 teaspoon coconut sugar
- 1/4 teaspoon ground cloves
- 1/4 teaspoon ground cardamom
- 1/2 teaspoon ground cinnamon
- 3/4 cup oat milk
- 1/2 cup applesauce, unsweetened
- 2 tablespoons coconut oil
- 8 tablespoons coconut, shredded
- 8 tablespoons pure maple syrup

Directions:

1. In a mixing bowl, thoroughly combine the flour, baking powder, salt, sugar and spices. Gradually add in the milk and applesauce.
2. Heat a frying pan over a moderately high flame and add a small amount of the coconut oil.
3. Once hot, pour the batter into the frying pan. Cook for approximately 3 minutes until the bubbles form; flip it and cook on the other side for 3 minutes longer until browned on the underside. Repeat with the remaining oil and batter.
4. Serve with shredded coconut and maple syrup. Bon appétit!

Cinnamon Buckwheat With Almonds

Servings:4
Cooking Time:20 Minutes
Ingredients:
- 1 cup almond milk
- 1 cup water
- 1 cup buckwheat groats, rinsed
- 1 tsp cinnamon
- ¼ cup chopped almonds
- 2 tbsp pure date syrup

Directions:
1. Place almond milk, water, and buckwheat in a pot over medium heat and bring to a boil. Lower the heat and simmer covered for 15 minutes. Allow sitting covered for 5 minutes. Mix in the cinnamon, almonds, and date syrup. Serve warm.

Sweet Kiwi Oatmeal Bars

Servings:12
Cooking Time:50 Minutes
Ingredients:
- 2 cups uncooked rolled oats
- 2 cups all-purpose flour
- 1 ½ cups pure date sugar
- 1 ½ tsp baking soda
- ½ tsp ground cinnamon
- 1 cup plant butter, melted
- 4 cups kiwi, chopped
- ¼ cup organic cane sugar
- 2 tbsp cornstarch

Directions:
1. Preheat oven to 380 F. Grease a baking dish.
2. In a bowl, mix the oats, flour, date sugar, baking soda, salt, and cinnamon. Put in butter and whisk to combine. In another bowl, combine the kiwis, cane sugar, and cornstarch until the kiwis are coated. Spread 3 cups of oatmeal mixture on a greased baking dish and top with kiwi mixture and finally put the remaining oatmeal mixture on top. Bake for 40 minutes. Allow cooling and slice into bars.

Lemon-almond Waffles

Servings:4
Cooking Time:20 Minutes
Ingredients:
- 2 tbsp flax seed powder
- 2/3 cup almond flour
- 2 ½ tsp baking powder
- A pinch salt

- 1 ½ cups almond milk
- 2 tbsp plant butter
- 1 cup fresh almond butter
- 2 tbsp pure maple syrup
- 1 tsp fresh lemon juice

Directions:

1. In a medium bowl, mix the flaxseed powder with 6 tbsp water and allow soaking for 5 minutes. Add the almond flour, baking powder, salt, and almond milk. Mix until well combined. Preheat a waffle iron and brush with some plant butter. Pour in a quarter cup of the batter, close the iron and cook until the waffles are golden and crisp, 2-3 minutes.
2. Transfer the waffles to a plate and make more waffles using the same process and ingredient proportions. In a bowl, mix the almond butter with the maple syrup and lemon juice. Spread the top with the almond-lemon mixture and serve.

Blackberry Waffles

Servings:4
Cooking Time:15 Minutes
Ingredients:

- 1 ½ cups whole-heat flour
- ½ cup old-fashioned oats
- ¼ cup date sugar
- 3 tsp baking powder
- ½ tsp salt
- 1 tsp ground cinnamon
- 2 cups soy milk
- 1 tbsp fresh lemon juice
- 1 tsp lemon zest
- ¼ cup plant butter, melted
- ½ cup fresh blackberries

Directions:

1. Preheat the waffle iron.
2. In a bowl, mix flour, oats, sugar, baking powder, salt, and cinnamon. Set aside. In another bowl, combine milk, lemon juice, lemon zest, and butter. Pour into the wet ingredients and whisk to combine. Add the batter to the hot greased waffle iron, using approximately a ladleful for each waffle. Cook for 3-5 minutes, until golden brown. Repeat the process until no batter is left. Serve topped with blackberries.

Yogurt Carrot Griddle Cakes

Servings: 4
Cooking Time: 25 Minutes
Ingredients:

- 1/2 cup oat flour
- 1/2 teaspoon baking powder
- 1 teaspoon coconut sugar
- 1/4 teaspoon ground allspice
- 1/4 teaspoon vanilla extract
- 1 large-sized carrot, trimmed and grated
- 1 cup banana, mashed
- 1/2 cup coconut yogurt
- 4 teaspoons coconut oil, at room temperature
- 4 tablespoons icing sugar
- 1 teaspoon ground cinnamon

Directions:

1. In a mixing bowl, thoroughly combine the flour, baking powder, coconut sugar, ground allspice and vanilla.
2. Gradually add in the carrot, banana and coconut yogurt.
3. Heat an electric griddle on medium and lightly slick it with the coconut oil.
4. Spoon about 1/4 of the batter onto the preheated griddle. Cook your cake for approximately 3 minutes until the bubbles form; flip it and cook on the other side for 3 minutes longer until browned on the underside.
5. Repeat with the remaining oil and batter. In a small bowl, mix the icing sugar and ground cinnamon.
6. Dust each griddle cake with the cinnamon sugar and serve hot. Enjoy!

Mixed Berry And Almond Butter Swirl Bowl

Servings: 3
Cooking Time: 10 Minutes
Ingredients:

- 1 ½ cups almond milk
- 2 small bananas
- 2 cups mixed berries, fresh or frozen
- 3 dates, pitted
- 3 scoops hemp protein powder
- 3 tablespoons smooth almond butter
- 2 tablespoons pepitas

Directions:

1. In your blender or food processor, mix the almond milk with the bananas, berries and dates.
2. Process until everything is well combined. Divide the smoothie between three bowls.
3. Top each smoothie bowl with almond butter and use a butter knife to swirl the almond butter into the top of each smoothie bowl.
4. Afterwards, garnish each smoothie bowl with pepitas, serve well-chilled and enjoy!

Traditional Indian Roti

Servings: 5
Cooking Time: 30 Minutes
Ingredients:

- 2 cups bread flour
- 1 teaspoon baking powder
- 1/2 teaspoon salt
- 3/4 warm water
- 1 cup vegetable oil, for frying

Directions:

1. Thoroughly combine the flour, baking powder and salt in a mixing bowl. Gradually add in the water until the dough comes together.
2. Divide the dough into five balls; flatten each ball to create circles.
3. Heat the olive oil in a frying pan over a moderately high flame. Fry the first bread, turning it over to promote even cooking; fry it for about 10 minutes or until golden brown.
4. Repeat with the remaining dough. Transfer each roti to a paper towel-lined plate to drain the excess oil.
5. Bon appétit!

Thyme Pumpkin Stir-fry

Servings:2
Cooking Time:25 Minutes
Ingredients:
- 1 cup pumpkin, shredded
- 1 tbsp olive oil
- ½ onion, chopped
- 1 carrot, peeled and chopped
- 2 garlic cloves, minced
- ½ tsp dried thyme
- 1 cup chopped kale
- Salt and black pepper to taste

Directions:
1. Heat the oil in a skillet over medium heat. Sauté onion and carrot for 5 minutes. Add in garlic and thyme, cook for 30 seconds until the garlic is fragrant. Place in the pumpkin and cook for 10 minutes until tender. Stir in kale, cook for 4 minutes until the kale wilts. Season with salt and pepper. Serve hot.

Banana French Toast With Strawberry Syrup

Servings:8
Cooking Time:40 Minutes
Ingredients:
- 1 banana, mashed
- 1 cup coconut milk
- 1 tsp pure vanilla extract
- ¼ tsp ground nutmeg
- ½ tsp ground cinnamon
- 1 ½ tsp arrowroot powder
- A pinch of salt
- 8 slices whole-grain bread
- 1 cup strawberries
- 2 tbsp water
- 2 tbsp maple syrup

Directions:
1. Preheat oven to 350 F.
2. In a bowl, stir banana, coconut milk, vanilla, nutmeg, cinnamon, arrowroot, and salt. Dip each bread slice in the banana mixture and arrange on a baking tray. Spread the remaining banana mixture over the top. Bake for 30 minutes until the tops are lightly browned. In a pot over medium heat, put the strawberries, water, and maple syrup. Simmer for 15-10 minutes until the berries breaking up and the liquid has reduced. Serve topped with strawberry syrup.

Berry Quinoa Bowl

Servings:4
Cooking Time:5 Minutes
Ingredients:
- 3 cups cooked quinoa
- 1 ⅓ cups unsweetened almond milk
- 2 bananas, sliced
- 2 cups berries
- ½ cup chopped raw hazelnuts
- ¼ cup agave syrup

Directions:
1. In a large bowl, combine the quinoa, milk, banana, raspberries, blueberries, and hazelnuts. Divide between serving bowls and top with agave syrup to serve.

Classic Tofu Scramble

Servings: 2
Cooking Time: 15 Minutes
Ingredients:
- 1 tablespoon olive oil
- 6 ounces extra-firm tofu, pressed and crumbled
- 1 cup baby spinach
- Sea salt and ground black pepper to taste
- 1/2 teaspoon turmeric powder
- 1/4 teaspoon cumin powder
- 1/2 teaspoon garlic powder
- 1 handful fresh chives, chopped

Directions:
1. Heat the olive oil in a frying skillet over medium heat. When it's hot, add the tofu and sauté for 8 minutes, stirring occasionally to promote even cooking.
2. Add in the baby spinach and aromatics and continue sautéing an additional 1 to 2 minutes.
3. Garnish with fresh chives and serve warm. Bon appétit!

Buckwheat Porridge With Apples And Almonds

Servings: 3
Cooking Time: 20 Minutes
Ingredients:
- 1 cup buckwheat groats, toasted
- 3/4 cup water
- 1 cup rice milk
- 1/4 teaspoon sea salt
- 3 tablespoons agave syrup
- 1 cup apples, cored and diced
- 3 tablespoons almonds, slivered
- 2 tablespoons coconut flakes
- 2 tablespoons hemp seeds

Directions:
1. In a saucepan, bring the buckwheat groats, water, milk and salt to a boil. Immediately turn the heat to a simmer; let it simmer for about 13 minutes until it has softened.
2. Stir in the agave syrup. Divide the porridge between three serving bowls.
3. Garnish each serving with the apples, almonds, coconut and hemp seeds. Bon appétit!

Coconut Fruit Smoothie

Servings:3
Cooking Time:5 Minutes
Ingredients:
- 1 cup strawberries
- 1 cup chopped watermelon
- 1 cup cranberries
- 1 tbsp chia seeds
- ½ cup coconut milk
- 1 cup water

- 1 tsp goji berries
- 2 tbsp fresh mint, chopped

Directions:

1. In a food processor, put the strawberries, watermelon, cranberries, chia seeds, coconut milk, water, goji berries, and mint. Pulse until smooth, adding more water or milk if needed. Divide between 3 glasses and serve.

Autumn Pumpkin Griddle Cakes

Servings: 4
Cooking Time: 30 Minutes
Ingredients:

- 1/2 cup oat flour
- 1/2 cup whole-wheat white flour
- 1 teaspoon baking powder
- 1/4 teaspoon Himalayan salt
- 1 teaspoon sugar
- 1/2 teaspoon ground allspice
- 1/2 teaspoon ground cinnamon
- 1/2 teaspoon crystalized ginger
- 1 teaspoon lemon juice, freshly squeezed
- 1/2 cup almond milk
- 1/2 cup pumpkin puree
- 2 tablespoons coconut oil

Directions:

1. In a mixing bowl, thoroughly combine the flour, baking powder, salt, sugar and spices. Gradually add in the lemon juice, milk and pumpkin puree.
2. Heat an electric griddle on medium and lightly slick it with the coconut oil.
3. Cook your cake for approximately 3 minutes until the bubbles form; flip it and cook on the other side for 3 minutes longer until browned on the underside.
4. Repeat with the remaining oil and batter. Serve dusted with cinnamon sugar, if desired. Bon appétit!

Scrambled Tofu With Swiss Chard

Servings:5
Cooking Time:35 Minutes
Ingredients:

- 1 package tofu, crumbled
- 2 tsp olive oil
- 1 onion, chopped
- 3 cloves minced garlic
- 1 celery stalk, chopped
- 2 large carrots, chopped
- 1 tsp chili powder
- ½ tsp ground cumin
- ½ tsp ground turmeric
- Salt and black pepper to taste
- 5 cups Swiss chard

Directions:

1. Heat the oil in a skillet over medium heat. Add in the onion, garlic, celery, and carrots. Sauté for 5 minutes. Stir in tofu, chili powder, cumin, turmeric, salt, and pepper, cook for 7-8 minutes more. Mix in the Swiss chard and cook until wilted, about 3 minutes. Allow cooling and seal, and serve.

Orange Granola With Hazelnuts

Servings:5
Cooking Time:50 Minutes
Ingredients:

- 2 cups rolled oats
- ¾ cup whole-wheat flour
- 1 tbsp ground cinnamon
- 1 tsp ground ginger
- ½ cup sunflower seeds
- ½ cup hazelnuts, chopped
- ½ cup pumpkin seeds
- ½ cup shredded coconut
- 1 ¼ cups orange juice
- ½ cup dried cherries
- ½ cup goji berries

Directions:

1. Preheat oven to 350 F.
2. In a bowl, combine the oats, flour, cinnamon, ginger, sunflower seeds, hazelnuts, pumpkin seeds, and coconut. Pour in the orange juice, toss to mix well.
3. Transfer to a baking sheet and bake for 15 minutes. Turn the granola and continue baking until it is crunchy, about 30 minutes. Stir in the cherries and goji berries and store in the fridge for up to 14 days.

Homemade Toast Crunch

Servings: 8
Cooking Time: 15 Minutes
Ingredients:

- 1 cup almond flour
- 1 cup coconut flour
- 1/2 cup all-purpose flour
- 1 cup sugar
- 1 teaspoon kosher salt
- 1 teaspoon cardamom
- 1/4 teaspoon grated nutmeg
- 1 tablespoon cinnamon
- 3 tablespoons flax seeds, ground
- 1/2 cup coconut oil, melted
- 8 tablespoons coconut milk

Directions:

1. Begin by preheating the oven to 340 degrees F. In a mixing bowl, thoroughly combine all the dry ingredients.
2. Gradually pour in the oil and milk; mix to combine well.
3. Shape the dough into a ball and roll out between 2 sheets of a parchment paper. Cut into small squares and prick them with a fork to prevent air bubbles.
4. Bake in the preheated oven for about 15 minutes. They will continue to crisp as they cool. Bon appétit!

Mushroom Crepes

Servings:4
Cooking Time:25 Minutes
Ingredients:

- 1 cup whole-wheat flour
- 1 tsp onion powder
- ½ tsp baking soda

- ¼ tsp salt
- 1 cup pressed, crumbled tofu
- ⅓ cup plant-based milk
- ¼ cup lemon juice
- 2 tbsp extra-virgin olive oil
- ½ cup finely chopped mushrooms
- ½ cup finely chopped onion
- 2 cups collard greens

Directions:

1. Combine the flour, onion powder, baking soda, and salt in a bowl. Blitz the tofu, milk, lemon juice, and oil in a food processor over high speed for 30 seconds. Pour over the flour mixture and mix to combine well. Add in the mushrooms, onion, and collard greens.

2. Heat a skillet and grease with cooking spray. Lower the heat and spread a ladleful of the batter across the surface of the skillet. Cook for 4 minutes on both sides or until set. Remove to a plate. Repeat the process until no batter is left, greasing with a little more oil, if needed. Serve.

Apple Chocolate Smoothie

Servings:4
Cooking Time:5 Minutes
Ingredients:

- 1 cup applesauce
- 2 tbsp plant protein powder
- 1 tbsp flaxseed
- 1 tbsp unsweetened cacao powder
- 1 tbsp peanut butter
- 1 tbsp maple syrup
- 1 cup spinach, chopped
- ½ cup non-dairy milk
- 1 cup water
- 1 tsp matcha powder
- 1 tsp cocoa nibs

Directions:

1. Put in a food processor the applesauce, protein powder, flaxseed, cacao powder, peanut butter, maple syrup, spinach, milk, water, matcha powder, and cocoa nibs. Pulse until smooth. Divide between glasses and serve.

Potato & Cauliflower Hash Browns

Servings:4
Cooking Time:35 Minutes
Ingredients:

- 3 tbsp flax seed powder
- 2 large potatoes, shredded
- 1 big head cauliflower, riced
- ½ white onion, grated
- Salt and black pepper to taste
- 4 tbsp plant butter

Directions:

1. In a medium bowl, mix the flaxseed powder and 9 tbsp water. Allow thickening for 5 minutes for the vegan "flax egg." Add the potatoes, cauliflower, onion, salt, and black pepper to the vegan "flax egg" and mix until well combined. Allow sitting for 5 minutes to thicken.

2. Working in batches, melt 1 tbsp of plant butter in a non-stick skillet and add 4 scoops of the hashbrown mixture to the skillet. Make sure to have 1 to 2-inch intervals between each scoop.

3. Use the spoon to flatten the batter and cook until compacted and golden brown on the bottom part, 2 minutes. Flip the hashbrowns and cook further for 2 minutes or until the vegetable cook and is golden brown. Transfer to a paper-towel-lined plate to drain grease. Make the remaining hashbrowns using the remaining ingredients. Serve warm.

Energy Chia-peach Smoothie

Servings:2
Cooking Time:5 Minutes
Ingredients:

- 1 banana, sliced
- 1 peach, chopped
- 1 cup almond milk
- 1 scoop plant-based protein powder
- 1 tbsp chia seeds
- 1 cucumber, chopped

Directions:

1. Purée the banana, peach, almond milk, protein powder, chia seeds, and cucumber for 50 seconds until smooth in a food processor. Serve immediately in glasses.

Morning Green Smoothie

Servings:2
Cooking Time:5 Minutes
Ingredients:

- 1 avocado
- 1 cup chopped cucumber
- 2 cups curly endive
- 2 apples, peeled and cored
- 2 tbsp lime juice
- 2 cups soy milk
- ½-inch piece peeled fresh ginger
- 2 tbsp chia seeds
- 1 cup unsweetened coconut yogurt

Directions:

1. Put in a food processor the avocado, cucumber, curly endive, apple, lime juice, soy milk, ginger, chia seeds, and coconut yogurt. Blend until smooth. Serve.

Almond Oatmeal Porridge

Servings:4
Cooking Time:25 Minutes
Ingredients:

- 2 ½ cups vegetable broth
- 2 ½ cups almond milk
- ½ cup steel-cut oats
- 1 tbsp pearl barley
- ½ cup slivered almonds
- ¼ cup nutritional yeast
- 2 cups old-fashioned rolled oats

Directions:

1. Pour the broth and almond milk in a pot over medium heat and bring to a boil. Stir in oats, pearl barley, almond

slivers, and nutritional yeast. Reduce the heat and simmer for 20 minutes. Add in the rolled oats, cook for an additional 5 minutes, until creamy. Allow cooling before serving.

Spicy Quinoa Bowl With Black Beans

Servings:4
Cooking Time:25 Minutes
Ingredients:
- 1 cup brown quinoa, rinsed
- 3 tbsp plant-based yogurt
- ½ lime, juiced
- 2 tbsp chopped fresh cilantro
- 1 can black beans, drained
- 3 tbsp tomato salsa
- ¼ avocado, sliced
- 2 radishes, shredded
- 1 tbsp pepitas (pumpkin seeds)

Directions:
1. Cook the quinoa with 2 cups of slightly salted water in a medium pot over medium heat or until the liquid absorbs, 15 minutes. Spoon the quinoa into serving bowls and fluff with a fork.
2. In a small bowl, mix the yogurt, lime juice, cilantro, and salt. Divide this mixture on the quinoa and top with beans, salsa, avocado, radishes, and pepitas. Serve immediately.

Cheddar Grits With Soy Chorizo

Servings:6
Cooking Time:25 Minutes
Ingredients:
- 1 cup quick-cooking grits
- ½ cup grated plant-based cheddar
- 2 tbsp peanut butter
- 1 cup soy chorizo, chopped
- 1 cup corn kernels
- 2 cups vegetable broth

Directions:
1. Preheat oven to 380 F.
2. Pour the broth in a pot and bring to a boil over medium heat. Stir in salt and grits. Lower the heat and cook until the grits are thickened, stirring often. Turn the heat off, put in the plant-based cheddar cheese, peanut butter, soy chorizo, and corn and mix well. Spread the mixture into a greased baking dish and bake for 45 minutes until slightly puffed and golden brown. Serve right away.

Veggie Panini

Servings:4
Cooking Time:30 Minutes
Ingredients:
- 1 tbsp olive oil
- 1 cup sliced button mushrooms
- Salt and black pepper to taste
- 1 ripe avocado, sliced
- 2 tbsp freshly squeezed lemon juice
- 1 tbsp chopped parsley
- ½ tsp pure maple syrup
- 8 slices whole-wheat ciabatta

- 4 oz sliced plant-based Parmesan

Directions:
1. Heat the olive oil in a medium skillet over medium heat and sauté the mushrooms until softened, 5 minutes. Season with salt and black pepper. Turn the heat off.
2. Preheat a panini press to medium heat, 3 to 5 minutes. Mash the avocado in a medium bowl and mix in the lemon juice, parsley, and maple syrup. Spread the mixture on 4 bread slices, divide the mushrooms and plant-based Parmesan cheese on top. Cover with the other bread slices and brush the top with olive oil. Grill the sandwiches one after another in the heated press until golden brown, and the cheese is melted. Serve.

Morning Pecan & Pear Farro

Servings:4
Cooking Time:20 Minutes
Ingredients:
- 2 cups water
- ½ tsp salt
- 1 cup farro
- 1 tbsp plant butter
- 2 pears, peeled, cored, and chopped
- ¼ cup chopped pecans

Directions:
1. Bring water to a boil in a pot over high heat. Stir in salt and farro. Lower the heat, cover, and simmer for 15 minutes until the farro is tender and the liquid has absorbed. Turn the heat off and add in the butter, pears, and pecans. Cover and rest for 12-15 minutes. Serve immediately.

Frosty Hemp And Blackberry Smoothie Bowl

Servings: 2
Cooking Time: 10 Minutes
Ingredients:
- 2 tablespoons hemp seeds
- 1/2 cup coconut milk
- 1 cup coconut yogurt
- 1 cup blackberries, frozen
- 2 small-sized bananas, frozen
- 4 tablespoons granola

Directions:
1. In your blender, mix all ingredients, trying to keep the liquids at the bottom of the blender to help it break up the fruits.
2. Divide your smoothie between serving bowls.
3. Garnish each bowl with granola and some extra frozen berries, if desired. Serve immediately!

Pecan & Pumpkin Seed Oat Jars

Servings:5
Cooking Time:10 Minutes + Chilling Time
Ingredients:
- 2 ½ cups old-fashioned rolled oats
- 5 tbsp pumpkin seeds
- 5 tbsp chopped pecans
- 5 cups unsweetened soy milk
- 2 ½ tsp agave syrup
- Salt to taste
- 1 tsp ground cardamom
- 1 tsp ground ginger

Directions:
1. In a bowl, put oats, pumpkin seeds, pecans, soy milk, agave syrup, salt, cardamom, and ginger and toss to combine. Divide the mixture between mason jars. Seal the lids and transfer to the fridge to soak for 10-12 hours.

Creamy Sesame Bread

Servings:6
Cooking Time:40 Minutes
Ingredients:
- 4 tbsp flax seed powder
- 2/3 cup cashew cream cheese
- 4 tbsp sesame oil + for brushing
- 1 cup coconut flour
- 2 tbsp psyllium husk powder
- 1 tsp salt
- 1 tsp baking powder
- 1 tbsp sesame seeds

Directions:
1. In a bowl, mix the flax seed powder with 1 ½ cups water until smoothly combined and set aside to soak for 5 minutes. Preheat oven to 400 F. When the vegan "flax egg" is ready, beat in the cream cheese and sesame oil until well mixed.
2. Whisk in the coconut flour, psyllium husk powder, salt, and baking powder until adequately blended.
3. Grease a 9 x 5 inches baking tray with cooking spray, and spread the dough in the tray. Allow the mixture to stand for 5 minutes and then brush with some sesame oil.
4. Sprinkle with the sesame seeds and bake the dough for 30 minutes or until golden brown on top and set within. Take out the bread and allow cooling for a few minutes. Slice and serve.

Chapter 3. Snacks, Appetizers & Side Dishes

Asian-style Mushrooms

Servings: 7
Cooking Time: 25 Minutes
Ingredients:
- 8 ounces tempeh, crumbled
- 1 tablespoon tahini
- 2 tablespoons soy sauce
- 1 teaspoon agave syrup
- 1 tablespoon rice vinegar
- 1 teaspoon paprika
- 2 tablespoons fresh cilantro, chopped
- 1 tablespoon fresh mint, chopped
- 1/2 cup breadcrumbs
- 1 tablespoon sesame oil
- 20 button mushrooms

Directions:
1. Thoroughly combine the tempeh, tahini, soy sauce, agave syrup, vinegar, paprika, cilantro and mint.
2. Divide the mixture between your mushrooms. Top them with breadcrumbs. Brush your mushrooms with the sesame oil.
3. Bake the mushrooms in the preheated oven at 350 degrees F for about 20 minutes or until tender and cooked through. Bon appétit!

Crunchy Sweet Potato Bites

Servings: 4
Cooking Time: 25 Minutes
Ingredients:
- 4 sweet potatoes, peeled and grated
- 2 chia eggs
- 1/4 cup nutritional yeast
- 2 tablespoons tahini
- 2 tablespoons chickpea flour
- 1 teaspoon shallot powder
- 1 teaspoon garlic powder
- 1 teaspoon paprika
- Sea salt and ground black pepper, to taste

Directions:
1. Start by preheating your oven to 395 degrees F. Line a baking pan with parchment paper or Silpat mat.
2. Thoroughly combine all the ingredients until everything is well incorporated.
3. Roll the batter into equal balls and place them in your refrigerator for about 1 hour.
4. Bake these balls for approximately 25 minutes, turning them over halfway through the cooking time. Bon appétit!

Guacamole With Daikon

Servings:4
Cooking Time:15 Minutes
Ingredients:
- Juice of 1 lime
- 1 avocado, cubed
- ½ red onion, sliced
- 1 garlic clove, minced
- ¼ cup chopped cilantro
- 1 daikon, cut into matchsticks

Directions:
1. Place the avocado in a bowl and squeeze the lime juice. Sprinkle with salt. Mash the avocado using a fork, stir in onion, garlic, and cilantro. Serve with daikon slices.

Traditional Lebanese Mutabal

Servings: 6
Cooking Time: 10 Minutes
Ingredients:
- 1 pound eggplant
- 1 onion, chopped
- 1 tablespoon garlic paste
- 4 tablespoons tahini
- 1 tablespoon coconut oil
- 2 tablespoons lemon juice
- 1/2 teaspoon ground coriander
- 1/4 cup ground cloves
- 1 teaspoon red pepper flakes
- 1 teaspoon smoked peppers
- Sea salt and ground black pepper, to taste

Directions:
1. Roast the eggplant until the skin turns black; peel the eggplant and transfer it to the bowl of your food processor.
2. Add in the remaining ingredients. Blend until everything is well incorporated.
3. Serve with crostini or pita bread, if desired. Bon appétit!

Beet & Carrot Stir-fry

Servings:4
Cooking Time:20 Minutes
Ingredients:
- 2 beets, peeled and cut into wedges
- 3 small carrots, cut crosswise
- 2 tbsp plant butter
- 1 red onion, cut into wedges
- ½ tsp dried oregano
- 1/8 tsp salt

Directions:
1. Steam the beets and carrots in a medium safe microwave bowl until softened, 6 minutes.
2. Meanwhile, melt the butter in a large skillet and sauté the onion until softened, 3 minutes. Stir in the carrots, beets, oregano, and salt. Mix well and cook for 5 minutes. Serve warm.

Creamy Rosemary Broccoli Mash

Servings: 4
Cooking Time: 15 Minutes

Ingredients:
- 1 ½ pounds broccoli florets
- 3 tablespoons vegan butter
- 4 cloves garlic, chopped
- 2 sprigs fresh rosemary, leaves picked and chopped
- Sea salt and red pepper, to taste
- 1/4 cup soy milk, unsweetened

Directions:
1. Steam the broccoli florets for about 10 minutes; set it aside to cool.
2. In a saucepan, melt the vegan butter over a moderately high heat; now, sauté the garlic and rosemary for about 1 minute or until they are fragrant.
3. Add the broccoli florets to your food processor followed by the sautéed garlic/rosemary mixture, salt, pepper and milk. Puree until everything is well incorporated.
4. Garnish with some extra fresh herbs, if desired and serve hot. Bon appétit!

Dijon Roasted Asparagus

Servings:4
Cooking Time:35 Minutes
Ingredients:
- 2 tbsp plant butter
- 1 lb asparagus, hard part trimmed
- 2 garlic cloves, minced
- 1 tsp Dijon mustard
- 1 tbsp freshly squeezed lemon juice

Directions:
1. Melt the butter in a large skillet and sauté the asparagus until softened with some crunch, 7 minutes. Mix in the garlic and cook until fragrant, 30 seconds.
2. Meanwhile, in a small bowl, quickly whisk the mustard, lemon juice and pour the mixture over the asparagus. Cook for 2 minutes. Plate the asparagus. Serve warm.

Hummus Avocado Boats

Servings: 4
Cooking Time: 10 Minutes
Ingredients:
- 1 tablespoon fresh lemon juice
- 2 ripe avocados, halved and pitted
- 8 ounces hummus
- 1 garlic clove, minced
- 1 medium tomato, chopped
- Sea salt and ground black pepper, to taste
- 1/2 teaspoon turmeric powder
- 1/2 teaspoon cayenne pepper
- 1 tablespoon tahini

Directions:
1. Drizzle the fresh lemon juice over the avocado halves.
2. Mix the hummus, garlic, tomato, salt, black pepper, turmeric powder, cayenne pepper and tahini. Spoon the filling into your avocados.
3. Serve immediately.

Greek-style Eggplant Skillet

Servings: 4
Cooking Time: 15 Minutes
Ingredients:

- 4 tablespoons olive oil
- 1 ½ pounds eggplant, peeled and sliced
- 1 teaspoon garlic, minced
- 1 tomato, crushed
- Sea salt and ground black pepper, to taste
- 1 teaspoon cayenne pepper
- 1/2 teaspoon dried oregano
- 1/4 teaspoon ground bay leaf
- 2 ounces Kalamata olives, pitted and sliced

Directions:
1. Heat the oil in a sauté pan over medium-high flame.
2. Then, sauté the eggplant for about 9 minutes or until just tender.
3. Add in the remaining ingredients, cover and continue to cook for 2 to 3 minutes more or until thoroughly cooked. Serve warm.

Yukon Gold Mashed Potatoes

Servings: 5
Cooking Time: 25 Minutes
Ingredients:

- 2 pounds Yukon Gold potatoes, peeled and diced
- 1 clove garlic, pressed
- Sea salt and red pepper flakes, to taste
- 3 tablespoons vegan butter
- 1/2 cup soy milk
- 2 tablespoons scallions, sliced

Directions:
1. Cover the potatoes with an inch or two of cold water. Cook the potatoes in gently boiling water for about 20 minutes.
2. Then, puree the potatoes, along with the garlic, salt, red pepper, butter and milk, to your desired consistency.
3. Serve garnished with fresh scallions. Bon appétit!

Easy Lebanese Toum

Servings: 6
Cooking Time: 10 Minutes
Ingredients:

- 2 heads garlic
- 1 teaspoon coarse sea salt
- 1 ½ cups olive oil
- 1 lemon, freshly squeezed
- 2 cups carrots, cut into matchsticks

Directions:
1. Puree the garlic cloves and salt in your food processor of a high-speed blender until creamy and smooth, scraping down the sides of the bowl.
2. Gradually and slowly, add in the olive oil and lemon juice, alternating between these two ingredients to create a fluffy sauce.
3. Blend until the sauce has thickened. Serve with carrot sticks and enjoy!

Muhammara Dip With A Twist

Servings: 9
Cooking Time: 35 Minutes
Ingredients:

- 3 red bell peppers
- 5 tablespoons olive oil
- 2 garlic cloves, chopped
- 1 tomato, chopped
- 3/4 cup bread crumbs
- 2 tablespoons molasses
- 1 teaspoon ground cumin
- 1/4 sunflower seeds, toasted
- 1 Maras pepper, minced
- 2 tablespoons tahini
- Sea salt and red pepper, to taste

Directions:
1. Start by preheating your oven to 400 degrees F.
2. Place the peppers on a parchment-lined baking pan. Bake for about 30 minutes; peel the peppers and transfer them to your food processor.
3. Meanwhile, heat 2 tablespoons of the olive oil in a frying pan over medium-high heat. Sauté the garlic and tomatoes for about 5 minutes or until they've softened.
4. Add the sautéed vegetables to your food processor. Add in the remaining ingredients and process until creamy and smooth.
5. Bon appétit!

Mediterranean-style Green Beans

Servings: 4
Cooking Time: 20 Minutes
Ingredients:

- 2 tablespoons olive oil
- 1 red bell pepper, seeded and diced
- 1 ½ pounds green beans
- 4 garlic cloves, minced
- 1/2 teaspoon mustard seeds
- 1/2 teaspoon fennel seeds
- 1 teaspoon dried dill weed
- 2 tomatoes, pureed
- 1 cup cream of celery soup
- 1 teaspoon Italian herb mix
- 1 teaspoon cayenne pepper
- Salt and freshly ground black pepper

Directions:
1. Heat the olive oil in a saucepan over medium flame. Once hot, fry the peppers and green beans for about 5 minutes, stirring periodically to promote even cooking.
2. Add in the garlic, mustard seeds, fennel seeds and dill and continue sautéing an additional 1 minute or until fragrant.
3. Add in the pureed tomatoes, cream of celery soup, Italian herb mix, cayenne pepper, salt and black pepper. Continue to simmer, covered, for about 9 minutes or until the green beans are tender.
4. Taste, adjust the seasonings and serve warm. Bon appétit!

Sautéed Cauliflower With Sesame Seeds

Servings: 4
Cooking Time: 15 Minutes
Ingredients:
- 1 cup vegetable broth
- 1 ½ pounds cauliflower florets
- 4 tablespoons olive oil
- 2 scallion stalks, chopped
- 4 garlic cloves, minced
- Sea salt and freshly ground black pepper, to taste
- 2 tablespoons sesame seeds, lightly toasted

Directions:
1. In a large saucepan, bring the vegetable broth to a boil; then, add in the cauliflower and cook for about 6 minutes or until fork-tender; reserve.
2. Then, heat the olive oil until sizzling; now, sauté the scallions and garlic for about 1 minute or until tender and aromatic.
3. Add in the reserved cauliflower, followed by salt and black pepper; continue to simmer for about 5 minutes or until heated through
4. Garnish with toasted sesame seeds and serve immediately. Bon appétit!

Aromatic Sautéed Swiss Chard

Servings: 4
Cooking Time: 15 Minutes
Ingredients:
- 2 tablespoons vegan butter
- 1 onion, chopped
- 2 cloves garlic, sliced
- Sea salt and ground black pepper, to season
- 1 ½ pounds Swiss chard, torn into pieces, tough stalks removed
- 1 cup vegetable broth
- 1 bay leaf
- 1 thyme sprig
- 2 rosemary sprigs
- 1/2 teaspoon mustard seeds
- 1 teaspoon celery seeds

Directions:
1. In a saucepan, melt the vegan butter over medium-high heat.
2. Then, sauté the onion for about 3 minutes or until tender and translucent; sauté the garlic for about 1 minute until aromatic.
3. Add in the remaining ingredients and turn the heat to a simmer; let it simmer, covered, for about 10 minutes or until everything is cooked through. Bon appétit!

Carrot Nori Rolls

Servings:4
Cooking Time:15 Minutes
Ingredients:
- 2 tbsp almond butter
- 2 tbsp tamari
- 4 standard nori sheets

- 1 green bell pepper, sliced
- 1 tbsp pickled ginger
- ½ cup grated carrots

Directions:
1. Preheat oven to 350 F.
2. Whisk the almond butter and tamari until smooth and thick.
3. Place a nori sheet on a flat surface with the rough side facing up. Spoon a bit of the tamari mixture at the other side of the nori sheet, and spread on all sides. Put bell pepper slices, carrots, and ginger in a layer at the other end of the sheet. Fold up in the tahini direction to seal. Repeat the process with the remaining sheets. Arrange on a baking tray and bake for about 10 minutes until browned and crispy. Allow cooling for a few minutes before slicing into 4 pieces.

Roman Balsamic Tomato Bruschetta

Servings:12
Cooking Time:20 Minutes
Ingredients:
- 3 tomatoes, chopped
- ¼ cup chopped fresh basil
- 1 tbsp olive oil
- 1 whole-wheat baguette, sliced
- 1 garlic clove, halved
- Balsamic vinegar for garnish

Directions:
1. Preheat oven to 420 F.
2. Mix the tomatoes, basil, olive oil, and salt in a bowl. Set aside. Arrange baguette slices on a baking sheet and toast for 6 minutes on both sides until brown. Spread the garlic over the bread and top with the tomato mixture. Serve right away.

Parmesan Broccoli Tots

Servings:4
Cooking Time:30 Minutes
Ingredients:
- 1 tbsp flaxseed powder
- 1 head broccoli, cut into florets
- 2/3 cup toasted almond flour
- 2 garlic cloves, minced
- 2 cups grated plant-based Parmesan
- Salt to taste

Directions:
1. Preheat the oven to 350 F and line a baking sheet with parchment paper.
2. In a small bowl, mix the flaxseed powder with the 3 tbsp water and allow thickening for 5 minutes to make the vegan "flax egg". Place the broccoli in a safe microwave bowl, sprinkle with 2 tbsp of water, and steam in the microwave for 1 minute or until softened. Transfer the broccoli to a food processor and add the vegan "flax egg," almond flour, garlic, plant cheese, and salt. Blend until coarsely smooth.
3. Pour the mixture into a bowl and form 2-inch oblong balls from the mixture. Place the tots on the baking sheet and bake in the oven for 15 to 20 minutes or until firm and compacted. Remove the tots from the oven and serve warm with tomato dipping sauce.

Easy Roasted Kohlrabi

Servings: 4
Cooking Time: 30 Minutes
Ingredients:
- 1 pound kohlrabi bulbs, peeled and sliced
- 4 tablespoons olive oil
- 1/2 teaspoon mustard seeds
- 1 teaspoon celery seeds
- 1 teaspoon dried marjoram
- 1 teaspoon granulated garlic, minced
- Sea salt and ground black pepper, to taste
- 2 tablespoons nutritional yeast

Directions:
1. Start by preheating your oven to 450 degrees F.
2. Toss the kohlrabi with the olive oil and spices until well coated. Arrange the kohlrabi in a single layer on a parchment-lined roasting pan.
3. Bake the kohlrabi in the preheated oven for about 15 minutes; stir them and continue to cook an additional 15 minutes.
4. Sprinkle nutritional yeast over the warm kohlrabi and serve immediately. Bon appétit!

Louisiana-style Sweet Potato Chips

Servings:4
Cooking Time:55 Minutes
Ingredients:
- 2 sweet potatoes, peeled and sliced
- 2 tbsp melted plant butter
- 1 tbsp Cajun seasoning

Directions:
1. Preheat the oven to 400 F and line a baking sheet with parchment paper.
2. In a medium bowl, add the sweet potatoes, salt, plant butter, and Cajun seasoning. Toss well. Spread the chips on the baking sheet, making sure not to overlap, and bake in the oven for 50 minutes to 1 hour or until crispy. Remove the sheet and pour the chips into a large bowl. Allow cooling and enjoy.

Grilled Tofu Mayo Sandwiches

Servings:2
Cooking Time:15 Minutes
Ingredients:
- ¼ cup tofu mayonnaise
- 2 slices whole-grain bread
- ¼ cucumber, sliced
- ½ cup lettuce, chopped
- ½ tomato, sliced
- 1 tsp olive oil, divided

Directions:
1. Spread the vegan mayonnaise over a bread slice, top with the cucumber, lettuce, and tomato and finish with the other slice. Heat the oil in a skillet over medium heat. Place the sandwich and grill for 3 minutes, then flip over and cook for a further 3 minutes. Cut the sandwich in half and serve.

Strawberries Stuffed With Banana Cream

Servings:4
Cooking Time:10 Minutes
Ingredients:
- 12 strawberries, heads removed
- ¼ cup cashew cream
- ¼ tsp banana extract
- 1 tbsp unsweetened coconut flakes

Directions:
1. Use a teaspoon to scoop out some of the strawberries pulp to create a hole within. In a small bowl, mix the cashew cream, banana extract, and maple syrup. Spoon the mixture into the strawberries and garnish with the coconut flakes. Serve.

Olive Oil Garlic Crostini

Servings: 4
Cooking Time: 10 Minutes
Ingredients:
- 1 whole-grain baguette, sliced
- 4 tablespoons extra-virgin olive oil
- 1/2 teaspoon sea salt
- 3 cloves garlic, halved

Directions:
1. Preheat your broiler.
2. Brush each slice of bread with the olive oil and sprinkle with sea salt. Place under the preheated broiler for about 2 minutes or until lightly toasted.
3. Rub each slice of bread with the garlic and serve. Bon appétit!

Easy Za'atar Popcorn

Servings: 2
Cooking Time: 10 Minutes
Ingredients:
- 2 tablespoons coconut oil
- 1/4 cup of popcorn kernels
- 1 tablespoon za'atar spice blend
- Sea salt, to taste

Directions:
1. Heat the oil in a thick-bottomed saucepan over medium-high heat.
2. Once hot, add the popcorn kernels in an even layer.
3. Cover the saucepan, remove from the heat and wait for 30 seconds.
4. Return the saucepan to the heat, shaking it occasionally. Toss the prepared popcorn with the spices. Bon appétit!

Green Salsa

Servings:4
Cooking Time:15 Minutes
Ingredients:
- 3 large heirloom tomatoes, chopped
- 1 green onion, finely chopped
- ½ bunch parsley, chopped
- 2 garlic cloves, minced
- 1 Jalapeño pepper, minced

- Juice of 1 lime
- ¼ cup olive oil Salt to taste
- Whole-grain tortilla chips

Directions:
1. Combine the tomatoes, green onion, parsley, garlic, jalapeño pepper, lime juice, olive oil, and salt in a bowl. Let it rest for 10 minutes at room temperature. Serve with tortilla chips.

Kale & Hummus Pinwheels

Servings:4
Cooking Time:10 Minutes
Ingredients:
- 3 whole-grain flour tortillas
- 1 cup kale, chopped
- ¾ cup hummus
- ¾ cup shredded carrots

Directions:
1. Spread the hummus over the tortillas and top with kale and carrots. Fold the edges over the filling and roll up to make burritos. Cut into pinwheels and serve.

Avocado With Tangy Ginger Dressing

Servings: 4
Cooking Time: 10 Minutes
Ingredients:
- 2 avocados, pitted and halved
- 1 clove garlic, pressed
- 1 teaspoon fresh ginger, peeled and minced
- 2 tablespoons balsamic vinegar
- 4 tablespoons extra-virgin olive oil
- Kosher salt and ground black pepper, to taste

Directions:
1. Place the avocado halves on a serving platter.
2. Mix the garlic, ginger, vinegar, olive oil, salt and black pepper in a small bowl. Divide the sauce between the avocado halves.
3. Bon appétit!

Roasted Pepper And Tomato Dip

Servings: 10
Cooking Time: 35 Minutes
Ingredients:
- 4 red bell peppers
- 4 tomatoes
- 4 tablespoons olive oil
- 1 red onion, chopped
- 4 garlic cloves
- 4 ounces canned garbanzo beans, drained
- Sea salt and ground black pepper, to taste

Directions:
1. Start by preheating your oven to 400 degrees F.
2. Place the peppers and tomatoes on a parchment-lined baking pan. Bake for about 30 minutes; peel the peppers and transfer them to your food processor along with the roasted tomatoes.
3. Meanwhile, heat 2 tablespoons of the olive oil in a frying pan over medium-high heat. Sauté the onion and garlic for about 5 minutes or until they've softened.

4. Add the sautéed vegetables to your food processor. Add in the garbanzo beans, salt, pepper and the remaining olive oil; process until creamy and smooth.
5. Bon appétit!

French Haricots Verts

Servings: 4
Cooking Time: 10 Minutes
Ingredients:
- 1 ½ cups vegetable broth
- 1 Roma tomato, pureed
- 1 ½ pounds Haricots Verts, trimmed
- 4 tablespoons olive oil
- 2 garlic cloves, minced
- 1/2 teaspoon red pepper
- 1/2 teaspoon cumin seeds
- 1/2 teaspoon dried oregano
- Sea salt and freshly ground black pepper, to taste
- 1 tablespoon fresh lemon juice

Directions:
1. Bring the vegetable broth and pureed tomato to a boil. Add in the Haricots Verts and let it cook for about 5 minutes until Haricots Verts are crisp-tender; reserve.
2. In a saucepan, heat the olive oil over medium-high heat; sauté the garlic for 1 minute or until aromatic.
3. Add in the spices and reserved green beans; let it cook for about 3 minutes until cooked through.
4. Serve with a few drizzles of the fresh lemon juice. Bon appétit!

Lettuce Boats With Avocado Salsa

Servings: 5
Cooking Time: 10 Minutes
Ingredients:
- 1 large avocado, pitted, peeled and diced
- 1 large tomato, peeled and chopped
- 1 small onion, chopped
- 1/4 cup fresh cilantro, chopped
- 1 poblano pepper, minced
- 1/2 teaspoon Mexican oregano
- Sea salt and red pepper, to taste
- 1 head Romaine lettuce, leaves separated
- 1 tablespoon fresh lime juice

Directions:
1. Thoroughly combine the avocado, tomato, onion, cilantro, poblano pepper, Mexican oregano, salt and black pepper.
2. Divide the filling between lettuce leaves, drizzle lime juice over them and serve immediately.
3. Bon appétit!

Roasted Carrots With Herbs

Servings: 4
Cooking Time: 25 Minutes
Ingredients:
- 2 pounds carrots, trimmed and halved lengthwise
- 4 tablespoons olive oil
- 1 teaspoon granulated garlic

- 1 teaspoon paprika
- Sea salt and freshly ground black pepper
- 2 tablespoons fresh cilantro, chopped
- 2 tablespoons fresh parsley, chopped
- 2 tablespoons fresh chives, chopped

Directions:
1. Start by preheating your oven to 400 degrees F.
2. Toss the carrots with the olive oil, granulated garlic, paprika, salt and black pepper. Arrange them in a single layer on a parchment-lined roasting sheet.
3. Roast the carrots in the preheated oven for about 20 minutes, until fork-tender.
4. Toss the carrots with the fresh herbs and serve immediately. Bon appétit!

Mixed Seed Crackers

Servings:6
Cooking Time:57 Minutes
Ingredients:
- 1⁄3 cup sesame seed flour
- 1⁄3 cup pumpkin seeds
- 1⁄3 cup sunflower seeds
- 1⁄3 cup sesame seeds
- 1⁄3 cup chia seeds
- 1 tbsp psyllium husk powder
- 1 tsp salt
- ¼ cup plant butter, melted
- 1 cup boiling water

Directions:
1. Preheat oven to 300 F.
2. Combine the sesame seed flour with pumpkin seeds, sunflower seeds, sesame seeds, chia seeds, psyllium husk powder, and salt. Pour in the plant butter and hot water and mix the ingredients until a dough forms with a gel-like consistency.
3. Line a baking sheet with parchment paper and place the dough on the sheet. Cover the dough with another parchment paper and, with a rolling pin, flatten the dough into the baking sheet. Remove the parchment paper on top.
4. Tuck the baking sheet in the oven and bake for 45 minutes. Allow the crackers to cool and dry in the oven, about 10 minutes. After, remove the sheet and break the crackers into small pieces. Serve.

Baked Zucchini Chips

Servings: 7
Cooking Time: 1 Hour 30 Minutes
Ingredients:
- 1 pound zucchini, cut into 1/8-inch thick slices
- 2 tablespoons olive oil
- 1/2 teaspoon dried oregano
- 1/2 teaspoon dried basil
- 1/2 teaspoon red pepper flakes
- Sea salt and ground black pepper, to taste

Directions:
1. Toss the zucchini with the remaining ingredients.
2. Lay the zucchini slices in a single layer on a parchment-lined baking pan.

3. Bake at 235 degrees F for about 90 minutes until crisp and golden. Zucchini chips will crisp up as it cools.
4. Bon appétit!

Primavera Lettuce Rolls

Servings:4
Cooking Time:20 Minutes
Ingredients:
- 1 tbsp olive oil
- 2 oz rice noodles
- 2 tbsp Thai basil, chopped
- 2 tbsp cilantro, chopped
- 1 garlic clove, minced
- 1 tbsp minced fresh ginger
- Juice of ½ lime
- 2 tbsp soy sauce
- 1 avocado, sliced
- 2 carrots, peeled and julienned
- 8 leaves butter lettuce

Directions:
1. In a bowl, place the noodles in hot water and let them sit for 4 minutes. Drain and mix with the olive oil. Allow cooling.
2. Combine the basil, cilantro, garlic, ginger, lime juice, and soy sauce in another bowl. Add in cooked noodles, avocado, and carrots. Divide the mixture between the lettuce leaves. Fold in and secure with toothpicks. Serve right away.

Curry Mango-tofu Pitas

Servings:4
Cooking Time:15 Minutes
Ingredients:
- 4 pieces of whole-wheat pita bread, halved
- 1 lb extra-firm tofu, crumbled
- ½ cup tofu mayonnaise
- ¼ cup chopped mango chutney
- 2 tsp Dijon mustard
- 1 tbsp curry powder
- Salt to taste
- ⅛ tsp ground cayenne
- ¾ cup shredded carrots
- 1 fennel bulb, sliced
- ¼ cup minced red onion
- 4 lettuce leaves

Directions:
1. In a bowl, place tofu, mayonnaise, chutney, mustard, curry powder, salt, and cayenne pepper and stir to combine. Mix in the carrots, fennel, and onion. Let sit in the fridge for 20 minutes. Cover the pieces of the pita bread with lettuce leaves and scoop some of the tofu mixture in. Serve immediately.

Spicy Nut Burgers

Servings:4
Cooking Time:20 Minutes
Ingredients:
- ¾ cup chopped walnuts
- ¾ cup chopped cashews
- 1 medium carrot, grated
- 1 small onion, chopped
- 1 garlic clove, minced
- 1 serrano pepper, minced
- ¾ cup old-fashioned oats
- ¾ cup breadcrumbs
- 2 tbsp minced fresh cilantro
- ½ tsp ground coriander
- Salt and black pepper to taste
- 2 tsp fresh lime juice
- Canola oil for frying
- 4 sandwich rolls
- Lettuce leaves for garnish

Directions:
1. Pulse walnuts, cashews, carrot, onion, garlic, serrano pepper, oats, breadcrumbs, cilantro, coriander, lime juice, salt, and pepper in a food processor until well mixed. Remove and form into 4 burgers.
2. Warm the oil in a skillet over medium heat. Cook the burgers for 5 minutes per side, until golden brown. Serve in sandwich rolls with lettuce and a dressing of your choice.

Maple-pumpkin Cookies

Servings:12
Cooking Time:70 Minutes
Ingredients:
- 1 pumpkin, sliced
- 3 tbsp melted coconut oil, divided
- 1 tbsp maple syrup
- 1 cup whole-wheat flour
- 2 tsp baking powder
- Sea salt to taste

Directions:
1. Preheat oven to 360 F.
2. Place the pumpkin in a greased tray and bake for 45 minutes until tender. Let cool before mashing it. Mix the mashed pumpkin, 1 ½ tbsp of coconut oil, and maple syrup in a bowl.
3. Combine the flour and baking powder in another bowl. Fold in the pumpkin mixture and whisk with a fork until smooth.
4. Divide the mixture into balls. Arrange spaced out on a lined with a wax paper baking sheet; flatten the balls until a cookie shape is formed. Brush with the remaining melted coconut oil. Bake for 10 minutes, until they rise and become gold. Serve.

Spicy Pistachio Dip

Servings:4
Cooking Time:10 Minutes
Ingredients:
- 3 oz toasted pistachios + for garnish

- 3 tbsp coconut cream
- ¼ cup water
- Juice of half a lemon
- ½ tsp smoked paprika
- Cayenne pepper to taste
- ½ tsp salt
- ½ cup olive oil

Directions:
1. Pour the pistachios, coconut cream, water, lemon juice, paprika, cayenne pepper, and salt. Puree the ingredients at high speed until smooth. Add the olive oil and puree a little further. Manage the consistency of the dip by adding more oil or water. Spoon the dip into little bowls, garnish with some pistachios, and serve with julienned celery and carrots.

Thai-style Braised Kale

Servings: 4
Cooking Time: 10 Minutes
Ingredients:
- 1 cup water
- 1 ½ pounds kale, tough stems and ribs removed, torn into pieces
- 2 tablespoons sesame oil
- 1 teaspoon fresh garlic, pressed
- 1 teaspoon ginger, peeled and minced
- 1 Thai chili, chopped
- 1/2 teaspoon turmeric powder
- 1/2 cup coconut milk
- Kosher salt and ground black pepper, to taste

Directions:
1. In a large saucepan, bring the water to a rapid boil. Add in the kale and let it cook until bright, about 3 minutes. Drain, rinse and squeeze dry.
2. Wipe the saucepan with paper towels and preheat the sesame oil over a moderate heat. Once hot, cook the garlic, ginger and chili for approximately 1 minute or so, until fragrant.
3. Add in the kale and turmeric powder and continue to cook for a further 1 minute or until heated through.
4. Gradually pour in the coconut milk, salt and black pepper; continue to simmer until the liquid has thickened. Taste, adjust the seasonings and serve hot. Bon appétit!

Soy Chorizo Stuffed Cabbage Rolls

Servings:4
Cooking Time:35 Minutes
Ingredients:
- ¼ cup coconut oil, divided
- 1 large white onion, chopped
- 3 cloves garlic, minced, divided
- 1 cup crumbled soy chorizo
- 1 cup cauliflower rice
- 1 can tomato sauce
- 1 tsp dried oregano
- 1 tsp dried basil
- 8 full green cabbage leaves

Directions:

1. Heat half of the coconut oil in a saucepan over medium heat.
2. Add half of the onion, half of the garlic, and all of the soy chorizo. Sauté for 5 minutes or until the chorizo has browned further, and the onion softened. Stir in the cauli rice, season with salt and black pepper, and cook for 3 to 4 minutes. Turn the heat off and set the pot aside.
3. Heat the remaining oil in a saucepan over medium heat, add, and sauté the remaining onion and garlic until fragrant and soft. Pour in the tomato sauce, and season with salt, black pepper, oregano, and basil. Add ¼ cup water and simmer the sauce for 10 minutes.
4. While the sauce cooks, lay the cabbage leaves on a flat surface and spoon the soy chorizo mixture into the middle of each leaf. Roll the leaves to secure the filling. Place the cabbage rolls in the tomato sauce and cook further for 10 minutes. When ready, serve the cabbage rolls with sauce over mashed broccoli or with mixed seed bread.

Paprika Roasted Nuts

Servings:4
Cooking Time:10 Minutes
Ingredients:
- 8 oz walnuts and pecans
- 1 tsp salt
- 1 tbsp coconut oil
- 1 tsp cumin powder
- 1 tsp paprika powder

Directions:
1. In a bowl, mix walnuts, pecans, salt, coconut oil, cumin powder, and paprika powder until the nuts are well coated with spice and oil. Pour the mixture into a pan and toast while stirring continually. Once the nuts are fragrant and brown, transfer to a bowl. Allow cooling and serve with chilled berry juice.

Sautéed Carrots With Sesame Seeds

Servings: 4
Cooking Time: 10 Minutes
Ingredients:
- 1/3 cup vegetable broth
- 2 pounds carrots, trimmed and cut into sticks
- 4 tablespoons sesame oil
- 1 teaspoon garlic, chopped
- Himalayan salt and freshly ground black pepper, to taste
- 1 teaspoon cayenne pepper
- 2 tablespoons fresh parsley, chopped
- 2 tablespoons sesame seeds

Directions:
1. In a large saucepan, bring the vegetable broth to a boil. Turn the heat to medium-low. Add in the carrots and continue to cook, covered, for about 8 minutes, until the carrots are crisp-tender.
2. Heat the sesame oil over medium-high heat; now, sauté the garlic for 30 seconds or until aromatic. Add in the salt, black pepper and cayenne pepper.
3. In a small skillet, toast the sesame seeds for 1 minute or until just fragrant and golden.

4. To serve, garnish the sautéed carrots with parsley and toasted sesame seeds. Bon appétit!

Swiss Chard & Pecan Stuffed Mushrooms

Servings:4
Cooking Time:20 Minutes
Ingredients:
- 8 oz white mushrooms, stems chopped and reserved
- 2 tbsp olive oil
- 1 garlic clove, minced
- 1 cup cooked Swiss chard
- 1 cup finely chopped pecans
- ½ cup breadcrumbs
- Salt and black pepper to taste

Directions:
1. Preheat oven to 390 F.
2. Warm oil in a skillet over medium heat, add the mushroom stems and garlic and sauté for 3 minutes. Mix in chard, pecans, breadcrumbs, salt, and pepper. Cook for another 2 minutes, stirring occasionally.
3. Divide the resulting mixture between the mushroom caps and arrange on a greased baking dish. Bake for 15 minutes, until golden. Serve immediately.

Kentucky Cauliflower With Mashed Parsnips

Servings:6
Cooking Time:35 Minutes
Ingredients:
- ½ cup unsweetened almond milk
- ¼ cup coconut flour
- ¼ tsp cayenne pepper
- ½ cup whole-grain breadcrumbs
- ½ cup grated plant-based mozzarella
- 30 oz cauliflower florets
- 1 lb parsnips, peeled and quartered
- 3 tbsp melted plant butter
- A pinch of nutmeg
- 1 tsp cumin powder
- 1 cup coconut cream
- 2 tbsp sesame oil

Directions:
1. Preheat oven to 425 F and line a baking sheet with parchment paper.
2. In a small bowl, combine almond milk, coconut flour, and cayenne pepper. In another bowl, mix salt, breadcrumbs, and plant-based mozzarella cheese. Dip each cauliflower floret into the milk mixture, coating properly, and then into the cheese mixture. Place the breaded cauliflower on the baking sheet and bake in the oven for 30 minutes, turning once after 15 minutes.
3. Make slightly salted water in a saucepan and add the parsnips. Bring to boil over medium heat for 15 minutes or until the parsnips are fork-tender. Drain and transfer to a bowl. Add in melted plant butter, cumin powder, nutmeg, and coconut cream. Puree the ingredients using an immersion blender until smooth. Spoon the parsnip mash

into serving plates and drizzle with some sesame oil. Serve with the baked cauliflower when ready.

Roasted Asparagus With Sesame Seeds

Servings: 4
Cooking Time: 25 Minutes
Ingredients:
- 1 ½ pounds asparagus, trimmed
- 4 tablespoons extra-virgin olive oil
- Sea salt and ground black pepper, to taste
- 1/2 teaspoon dried oregano
- 1/2 teaspoon dried basil
- 1 teaspoon red pepper flakes, crushed
- 4 tablespoons sesame seeds
- 2 tablespoons fresh chives, roughly chopped

Directions:
1. Start by preheating the oven to 400 degrees F. Then, line a baking sheet with parchment paper.
2. Toss the asparagus with the olive oil, salt, black pepper, oregano, basil and red pepper flakes. Now, arrange your asparagus in a single layer on the prepared baking sheet.
3. Roast your asparagus for approximately 20 minutes.
4. Sprinkle sesame seeds over your asparagus and continue to bake an additional 5 minutes or until the asparagus spears are crisp-tender and the sesame seeds are lightly toasted.
5. Garnish with fresh chives and serve warm. Bon appétit!

Authentic Lebanese Dip

Servings: 12
Cooking Time: 10 Minutes
Ingredients:
- 2 can chickpeas/garbanzo beans
- 4 tablespoons lemon juice
- 4 tablespoons tahini
- 2 tablespoons olive oil
- 1 teaspoon ginger-garlic paste
- 1 teaspoon Lebanese 7 spice blend
- Sea salt and ground black pepper, to taste
- 1/3 cup chickpea liquid

Directions:
1. Blitz the chickpeas, lemon juice, tahini, olive oil, ginger-garlic paste and spices in your blender or food processor.
2. Blend until your desired consistency is reached, gradually adding the chickpea liquid.
3. Place in your refrigerator until ready to serve. Serve with veggie sticks, if desired. Bon appétit!

Mashed Root Vegetables

Servings: 5
Cooking Time: 25 Minutes
Ingredients:
- 1 pound russet potatoes, peeled and cut into chunks
- 1/2 pound parsnips, trimmed and diced
- 1/2 pound carrots, trimmed and diced
- 4 tablespoons vegan butter
- 1 teaspoon dried oregano
- 1/2 teaspoon dried dill weed

- 1/2 teaspoon dried marjoram
- 1 teaspoon dried basil

Directions:
1. Cover the vegetables with the water by 1 inch. Bring to a boil and cook for about 25 minutes until they've softened; drain.
2. Mash the vegetables with the remaining ingredients, adding cooking liquid, as needed.
3. Serve warm and enjoy!

Peanut Butter Date Bites

Servings: 2
Cooking Time: 5 Minutes
Ingredients:
- 8 fresh dates, pitted and cut into halves
- 8 teaspoons peanut butter
- 1/4 teaspoon ground cinnamon

Directions:
1. Divide the peanut butter between the date halves.
2. Dust with cinnamon and serve immediately. Bon appétit!

Za'atar Roasted Zucchini Sticks

Servings: 5
Cooking Time: 1 Hour 35 Minutes
Ingredients:
- 1 ½ pounds zucchini, cut into sticks lengthwise
- 2 garlic cloves, crushed
- 2 tablespoons extra-virgin olive oil
- 1 teaspoon za'atar spice
- Kosher salt and ground black pepper, to taste

Directions:
1. Toss the zucchini with the remaining ingredients.
2. Lay the zucchini sticks in a single layer on a parchment-lined baking pan.
3. Bake at 235 degrees F for about 90 minutes until crisp and golden. Zucchini sticks will crisp up as they cool.
4. Bon appétit!

Cannellini Bean Dipping Sauce

Servings: 6
Cooking Time: 10 Minutes
Ingredients:
- 10 ounces canned cannellini beans, drained
- 1 clove garlic, minced
- 2 roasted peppers, sliced
- Sea freshly ground black pepper, to taste
- 1/2 teaspoon ground cumin
- 1/2 teaspoon mustard seeds
- 1/2 teaspoon ground bay leaves
- 3 tablespoons tahini
- 2 tablespoons fresh Italian parsley, chopped

Directions:
1. Place all the ingredients, except for the parsley, in the bowl of your blender or food processor. Blitz until well blended.
2. Transfer the sauce to a serving bowl and garnish with fresh parsley.
3. Serve with pita wedges, tortilla chips, or veggie sticks, if desired. Enjoy!

Easy Zucchini Skillet

Servings: 4
Cooking Time: 10 Minutes
Ingredients:
- 2 tablespoons vegan butter
- 1 shallot, thinly sliced
- 1 teaspoon garlic, minced
- 1 ½ pounds zucchini, sliced
- Flaky sea salt and ground black pepper, to taste
- 1 teaspoon paprika
- 1/2 teaspoon cayenne pepper
- 1/2 teaspoon dried thyme
- 1/2 teaspoon celery seeds
- 1/2 teaspoon coriander pepper
- 2 tablespoons nutritional yeast

Directions:
1. In a saucepan, melt the vegan butter over medium-high heat.
2. Once hot, sauté the shallot for about 3 minutes or until tender. Then, sauté the garlic for about 1 minute until aromatic.
3. Add in the zucchini, along with the spices and continue to sauté for 6 minutes more until tender.
4. Taste and adjust the seasonings. Top with nutritional yeast and serve. Bon appétit!

Indian-style Roasted Chickpeas

Servings: 8
Cooking Time: 10 Minutes
Ingredients:
- 2 cups canned chickpeas, drained
- 2 tablespoons olive oil
- 1/2 teaspoon garlic powder
- 1/2 teaspoon paprika
- 1 teaspoon curry powder
- 1 teaspoon garam masala
- Sea salt and red pepper, to taste

Directions:
1. Pat the chickpeas dry using paper towels. Drizzle olive oil over the chickpeas.
2. Roast the chickpeas in the preheated oven at 400 degrees F for about 25 minutes, tossing them once or twice.
3. Toss your chickpeas with the spices and enjoy!

Homemade Seedy Bars

Servings:6
Cooking Time:55 Minutes
Ingredients:
- ¾ cup pumpkin seeds
- ½ cup sunflower seeds
- ½ cup sesame seeds
- ¼ cup poppy seeds
- 1 tsp minced garlic
- 1 tsp tamari sauce
- 1 tsp vegan Worcestershire sauce
- ½ tsp ground cayenne pepper
- ½ tsp dried oregano

Directions:
1. Preheat oven to 320 F. Line with parchment paper a baking sheet. Mix the pumpkin seeds, sunflower seeds, sesame seeds, poppy seeds, garlic, tamari, Worcestershire sauce, cayenne, oregano, and ½ cup water in a bowl. Spread on the baking sheet and bake for 25 minutes. Turn the seeds and bake for another 20-25 minutes. Allow cooling before slicing into bars.

Thai Stir-fried Spinach

Servings: 4
Cooking Time: 15 Minutes
Ingredients:
- 2 tablespoons sesame oil
- 1 onion, chopped
- 1 carrot, trimmed and chopped
- 1 Bird's eye chili pepper, minced
- 2 cloves garlic, minced
- 1 ½ pounds spinach leaves, torn into pieces
- 1/3 cup vegetable broth
- 2/3 cup coconut milk, unsweetened

Directions:
1. In a saucepan, heat the sesame oil over medium-high heat.
2. Then, sauté the onion and carrot for about 3 minutes or until tender. Then, sauté the garlic and Bird's eye chili for about 1 minute until aromatic.
3. Add in the broth and spinach and bring to a boil.
4. Turn the heat to a simmer and continue to cook for 5 minutes longer.
5. Add in the coconut milk and simmer for a further 5 minutes or until everything is cooked through. Bon appétit!

Chickpea & Pecan Balls

Servings:6
Cooking Time:35 Minutes
Ingredients:
- 1 can chickpeas
- ½ cup chopped pecans
- ¼ cup minced green onions
- 1 garlic clove, minced
- 3 tbsp whole-wheat flour
- 3 tbsp breadcrumbs
- 4 tbsp hot sauce ¼ tsp salt
- ⅛ tsp ground cayenne pepper
- ¼ cup plant butter, melted

Directions:
1. Preheat oven to 350 F.
2. In a food processor, put the chickpeas, pecans, green onions, garlic, flour, breadcrumbs, 2 tbsp of hot sauce, salt, and cayenne pepper. Pulse until chunky texture is formed.
3. Shape the mixture into 1-inch balls. Arrange on a greased baking pan and bake for 25-30 minutes, turning halfway through to ensure they cook evenly. In a bowl, whisk the remaining hot sauce with melted plant butter. Remove the balls to a serving plate and pour the hot butter all over and serve.

Onion Rings & Kale Dip

Servings:4
Cooking Time:35 Minutes
Ingredients:
- 1 onion, sliced into rings
- 1 tbsp flaxseed meal + 3 tbsp water
- 1 cup almond flour
- ½ cup grated plant-based Parmesan
- 2 tsp garlic powder
- ½ tbsp sweet paprika powder
- 2 oz chopped kale
- 2 tbsp olive oil
- 2 tbsp dried cilantro
- 1 tbsp dried oregano
- Salt and black pepper to taste
- 1 cup tofu mayonnaise
- 4 tbsp coconut cream
- Juice of ½ a lemon

Directions:
1. Preheat oven to 400 F. In a bowl, mix the flaxseed meal and water and leave the mixture to thicken and fully absorb for 5 minutes. In another bowl, combine almond flour, plant-based Parmesan cheese, half of the garlic powder, sweet paprika, and salt. Line a baking sheet with parchment paper in readiness for the rings. When the vegan "flax egg" is ready, dip in the onion rings one after another and then into the almond flour mixture. Place the rings on the baking sheet and grease with cooking spray. Bake for 15-20 minutes or until golden brown and crispy. Remove the onion rings into a serving bowl.
2. Put kale in a food processor. Add in olive oil, cilantro, oregano, remaining garlic powder, salt, black pepper, tofu mayonnaise, coconut cream, and lemon juice; puree until nice and smooth. Allow the dip to sit for about 10 minutes for the flavors to develop. After, serve the dip with the crispy onion rings.

Classic Vegan Meatballs

Servings: 4
Cooking Time: 15 Minutes
Ingredients:
- 1 cup brown rice, cooked and cooled
- 1 cup canned or boiled red kidney beans, drained
- 1 teaspoon fresh garlic, minced
- 1 small onion, chopped
- Sea salt and ground black pepper, to taste
- 1/2 teaspoon cayenne pepper
- 1/2 teaspoon smoked paprika
- 1/2 teaspoon coriander seeds
- 1/2 teaspoon coriander mustard seeds
- 2 tablespoons olive oil

Directions:
1. In a mixing bowl, thoroughly combine all the ingredients, except for the olive oil. Mix to combine well and then, shape the mixture into equal balls using oiled hands.

2. Then, heat the olive oil in a nonstick skillet over medium heat. Once hot, fry the meatballs for about 10 minutes until golden brown on all sides.
3. Serve with cocktail sticks and enjoy!

Roasted Root Vegetables

Servings: 6
Cooking Time: 35 Minutes
Ingredients:
- 1/4 cup olive oil
- 2 carrots, peeled and cut into 1 ½-inch pieces
- 2 parsnips, peeled and cut into 1 ½-inch pieces
- 1 celery stalk, peeled and cut into 1 ½-inch pieces
- 1 pound sweet potatoes, peeled and cut into 1 ½-inch pieces
- 1/4 cup olive oil
- 1 teaspoon mustard seeds
- 1/2 teaspoon basil
- 1/2 teaspoon oregano
- 1 teaspoon red pepper flakes
- 1 teaspoon dried thyme
- Sea salt and ground black pepper, to taste

Directions:
1. Toss the vegetables with the remaining ingredients until well coated.
2. Roast the vegetables in the preheated oven at 400 degrees F for about 35 minutes, stirring halfway through the cooking time.
3. Taste, adjust the seasonings and serve warm. Bon appétit!

Sautéed Turnip Greens

Servings: 4
Cooking Time: 15 Minutes
Ingredients:
- 2 tablespoons olive oil
- 1 onion, sliced
- 2 garlic cloves, sliced
- 1 ½ pounds turnip greens cleaned and chopped
- 1/4 cup vegetable broth
- 1/4 cup dry white wine
- 1/2 teaspoon dried oregano
- 1 teaspoon dried parsley flakes
- Kosher salt and ground black pepper, to taste

Directions:
1. In a sauté pan, heat the olive oil over a moderately high heat.
2. Now, sauté the onion for 3 to 4 minutes or until tender and translucent. Add in the garlic and continue to cook for 30 seconds more or until aromatic.
3. Stir in the turnip greens, broth, wine, oregano and parsley; continue sautéing an additional 6 minutes or until they have wilted completely.
4. Season with salt and black pepper to taste and serve warm. Bon appétit!

Mustard Mac & Cheese

Servings:4
Cooking Time:35 Minutes
Ingredients:
- 8 oz elbow macaroni
- 2 tbsp olive oil
- ½ tsp dry mustard powder
- 2 cups almond milk
- 2 cups plant-based cheddar, grated
- Salt and black pepper to taste
- ¼ cup flour
- 2 tbsp parsley, chopped

Directions:
1. Cook elbow macaroni in boiling water for 8-10 minutes until al dente. Drain.
2. Heat olive oil in a skillet over medium heat. Place flour, mustard powder, salt, and pepper and stir for about 3-5 minutes. Gradually pour in almond milk while stirring constantly with a spatula for another 5 minutes until the mixture is smooth. Turn off the heat and mix in cheddar cheese. When the cheese is melted, fold in macaroni and toss to coat. Sprinkle with parsley to serve.

Balsamic Roasted Red Pepper & Pecan Crostini

Servings:16
Cooking Time:15 Minutes
Ingredients:
- 2 jarred roasted red peppers
- 1 cup unsalted pecans
- ¼ cup water
- 1 tbsp soy sauce
- 2 tbsp chopped green onions
- ¼ cup nutritional yeast
- 2 tbsp balsamic vinegar
- 2 tbsp olive oil

Directions:
1. Cut 1 red pepper and set aside. Slice the remaining pepper into strips, reserve for garnish. Pulse the pecans in a food processor until a fine powder forms. Pour in water, chopped red pepper, and soy sauce. Pulse until smooth. Put in green onions, yeast, vinegar, and oil. Blend until well mixed. Spread mixture onto toasted bread slices topped with pepper strips.

Authentic Guacamole

Servings:2
Cooking Time:10 Minutes
Ingredients:
- 2 ripe avocados
- 2 garlic cloves, pressed
- Zest and juice of 1 lime
- 1 tsp ground cumin
- 1 tomato, chopped
- 1 tbsp cilantro, chopped

Directions:
1. Place the avocados in a bowl and mash them. Stir in garlic, lime juice, lime zest, cumin, tomato, cilantro, salt, and pepper. Serve immediately.

Spiced Roasted Cauliflower

Servings: 6
Cooking Time: 25 Minutes
Ingredients:
- 1 ½ pounds cauliflower florets
- 1/4 cup olive oil
- 4 tablespoons apple cider vinegar
- 2 cloves garlic, pressed
- 1 teaspoon dried basil
- 1 teaspoon dried oregano
- Sea salt and ground black pepper, to taste

Directions:
1. Begin by preheating your oven to 420 degrees F.
2. Toss the cauliflower florets with the remaining ingredients.
3. Arrange the cauliflower florets on a parchment-lined baking sheet. Bake the cauliflower florets in the preheated oven for about 25 minutes or until they are slightly charred.
4. Bon appétit!

Cinnamon-maple Popcorn

Servings:4
Cooking Time:15 Minutes
Ingredients:
- ½ cup popcorn kernels
- ¼ tsp cinnamon powder
- ½ tsp pure maple syrup
- 1 tsp plant butter, melted
- Salt to taste

Directions:
1. Pour the popcorn kernels into a large pot and set over medium heat. Cover the lid and let the kernels pop completely. Shake the pot a few times to ensure even popping, 10 minutes.
2. In a small bowl, mix the cinnamon powder, maple syrup, butter, and salt. When the popcorn is ready, turn the heat off, and toss in the cinnamon mixture until well distributed. Pour the popcorn into serving bowls, allow cooling, and enjoy.

Sautéed Zucchini With Herbs

Servings: 4
Cooking Time: 10 Minutes
Ingredients:
- 2 tablespoons olive oil
- 1 onion, sliced
- 2 garlic cloves, minced
- 1 ½ pounds zucchini, sliced
- Sea salt and fresh ground black pepper, to taste
- 1 teaspoon cayenne pepper
- 1/2 teaspoon dried basil
- 1/2 teaspoon dried oregano
- 1/2 teaspoon dried rosemary

Directions:
1. In a saucepan, heat the olive oil over medium-high heat.

2. Once hot, sauté the onion for about 3 minutes or until tender. Then, sauté the garlic for about 1 minute until aromatic.

3. Add in the zucchini, along with the spices and continue to sauté for 6 minutes more until tender.

4. Taste and adjust the seasonings. Bon appétit!

Winter Roasted Vegetables

Servings: 4
Cooking Time: 45 Minutes
Ingredients:
- 1/2 pound carrots, slice into 1-inch chunks
- 1/2 pound parsnips, slice into 1-inch chunks
- 1/2 pound celery, slice into 1-inch chunks
- 1/2 pound sweet potatoes, slice into 1-inch chunks
- 1 large onion, slice into wedges
- 1/4 cup olive oil
- 1 teaspoon red pepper flakes
- 1 teaspoon dried basil
- 1 teaspoon dried oregano
- 1 teaspoon dried thyme
- Sea salt and freshly ground black pepper

Directions:
1. Start by preheating your oven to 420 degrees F.
2. Toss the vegetables with the olive oil and spices. Arrange them on a parchment-lined roasting pan.
3. Roast for about 25 minutes. Stir the vegetables and continue to cook for 20 minutes more.
4. Bon appétit!

Indian-style Hummus Dip

Servings: 10
Cooking Time: 10 Minutes
Ingredients:
- 20 ounces canned or boiled chickpeas, drained
- 1 teaspoon garlic, sliced
- 1/4 cup tahini
- 1/4 cup olive oil
- 1 lime, freshly squeezed
- 1/4 teaspoon turmeric
- 1/2 teaspoon cumin powder
- 1 teaspoon curry powder
- 1 teaspoon coriander seeds
- 1/4 cup chickpea liquid, or more, as needed
- 2 tablespoons fresh cilantro, roughly chopped

Directions:
1. Blitz the chickpeas, garlic, tahini, olive oil, lime, turmeric, cumin, curry powder and coriander seeds in your blender or food processor.
2. Blend until your desired consistency is reached, gradually adding the chickpea liquid.
3. Place in your refrigerator until ready to serve. Garnish with fresh cilantro.
4. Serve with naan bread or veggie sticks, if desired. Bon appétit!

Traditional Baba Ganoush

Servings: 8

Cooking Time: 25 Minutes
Ingredients:
- 1 pound eggplant, cut into rounds
- 1 teaspoon coarse sea salt
- 3 tablespoons olive oil
- 3 tablespoons fresh lime juice
- 2 cloves garlic, minced
- 3 tablespoons tahini
- 1/4 teaspoon ground cloves
- 1/2 teaspoon ground cumin
- 2 tablespoons fresh parsley, roughly chopped

Directions:
1. Rub the sea salt all over the eggplant rounds. Then, place them in a colander and let it sit for about 15 minutes; drain, rinse and pat dry with kitchen towels.
2. Roast the eggplant until the skin turns black; peel the eggplant and transfer it to the bowl of your food processor.
3. Add in the olive oil, lime juice, garlic, tahini, cloves and cumin. Blend until everything is well incorporated.
4. Garnish with fresh parsley leaves and enjoy!

Sesame Cabbage Sauté

Servings:4
Cooking Time:15 Minutes
Ingredients:
- 2 tbsp soy sauce
- 1 tbsp toasted sesame oil
- 1 tbsp hot sauce
- ½ tbsp pure date sugar
- ½ tbsp olive oil
- 1 head green cabbage, shredded
- 2 carrots, julienned
- 3 green onions, thinly sliced
- 2 garlic cloves, minced
- 1 tbsp fresh grated ginger
- Salt and black pepper to taste
- 1 tbsp sesame seeds

Directions:
1. In a small bowl, mix the soy sauce, sesame oil, hot sauce, and date sugar.
2. Heat the olive oil in a large skillet and sauté the cabbage, carrots, green onion, garlic, and ginger until softened, 5 minutes. Mix in the prepared sauce and toss well. Cook for 1 to 2 minutes. Dish the food and garnish it with the sesame seeds.

Bell Pepper & Seitan Balls

Servings:4
Cooking Time:25 Minutes
Ingredients:
- 1 tbsp flaxseed powder
- 1 lb seitan, crumbled
- ¼ cup chopped mixed bell peppers
- Salt and black pepper to taste
- 1 tbsp almond flour
- 1 tsp garlic powder
- 1 tsp onion powder
- 1 tsp tofu mayonnaise

- Olive oil for brushing

Directions:
1. Preheat the oven to 400 F and line a baking sheet with parchment paper.
2. In a bowl, mix flaxseed powder with 3 tbsp water and allow thickening for 5 minutes. Add in seitan, bell peppers, salt, pepper, almond flour, garlic powder, onion powder, and tofu mayonnaise. Mix and form 1-inch balls from the mixture. Arrange on the baking sheet, brush with cooking spray, and bake in the oven for 15 to 20 minutes or until brown and compacted. Remove from the oven and serve.

Tarragon Potato Chips

Servings:4
Cooking Time:40 Minutes
Ingredients:
- 1 lb potato, peeled and sliced
- 1 tsp smoked paprika
- ½ tsp garlic powder
- 1 tbsp tarragon
- ¼ tsp onion powder
- ¼ tsp chili powder
- ⅛ tsp ground mustard
- 1 tsp canola oil
- ⅛ tsp liquid smoke

Directions:
1. Preheat oven to 390 F.
2. Combine the paprika, garlic powder, tarragon, onion powder, chili powder, salt, and mustard in a bowl. Mix the potatoes, canola oil, liquid smoke, and tarragon mixture in another bowl; toss to coat. Spread the potatoes on a lined with parchment paper baking tray and bake for 30 minutes, flipping once halfway through cooking until golden. Serve.

Grilled Vegetables With Romesco Dip

Servings:4
Cooking Time:35 Minutes
Ingredients:
- 1 jar roasted peppers, drained
- ½ cup toasted almonds
- 1 garlic clove, minced
- 1 tbsp red wine vinegar
- 1 tsp crushed red chili flakes
- 2 slices toasted bread, chopped
- ½ tsp sweet paprika
- 1 tbsp tomato paste
- ½ cup olive oil + 2 tbsp for brushing
- Salt and black pepper to taste
- 1 green bell pepper, julienned
- 1 yellow bell pepper, julienned
- 1 bunch of asparagus, trimmed

Directions:
1. In a food processor, place roasted peppers, almonds, garlic, vinegar, toasted bread, paprika, and tomato paste; pulse, pouring slowly ½ cup of olive oil until the desired consistency is reached. Season with salt and black pepper and set aside.

2. Heat a grill pan over medium heat. Toss the vegetables in the remaining olive oil, season with salt and pepper, and cook in the pan for 3-5 minutes per side. Serve with the dip.

Mediterranean Tahini Beans

Servings:4
Cooking Time:10 Minutes
Ingredients:
- 1 tbsp sesame oil
- 1 cup string beans, trimmed
- Salt to taste
- 2 tbsp pure tahini
- 2 tbsp coarsely chopped mint leaves
- ¼ tsp red chili flakes for topping

Directions:
1. Pour the string beans into a medium safe microwave dish, sprinkle with 1 tbsp of water, and steam in the microwave until softened, 1 minute.
2. Heat the sesame oil in a large skillet and toss in the string beans until well coated in the butter. Season with salt and mix in the tahini and mint leaves. Cook for 1 to 2 minutes and turn the heat off. Serve.

Avocado With Tahini Sauce

Servings: 4
Cooking Time: 10 Minutes
Ingredients:
- 2 large-sized avocados, pitted and halved
- 4 tablespoons tahini
- 4 tablespoons soy sauce
- 1 tablespoon lemon juice
- 1/2 teaspoon red pepper flakes
- Sea salt and ground black pepper, to taste
- 1 teaspoon garlic powder

Directions:
1. Place the avocado halves on a serving platter.
2. Mix the tahini, soy sauce, lemon juice, red pepper, salt, black pepper and garlic powder in a small bowl. Divide the sauce between the avocado halves.
3. Bon appétit!

Carrot Energy Balls

Servings: 8
Cooking Time: 10 Minutes
Ingredients:
- 1 large carrot, grated carrot
- 1 ½ cups old-fashioned oats
- 1 cup raisins
- 1 cup dates, pitied
- 1 cup coconut flakes
- 1/4 teaspoon ground cloves
- 1/2 teaspoon ground cinnamon

Directions:
1. In your food processor, pulse all ingredients until it forms a sticky and uniform mixture.
2. Shape the batter into equal balls.
3. Place in your refrigerator until ready to serve. Bon appétit!

Peppery Hummus Dip

Servings: 10
Cooking Time: 10 Minutes
Ingredients:
- 20 ounces canned or boiled chickpeas, drained
- 1/4 cup tahini
- 2 garlic cloves, minced
- 2 tablespoons lemon juice, freshly squeezed
- 1/2 cup chickpea liquid
- 2 red roasted peppers, seeded and sliced
- 1/2 teaspoon paprika
- 1 teaspoon dried basil
- Sea salt and ground black pepper, to taste
- 2 tablespoons olive oil

Directions:
1. Blitz all the ingredients, except for the oil, in your blender or food processor until your desired consistency is reached.
2. Place in your refrigerator until ready to serve.
3. Serve with toasted pita wedges or chips, if desired. Bon appétit!

Braised Wax Beans With Herbs

Servings: 4
Cooking Time: 10 Minutes
Ingredients:
- 1 cup water
- 1 ½ pounds wax beans
- 4 tablespoons olive oil
- 4 cloves garlic, minced
- 1/2 teaspoon ginger, peeled and minced
- 1/2 teaspoon ground bay leaf
- Kosher salt and ground black pepper, to taste
- 2 tablespoons fresh Italian parsley, chopped
- 2 tablespoons fresh basil, chopped

Directions:
1. Bring the water to a boil. Add in the wax beans and let it cook for about 5 minutes until they are crisp-tender; reserve.
2. In a saucepan, heat the olive oil over medium-high heat; sauté the garlic, ginger and ground bay leaf for 1 minute or until aromatic.
3. Add in the salt, black pepper and reserved green beans; let it cook for about 3 minutes until cooked through.
4. Serve with fresh parsley and basil. Bon appétit!

Berries, Nuts & Cream Bowl

Servings:6
Cooking Time:30 Minutes
Ingredients:
- 5 tbsp flaxseed powder
- 1 cup dairy-free dark chocolate
- 1 cup plant butter
- 2 tsp vanilla extract
- 2 cups fresh blueberries
- 4 tbsp lemon juice
- 2 cups coconut cream
- 4 oz walnuts, chopped

- ½ cup roasted coconut chips

Directions:
1. Preheat oven to 320 F. Grease a springform pan with cooking spray and line with parchment paper. In a bowl, mix the flaxseed powder with 2/3 cup water and allow thicken for 5 minutes. Break the chocolate and butter into a bowl and melt in the microwave for 1-2 minutes.
2. Share the vegan "flax egg" into two bowls; whisk 1 pinch of salt into one portion and then 1 teaspoon of vanilla into the other. Pour the chocolate mixture into the vanilla mixture and combine well. Fold into the other vegan "flax egg" mixture. Pour the batter into the springform pan and bake for 15-20 minutes. When ready, slice the cake into squares and share it into serving bowls. Set aside.
3. Pour blueberries, lemon juice, and the remaining vanilla into a bowl. Break blueberries and allow sitting for a few minutes. Whip the coconut cream with a whisk until a soft peak forms. Spoon the cream on the cakes, top with the blueberry mixture, and sprinkle with walnuts and coconut flakes. Serve.

Chipotle Sweet Potato Fries

Servings: 4
Cooking Time: 45 Minutes
Ingredients:
- 4 medium sweet potatoes, peeled and cut into sticks
- 2 tablespoons peanut oil
- Sea salt and ground black pepper, to taste
- 1 teaspoon chipotle pepper powder
- 1/4 teaspoon ground allspice
- 1 teaspoon brown sugar
- 1 teaspoon dried rosemary

Directions:
1. Toss the sweet potato fries with the remaining ingredients.
2. Bake your fries at 375 degrees F for about 45 minutes or until browned; make sure to stir the fries once or twice.
3. Serve with your favorite dipping sauce, if desired. Bon appétit!

Bell Pepper Boats With Mango Salsa

Servings: 4
Cooking Time: 5 Minutes
Ingredients:
- 1 mango, peeled, pitted, cubed
- 1 small shallot, chopped
- 2 tablespoons fresh cilantro, minced
- 1 red chile pepper, seeded and chopped
- 1 tablespoon fresh lime juice
- 4 bell peppers, seeded and halved

Directions:
1. Thoroughly combine the mango, shallot, cilantro, red chile pepper and lime juice.
2. Spoon the mixture into the pepper halves and serve immediately.
3. Bon appétit!

Spicy Cauliflower Steaks

Servings: 4
Cooking Time: 35 Minutes
Ingredients:
- 2 medium heads cauliflower, sliced lengthwise into "steaks"
- 1/2 cup olive oil
- 4 cloves garlic, minced
- 1 teaspoon red pepper flakes
- 1/2 teaspoon cumin seeds
- 1/3 teaspoon ground bay leaf
- Kosher salt and ground black pepper, to taste

Directions:
1. Begin by preheating the oven to 400 degrees F. Brush the cauliflower "steaks" with 1/4 of the olive oil and arrange them on a parchment-lined roasting pan.
2. Then, in a mixing bowl, mix the remaining 1/4 of the olive oil with the aromatics.
3. Then, roast the cauliflower steaks for about 20 minutes; brush them with the oil/garlic mixture and continue cooking an additional 10 to 15 minutes.
4. Bon appétit!

Mediterranean-style Sautéed Kale

Servings: 4
Cooking Time: 10 Minutes
Ingredients:
- 4 tablespoons olive oil
- 1 small red onion, chopped
- 2 cloves garlic, thinly sliced
- 1 ½ pounds kale, tough stems removed, torn into pieces
- 2 tomatoes, peeled and pureed
- 1 teaspoon dried oregano
- 1 teaspoon dried basil
- 1/2 teaspoon dried rosemary
- 1/2 teaspoon dried thyme
- Sea salt and freshly ground black pepper, to taste

Directions:
1. In a saucepan, heat the olive oil over a moderately high heat. Now, sauté the onion and garlic for about 2 minutes or until they are aromatic.
2. Add in the kale and tomatoes, stirring to promote even cooking.
3. Turn the heat to a simmer, add in the spices and let it cook for 5 to 6 minutes, until the kale leaves wilt.
4. Serve warm and enjoy!

Tamari Lentil Dip

Servings:2
Cooking Time:10 Minutes
Ingredients:
- 1 can lentils, drained
- Zest and juice of 1 lime
- 1 tbsp tamari sauce
- ¼ cup fresh cilantro, chopped
- 1 tsp ground cumin
- 1 tsp cayenne pepper

Directions:
1. In a blender, put the lentils, lime zest, lime juice, tamari sauce, and ¼ cup of water. Pulse until smooth. Transfer to a bowl and stir in cilantro, cumin and cayenne pepper. Serve.

Chinese Cabbage Stir-fry

Servings: 3
Cooking Time: 10 Minutes
Ingredients:
- 3 tablespoons sesame oil
- 1 pound Chinese cabbage, sliced
- 1/2 teaspoon Chinese five-spice powder
- Kosher salt, to taste
- 1/2 teaspoon Szechuan pepper
- 2 tablespoons soy sauce
- 3 tablespoons sesame seeds, lightly toasted

Directions:
1. In a wok, heat the sesame oil until sizzling. Stir fry the cabbage for about 5 minutes.
2. Stir in the spices and soy sauce and continue to cook, stirring frequently, for about 5 minutes more, until the cabbage is crisp-tender and aromatic.
3. Sprinkle sesame seeds over the top and serve immediately.

Paprika Tofu & Zucchini Skewers

Servings:4
Cooking Time:10 Minutes
Ingredients:
- 1 block tofu, pressed cubed
- 1 medium zucchini, cut into rounds
- 1 tbsp olive oil
- 2 tbsp freshly squeezed lemon juice
- 1 tsp smoked paprika
- 1 tsp cumin powder
- 1 tsp garlic powder
- Salt and black pepper to taste

Directions:
1. Preheat a grill to medium heat.
2. Meanwhile, thread the tofu and zucchini alternately on the wooden skewers.
3. In a small bowl, whisk the olive oil, lemon juice, paprika, cumin powder, and garlic powder. Brush the skewers all around with the mixture and place on the grill grate. Cook on both sides until golden brown, 5 minutes. Season with salt and pepper and serve afterward.

Arugula & Hummus Pitas

Servings:4
Cooking Time:15 Minutes
Ingredients:
- 4 pieces of whole-wheat pita bread, halved
- 1 garlic clove, chopped
- ¾ cup tahini
- 2 tbsp fresh lemon juice
- ⅛ tsp ground cayenne
- ¼ cup water
- 1 can chickpeas
- 2 medium carrots, grated

- 1 large ripe tomato, sliced
- 2 cups arugula

Directions:

1. In a food processor, add in garlic, tahini, lemon juice, salt, cayenne pepper, and water. Pulse until smooth. In a bowl, mash the chickpeas with a fork. Stir in carrots and tahini mixture; reserve. Spread the hummus over the pitas and top with a tomato slice and arugula. Serve immediately.

Minty Berry Cocktail

Servings:4
Cooking Time:15 Minutes

Ingredients:

- 2 tbsp pineapple juice
- 1 tbsp fresh lime juice
- 1 tbsp agave nectar
- 2 tsp minced fresh mint
- 2 cups pitted fresh prunes
- 1 cup fresh blueberries
- 1 cup fresh strawberries, halved
- ½ cup fresh raspberries

Directions:

1. Whisk the pineapple juice, lime juice, agave nectar, and mint in a bowl. Set aside.
2. In another bowl, combine the prunes, blueberries, strawberries, and raspberries. Pour over the dressing and toss to coat. Serve right away.

Classic Party Mix

Servings: 15
Cooking Time: 1 Hour 5 Minutes

Ingredients:

- 5 cups vegan corn cereal
- 3 cups vegan mini pretzels
- 1 cup almonds, roasted
- 1/2 cup pepitas, toasted
- 1 tablespoon nutritional yeast
- 1 tablespoon balsamic vinegar
- 1 tablespoon soy sauce
- 1 teaspoon garlic powder
- 1/3 cup vegan butter

Directions:

1. Start by preheating your oven to 250 degrees F. Line a large baking pan with parchment paper or Silpat mat.
2. Mix the cereal, pretzels, almonds and pepitas in a serving bowl.
3. In a small saucepan, melt the remaining ingredients over a moderate heat. Pour the sauce over the cereal/nut mixture.
4. Bake for about 1 hour, stirring every 15 minutes, until golden and fragrant. Transfer it to a wire rack to cool completely. Bon appétit!

Sweet Potato Poblano Poppers

Servings: 7
Cooking Time: 25 Minutes

Ingredients:

- 1/2 pound cauliflower, trimmed and diced
- 1 pound sweet potatoes, peeled and diced

- 1/2 cup cashew milk, unsweetened
- 1/4 cup vegan mayonnaise
- 1/2 teaspoon curry powder
- 1/2 teaspoon cayenne pepper
- 1/4 teaspoon dried dill
- Sea and ground black pepper, to taste
- 1/2 cup fresh breadcrumbs
- 14 fresh poblano chiles, cut into halves, seeds removed

Directions:

1. Steam the cauliflower and sweet potatoes for about 10 minutes or until they've softened. Now, mash them with the cashew milk.
2. Add in the vegan mayo, curry powder, cayenne pepper, dill, salt and black pepper.
3. Spoon the mixture into the peppers and top them with the breadcrumbs.
4. Bake in the preheated oven at 400 degrees F for about 13 minutes or until the peppers have softened.
5. Bon appétit!

Buttery Turnip Mash

Servings: 4
Cooking Time: 35 Minutes

Ingredients:

- 2 cups water
- 1 ½ pounds turnips, peeled and cut into small pieces
- 4 tablespoons vegan butter
- 1 cup oat milk
- 2 fresh rosemary sprigs, chopped
- 1 tablespoon fresh parsley, chopped
- 1 teaspoon ginger-garlic paste
- Kosher salt and freshly ground black pepper
- 1 teaspoon red pepper flakes, crushed

Directions:

1. Bring the water to a boil; turn the heat to a simmer and cook your turnip for about 30 minutes; drain.
2. Using an immersion blender, puree the turnips with the vegan butter, milk, rosemary, parsley, ginger-garlic paste, salt, black pepper, red pepper flakes, adding the cooking liquid, if necessary.
3. Bon appétit!

Traditional Moroccan Tagine

Servings: 4
Cooking Time: 30 Minutes

Ingredients:

- 3 tablespoons olive oil
- 1 large shallot, chopped
- 1 teaspoon ginger, peeled and minced
- 4 garlic cloves, chopped
- 2 medium carrots, trimmed and chopped
- 2 medium parsnips, trimmed and chopped
- 2 medium sweet potatoes, peeled and cubed
- Sea salt and ground black pepper, to taste
- 1 teaspoon hot sauce
- 1 teaspoon fenugreek
- 1/2 teaspoon saffron
- 1/2 teaspoon caraway

- 2 large tomatoes, pureed
- 4 cups vegetable broth
- 1 lemon, cut into wedges

Directions:

1. In a Dutch Oven, heat the olive oil over medium heat. Once hot, sauté the shallots for 4 to 5 minutes, until tender.
2. Then, sauté the ginger and garlic for about 40 seconds or until aromatic.
3. Add in the remaining ingredients, except for the lemon and bring to a boil. Immediately turn the heat to a simmer.
4. Let it simmer for about 25 minutes or until the vegetables have softened. Serve with fresh lemon wedges and enjoy!

Classic Avocado Tartines

Servings: 3
Cooking Time: 5 Minutes
Ingredients:

- 2 medium avocados, pitted, peeled and mashed
- 2 tablespoons fresh lime juice
- Sea salt and ground black pepper, to taste
- 1/2 teaspoon red pepper flakes, crushed
- 6 slices whole-wheat bread, toasted
- 1 large tomato, sliced
- 3 tablespoons sesame seeds, toasted

Directions:

1. Combine the mashed avocado with the lime juice, salt, black pepper and red pepper.
2. Spread the mixture onto the toast; top with tomatoes and sesame seeds.
3. Bon appétit!

Vegetable & Rice Vermicelli Lettuce Rolls

Servings: 4
Cooking Time: 15 Minutes
Ingredients:

- 2 green onions
- 2 tbsp sesame oil
- 2 tbsp soy sauce
- 2 tbsp balsamic vinegar
- 1 tsp pure date sugar
- ⅛ tsp crushed red pepper
- 3 oz rice vermicelli
- 6 soft green leaf lettuce leaves
- 1 medium carrot, shredded
- ½ cucumber, sliced lengthwise
- ½ red bell pepper, cut into strips
- 1 cup fresh cilantro leaves

Directions:

1. Separate the white part of the green onions, chop and transfer to a bowl. Stir in soy sauce, balsamic vinegar, date sugar, red pepper, and 3 tbsp water. Set aside. Slice the green part diagonally and set aside.
2. Submerge the vermicelli in a bowl with hot water for 4 minutes. Drain and mix in the sesame oil. Allow cooling. Put the lettuce leaves on a flat surface.

3. Divide rice noodles between each leaf, in the middle, add green onion slices, carrot, cucumber, bell pepper, and cilantro. Roll the leaves up from the smaller edges. Arrange the rolls seam facing down in a plate. Serve with the dipping sauce.

Pecan Tempeh Cakes

Servings: 4
Cooking Time: 20 Minutes
Ingredients:

- 8 oz tempeh, chopped
- 1 chopped onion
- 2 garlic cloves, minced
- ¾ cup chopped pecans
- ½ cup old-fashioned oats
- 1 tbsp minced fresh parsley
- ½ tsp dried oregano
- ½ tsp dried thyme
- Salt and black pepper to taste
- 3 tbsp olive oil
- 1 tbsp Dijon mustard
- 4 whole-grain burger buns
- Sliced red onion, tomato, lettuce, and avocado

Directions:

1. Place the tempeh in a pot with hot water. Cook for 30 minutes. Drain and let cool.
2. In a blender, add onion, garlic, tempeh, pecans, oats, parsley, oregano, thyme, salt, and pepper. Pulse until everything is well combined. Form the mixture into 4 balls; flatten to make burgers.

Sweet Potato Puree

Servings: 5
Cooking Time: 25 Minutes
Ingredients:

- 2 pounds sweet potatoes, peeled and cubed
- 2 tablespoons olive oil
- 1 shallot, chopped
- 2 garlic cloves, minced
- 1/4 cup coconut milk, unsweetened
- Sea salt and cayenne pepper, to taste
- 2 tablespoons fresh chives, roughly chopped
- 2 tablespoons fresh parsley, roughly chopped

Directions:

1. Cover the sweet potatoes with an inch or two of cold water. Cook the sweet potatoes in gently boiling water for about 20 minutes; drain well.
2. Meanwhile, heat the olive oil in a cast-iron skillet and sauté the shallot for about 3 minutes until tender; add in the garlic and continue to sauté an additional 30 seconds or until tender.
3. Then, puree the potatoes, along with the shallot mixture, gradually adding the milk, to your desired consistency.
4. Season with salt and pepper to taste. Serve garnished with the fresh chives and parsley. Bon appétit!

Mushroom And Cannellini Bean "meatballs"

Servings: 4
Cooking Time: 15 Minutes
Ingredients:
- 4 tablespoons olive oil
- 1 cup button mushrooms, chopped
- 1 shallot, chopped
- 2 garlic cloves, crushed
- 1 cup canned or boiled cannellini beans, drained
- 1 cup quinoa, cooked
- Sea salt and ground black pepper, to taste
- 1 teaspoon smoked paprika
- 1/2 teaspoon red pepper flakes
- 1 teaspoon mustard seeds
- 1/2 teaspoon dried dill

Directions:
1. Heat 2 tablespoons of the olive oil in a nonstick skillet. Once hot, cook the mushrooms and shallot for 3 minutes or until just tender.
2. Add in the garlic, beans, quinoa and spices. Mix to combine well and then, shape the mixture into equal balls using oiled hands.
3. Then, heat the remaining 2 tablespoons of the olive oil in a nonstick skillet over medium heat. Once hot, fry the meatballs for about 10 minutes until golden brown on all sides.
4. Serve with cocktail sticks. Bon appétit!

Tofu Stuffed Peppers

Servings:4
Cooking Time:25 Minutes
Ingredients:
- 1 cup red and yellow bell peppers
- 1 oz tofu, chopped into small bits
- 1 cup cashew cream cheese
- 1 tbsp chili paste, mild
- 2 tbsp melted plant butter
- 1 cup grated plant-based Parmesan

Directions:
1. Preheat oven to 400 F. Use a knife to cut the bell peppers into two (lengthwise) and remove the core.
2. In a bowl, mix tofu, cashew cream cheese, chili paste, and melted butter until smooth. Spoon the cheese mixture into the bell peppers and use the back of the spoon to level the filling in the peppers. Grease a baking sheet with cooking spray and arrange the stuffed peppers on the sheet.
3. Sprinkle the plant-based Parmesan cheese on top and bake the peppers for 15-20 minutes until the peppers are golden brown and the cheese melted. Remove onto a serving platter and serve warm.

Roasted Butternut Squash

Servings: 4
Cooking Time: 25 Minutes
Ingredients:
- 4 tablespoons olive oil
- 1/2 teaspoon ground cumin
- 1/2 teaspoon ground allspice
- 1 ½ pounds butternut squash, peeled, seeded and diced
- 1/4 cup dry white wine
- 2 tablespoons dark soy sauce
- 1 teaspoon mustard seeds
- 1 teaspoon paprika
- Sea salt and ground black pepper, to taste

Directions:
1. Start by preheating your oven to 420 degrees F. Toss the squash with the remaining ingredients.
2. Roast the butternut squash for about 25 minutes or until tender and caramelized.
3. Serve warm and enjoy!

Tangy Rosemary Broccoli Florets

Servings: 6
Cooking Time: 35 Minutes
Ingredients:
- 2 pounds broccoli florets
- 1/4 cup extra-virgin olive oil
- Sea salt and ground black pepper, to taste
- 1 teaspoon ginger-garlic paste
- 1 tablespoon fresh rosemary, chopped
- 1/2 teaspoon lemon zest

Directions:
1. Toss the broccoli with the remaining ingredients until well coated.
2. Roast the vegetables in the preheated oven at 400 degrees F for about 35 minutes, stirring halfway through the cooking time.
3. Taste, adjust the seasonings and serve warm. Bon appétit!

Gingery Carrot Mash

Servings: 4
Cooking Time: 25 Minutes
Ingredients:
- 2 pounds carrots, cut into rounds
- 2 tablespoons olive oil
- 1 teaspoon ground cumin
- Salt ground black pepper, to taste
- 1/2 teaspoon cayenne pepper
- 1/2 teaspoon ginger, peeled and minced
- 1/2 cup whole milk

Directions:
1. Begin by preheating your oven to 400 degrees F.
2. Toss the carrots with the olive oil, cumin, salt, black pepper and cayenne pepper. Arrange them in a single layer on a parchment-lined roasting sheet.
3. Roast the carrots in the preheated oven for about 20 minutes, until crisp-tender.
4. Add the roasted carrots, ginger and milk to your food processor; puree the ingredients until everything is well blended.
5. Bon appétit!

Chapter 4. Legumes, Rice & Grains

Potage Au Quinoa

Servings: 4
Cooking Time: 25 Minutes
Ingredients:
- 2 tablespoons olive oil
- 1 onion, chopped
- 4 medium potatoes, peeled and diced
- 1 carrot, trimmed and diced
- 1 parsnip, trimmed and diced
- 1 jalapeno pepper, seeded and chopped
- 4 cups vegetable broth
- 1 cup quinoa
- Sea salt and ground white pepper, to taste

Directions:
1. In a heavy-bottomed pot, heat the olive oil over medium-high heat. Sauté the onion, potatoes, carrots, parsnip and pepper for about 5 minutes or until they've softened.
2. Add in the vegetable broth and quinoa; bring to a boil.
3. Immediately turn the heat to a simmer for about 15 minutes or until the quinoa is tender.
4. Season with salt and pepper to taste. Puree your potage with an immersion blender. Reheat the potage just before serving and enjoy!

Freekeh Pilaf With Chickpeas

Servings: 4
Cooking Time: 40 Minutes
Ingredients:
- 4 tablespoons olive oil
- 1 cup shallots, chopped
- 1 celery stalks, chopped
- 1 carrot, chopped
- 1 teaspoon garlic, minced
- Sea salt and ground black pepper, to taste
- 1 teaspoon cayenne pepper
- 1 teaspoon dried basil
- 1 teaspoon dried oregano
- 1 cup freekeh
- 2 ½ cups water
- 1 cup boiled chickpeas, drained
- 2 tablespoons roasted peanuts, roughly chopped
- 2 tablespoons fresh mint, roughly chopped

Directions:
1. Heat the olive oil in a heavy-bottomed pot over medium-high heat. Once hot, sauté the shallot, celery and carrot for about 3 minutes until just tender.
2. Then, add in the garlic and continue to sauté for 30 seconds more or until aromatic. Add in the spices, freekeh and water.
3. Turn the heat to a simmer for 30 to 35 minutes, stirring occasionally to promote even cooking. Fold in the boiled chickpeas.

4. To serve, spoon into individual bowls and garnish with roasted peanuts and fresh mint. Bon appétit!

Creamed Chickpea Salad With Pine Nuts

Servings: 4
Cooking Time: 10 Minutes
Ingredients:
- 16 ounces canned chickpeas, drained
- 1 teaspoon garlic, minced
- 1 shallot, chopped
- 1 cup cherry tomatoes, halved
- 1 bell pepper, seeded and sliced
- 1/4 cup fresh basil, chopped
- 1/4 cup fresh parsley, chopped
- 1/2 cup vegan mayonnaise
- 1 tablespoon lemon juice
- 1 teaspoon capers, drained
- Sea salt and ground black pepper, to taste
- 2 ounces pine nuts

Directions:
1. Place the chickpeas, vegetables and herbs in a salad bowl.
2. Add in the mayonnaise, lemon juice, capers, salt and black pepper. Stir to combine.
3. Top with pine nuts and serve immediately. Bon appétit!

Rice Pudding With Currants

Servings: 4
Cooking Time: 45 Minutes
Ingredients:
- 1 ½ cups water
- 1 cup white rice
- 2 ½ cups oat milk, divided
- 1/2 cup white sugar
- A pinch of salt
- A pinch of grated nutmeg
- 1 teaspoon ground cinnamon
- 1/2 teaspoon vanilla extract
- 1/2 cup dried currants

Directions:
1. In a saucepan, bring the water to a boil over medium-high heat. Immediately turn the heat to a simmer, add in the rice and let it cook for about 20 minutes.
2. Add in the milk, sugar and spices and continue to cook for 20 minutes more, stirring constantly to prevent the rice from sticking to the pan.
3. Top with dried currants and serve at room temperature. Bon appétit!

Sweet Oatmeal "grits"

Servings: 4
Cooking Time: 20 Minutes
Ingredients:
- 1 ½ cups steel-cut oats, soaked overnight
- 1 cup almond milk
- 2 cups water
- A pinch of grated nutmeg
- A pinch of ground cloves
- A pinch of sea salt
- 4 tablespoons almonds, slivered
- 6 dates, pitted and chopped
- 6 prunes, chopped

Directions:
1. In a deep saucepan, bring the steel cut oats, almond milk and water to a boil.
2. Add in the nutmeg, cloves and salt. Immediately turn the heat to a simmer, cover and continue to cook for about 15 minutes or until they've softened.
3. Then, spoon the grits into four serving bowls; top them with the almonds, dates and prunes.
4. Bon appétit!

Pea Dip With Herbs

Servings: 8
Cooking Time: 1 Hour 5 Minutes
Ingredients:
- 2 cups black-eyed peas, soaked overnight and drained
- 1 lemon, freshly squeezed
- 2 cloves garlic, minced
- 1 teaspoon fresh dill
- 2 tablespoons fresh basil, chopped
- 2 tablespoons fresh parsley, chopped
- 3 tablespoons olive oil
- Sea salt and red pepper, to taste

Directions:
1. Cover the black-eyed peas with water by 2 inches and bring to a gentle boil. Let it boil for about 15 minutes.
2. Then, turn the heat to a simmer for about 45 minutes. Let it cool completely.
3. Add the peas to the bowl of your food processor. Add in the remaining ingredients and process until well combined.
4. Garnish with some extra herbs and serve with your favorite dippers. Bon appétit!

Brown Lentil Bowl

Servings: 4
Cooking Time: 20 Minutes
Ingredients:
- 1 cup brown lentils, soaked overnight and drained
- 3 cups water
- 2 cups brown rice, cooked
- 1 zucchini, diced
- 1 red onion, chopped
- 1 teaspoon garlic, minced
- 1 cucumber, sliced
- 1 bell pepper, sliced

- 4 tablespoons olive oil
- 1 tablespoon rice vinegar
- 2 tablespoons lemon juice
- 2 tablespoons soy sauce
- 1/2 teaspoon dried oregano
- 1/2 teaspoon ground cumin
- Sea salt and ground black pepper, to taste
- 2 cups arugula
- 2 cups Romaine lettuce, torn into pieces

Directions:
1. Add the brown lentils and water to a saucepan and bring to a boil over high heat. Then, turn the heat to a simmer and continue to cook for 20 minutes or until tender.
2. Place the lentils in a salad bowl and let them cool completely.
3. Add in the remaining ingredients and toss to combine well. Serve at room temperature or well-chilled. Bon appétit!

Easy Barley Risotto

Servings: 4
Cooking Time: 35 Minutes
Ingredients:
- 2 tablespoons vegan butter
- 1 medium onion, chopped
- 1 bell pepper, seeded and chopped
- 2 garlic cloves, minced
- 1 teaspoon ginger, minced
- 2 cups vegetable broth
- 2 cups water
- 1 cup medium pearl barley
- 1/2 cup white wine
- 2 tablespoons fresh chives, chopped

Directions:
1. Melt the vegan butter in a saucepan over medium-high heat.
2. Once hot, cook the onion and pepper for about 3 minutes until just tender.
3. Add in the garlic and ginger and continue to sauté for 2 minutes or until aromatic.
4. Add in the vegetable broth, water, barley and wine; cover and continue to simmer for about 30 minutes. Once all the liquid has been absorbed; fluff the barley with a fork.
5. Garnish with fresh chives and serve warm. Bon appétit!

Old-fashioned Pilaf

Servings: 4
Cooking Time: 45 Minutes
Ingredients:
- 2 tablespoons sesame oil
- 1 shallot, sliced
- 2 bell peppers, seeded and sliced
- 3 cloves garlic, minced
- 10 ounces oyster mushrooms, cleaned and sliced
- 2 cups brown rice
- 2 tomatoes, pureed
- 2 cups vegetable broth
- Salt and black pepper, to taste
- 1 cup sweet corn kernels

- 1 cup green peas

Directions:

1. Heat the sesame oil in a saucepan over medium-high heat.
2. Once hot, cook the shallot and peppers for about 3 minutes until just tender.
3. Add in the garlic and oyster mushrooms; continue to sauté for 1 minute or so until aromatic.
4. In a lightly oiled casserole dish, place the rice, flowed by the mushroom mixture, tomatoes, broth, salt, black pepper, corn and green peas.
5. Bake, covered, at 375 degrees F for about 40 minutes, stirring after 20 minutes. Bon appétit!

Amarant Grits With Walnuts

Servings: 4
Cooking Time: 35 Minutes
Ingredients:

- 2 cups water
- 2 cups coconut milk
- 1 cup amaranth
- 1 cinnamon stick
- 1 vanilla bean
- 4 tablespoons maple syrup
- 4 tablespoons walnuts, chopped

Directions:

1. Bring the water and coconut milk to a boil over medium-high heat; add in the amaranth, cinnamon and vanilla and turn the heat to a simmer.
2. Let it cook for about 30 minutes, stirring periodically to prevent the amaranth from sticking to the bottom of the pan.
3. Top with maple syrup and walnuts. Bon appétit!

Middle Eastern Chickpea Stew

Servings: 4
Cooking Time: 20 Minutes
Ingredients:

- 1 onion, chopped
- 1 chili pepper, chopped
- 2 garlic cloves, chopped
- 1 teaspoon mustard seeds
- 1 teaspoon coriander seeds
- 1 bay leaf
- 1/2 cup tomato puree
- 2 tablespoons olive oil
- 1 celery with leaves, chopped
- 2 medium carrots, trimmed and chopped
- 2 cups vegetable broth
- 1 teaspoon ground cumin
- 1 small-sized cinnamon stick
- 16 ounces canned chickpeas, drained
- 2 cups Swiss chard, torn into pieces

Directions:

1. In your blender or food processor, blend the onion, chili pepper, garlic, mustard seeds, coriander seeds, bay leaf and tomato puree into a paste.
2. In a stockpot, heat the olive oil until sizzling. Now, cook the celery and carrots for about 3 minutes or until they've

softened. Add in the paste and continue to cook for a further 2 minutes.
3. Then, add in the vegetable broth, cumin, cinnamon and chickpeas; bring to a gentle boil.
4. Turn the heat to simmer and let it cook for 6 minutes; fold in Swiss chard and continue to cook for 4 to 5 minutes more or until the leaves wilt. Serve hot and enjoy!

Classic Chickpea Curry

Servings: 4
Cooking Time: 15 Minutes
Ingredients:

- 1 onion, diced
- 1 Thai chili pepper
- 2 ripe tomatoes, diced
- 1 teaspoon fresh ginger, minced
- 2 garlic cloves, peeled
- 1 teaspoon cumin seeds
- 1/2 teaspoon mustard seeds
- 1 bay leaf
- 3 tablespoons coconut oil
- Sea salt and ground black pepper, to taste
- 1 tablespoon garam masala
- 1 teaspoon curry powder
- 14 ounces canned chickpeas, drained
- 1/2 cup vegetable broth
- 1 can coconut milk, unsweetened
- 1 lime, freshly squeezed

Directions:

1. In your blender or food processor, blend the onion, chili pepper, tomatoes, ginger, garlic, cumin, mustard and bay leaf into a paste.
2. In a saucepan, heat the coconut oil over medium heat. Once hot, cook the prepared paste for about 2 minutes or until aromatic.
3. Add in the salt, pepper, garam masala, curry powder canned, chickpeas, vegetable broth and coconut milk. Turn the heat to a simmer.
4. Continue to simmer for 8 minutes more or until cooked through.
5. Remove from the heat. Drizzle fresh lime juice over the top of each serving. Bon appétit!

Cremini Mushroom Risotto

Servings: 3
Cooking Time: 20 Minutes
Ingredients:

- 3 tablespoons vegan butter
- 1 teaspoon garlic, minced
- 1 teaspoon thyme
- 1 pound Cremini mushrooms, sliced
- 1 ½ cups white rice
- 2 ½ cups vegetable broth
- 1/4 cup dry sherry wine
- Kosher salt and ground black pepper, to taste
- 3 tablespoons fresh scallions, thinly sliced

Directions:

1. In a saucepan, melt the vegan butter over a moderately high flame. Cook the garlic and thyme for about 1 minute or until aromatic.
2. Add in the mushrooms and continue to sauté until they release the liquid or about 3 minutes.
3. Add in the rice, vegetable broth and sherry wine. Bring to a boil; immediately turn the heat to a gentle simmer.
4. Cook for about 15 minutes or until all the liquid has absorbed. Fluff the rice with a fork, season with salt and pepper and garnish with fresh scallions.
5. Bon appétit!

Indian Chaat Bean Salad

Servings: 3
Cooking Time: 1 Hour
Ingredients:
- 1/2 pound chawli (black-eyed) beans, soaked overnight and drained
- 2 tablespoons shallots, chopped
- 1 clove garlic, minced
- 1 bell pepper, seeded and chopped
- 1 green chili pepper, seeded and chopped
- 1 teaspoon turmeric powder
- 1/2 teaspoon turmeric powder
- Dressing:
- 1/4 cup olive oil
- 1/4 cup wine vinegar
- 1 tablespoon agave syrup
- 1 teaspoon chaat masala
- 1 teaspoon coriander seeds
- Kosher salt and ground black pepper, to season

Directions:
1. Cover the soaked beans with a fresh change of cold water and bring to a boil. Turn the heat to a simmer and continue to cook for 50 to 55 minutes or until tender.
2. Allow your beans to cool completely; then, transfer them to a salad bowl.
3. Add in the remaining ingredients for the salad and toss to combine well.
4. Mix all the dressing ingredients. Dress your salad and serve well-chilled. Bon appétit!

Authentic African Mielie-meal

Servings: 4
Cooking Time: 15 Minutes
Ingredients:
- 3 cups water
- 1 cup coconut milk
- 1 cup maize meal
- 1/3 teaspoon kosher salt
- 1/4 teaspoon grated nutmeg
- 1/4 teaspoon ground cloves
- 4 tablespoons maple syrup

Directions:
1. In a saucepan, bring the water and milk to a boil; then, gradually add in the maize meal and turn the heat to a simmer.

2. Add in the salt, nutmeg and cloves. Let it cook for 10 minutes.
3. Add in the maple syrup and gently stir to combine. Bon appétit!

Bulgur Pancakes With A Twist

Servings: 4
Cooking Time: 50 Minutes
Ingredients:
- 1/2 cup bulgur wheat flour
- 1/2 cup almond flour
- 1 teaspoon baking soda
- 1/2 teaspoon fine sea salt
- 1 cup full-fat coconut milk
- 1/2 teaspoon ground cinnamon
- 1/4 teaspoon ground cloves
- 4 tablespoons coconut oil
- 1/2 cup maple syrup
- 1 large-sized banana, sliced

Directions:
1. In a mixing bowl, thoroughly combine the flour, baking soda, salt, coconut milk, cinnamon and ground cloves; let it stand for 30 minutes to soak well.
2. Heat a small amount of the coconut oil in a frying pan.
3. Fry the pancakes until the surface is golden brown. Garnish with maple syrup and banana. Bon appétit!

Lentil Salad With Pine Nuts

Servings: 3
Cooking Time: 20 Minutes
Ingredients:
- 1/2 cup brown lentils
- 1 ½ cups vegetable broth
- 1 carrot, cut into matchsticks
- 1 small onion, chopped
- 1 cucumber, sliced
- 2 cloves garlic, minced
- 3 tablespoons extra-virgin olive oil
- 1 tablespoon red wine vinegar
- 2 tablespoons lemon juice
- 2 tablespoons basil, chopped
- 2 tablespoons parsley, chopped
- 2 tablespoons chives, chopped
- Sea salt and ground black pepper, to taste
- 2 tablespoons pine nuts, roughly chopped

Directions:
1. Add the brown lentils and vegetable broth to a saucepan and bring to a boil over high heat. Then, turn the heat to a simmer and continue to cook for 20 minutes or until tender.
2. Place the lentils in a salad bowl.
3. Add in the vegetables and toss to combine well. In a mixing bowl, whisk the oil, vinegar, lemon juice, basil, parsley, chives, salt and black pepper.
4. Dress your salad, garnish with pine nuts and serve at room temperature. Bon appétit!

Spiced Roasted Chickpeas

Servings: 6
Cooking Time: 25 Minutes
Ingredients:
- 2 cups canned chickpeas, drained
- 2 tablespoons olive oil
- Sea salt and red pepper, to taste
- 1 teaspoon chili powder
- 1/2 teaspoon curry powder
- 1/2 teaspoon garlic powder

Directions:
1. Pat the chickpeas dry using paper towels. Drizzle olive oil over the chickpeas.
2. Roast the chickpeas in the preheated oven at 400 degrees F for about 25 minutes, tossing them once or twice.
3. Toss your chickpeas with the spices and enjoy!

Mexican Chickpea Taco Bowls

Servings: 4
Cooking Time: 15 Minutes
Ingredients:
- 2 tablespoons sesame oil
- 1 red onion, chopped
- 1 habanero pepper, minced
- 2 garlic cloves, crushed
- 2 bell peppers, seeded and diced
- Sea salt and ground black pepper
- 1/2 teaspoon Mexican oregano
- 1 teaspoon ground cumin
- 2 ripe tomatoes, pureed
- 1 teaspoon brown sugar
- 16 ounces canned chickpeas, drained
- 4 flour tortillas
- 2 tablespoons fresh coriander, roughly chopped

Directions:
1. In a large skillet, heat the sesame oil over a moderately high heat. Then, sauté the onions for 2 to 3 minutes or until tender.
2. Add in the peppers and garlic and continue to sauté for 1 minute or until fragrant.
3. Add in the spices, tomatoes and brown sugar and bring to a boil. Immediately turn the heat to a simmer, add in the canned chickpeas and let it cook for 8 minutes longer or until heated through.
4. Toast your tortillas and arrange them with the prepared chickpea mixture.
5. Top with fresh coriander and serve immediately. Bon appétit!

Barley Pilaf With Wild Mushrooms

Servings: 4
Cooking Time: 45 Minutes
Ingredients:
- 2 tablespoons vegan butter
- 1 small onion, chopped
- 1 teaspoon garlic, minced
- 1 jalapeno pepper, seeded and minced
- 1 pound wild mushrooms, sliced
- 1 cup medium pearl barley, rinsed
- 2 ¾ cups vegetable broth

Directions:
1. Melt the vegan butter in a saucepan over medium-high heat.
2. Once hot, cook the onion for about 3 minutes until just tender.
3. Add in the garlic, jalapeno pepper, mushrooms; continue to sauté for 2 minutes or until aromatic.
4. Add in the barley and broth, cover and continue to simmer for about 30 minutes. Once all the liquid has absorbed, allow the barley to rest for about 10 minutes fluff with a fork.
5. Taste and adjust the seasonings. Bon appétit!

Basic Amaranth Porridge

Servings: 4
Cooking Time: 35 Minutes
Ingredients:
- 3 cups water
- 1 cup amaranth
- 1/2 cup coconut milk
- 4 tablespoons agave syrup
- A pinch of kosher salt
- A pinch of grated nutmeg

Directions:
1. Bring the water to a boil over medium-high heat; add in the amaranth and turn the heat to a simmer.
2. Let it cook for about 30 minutes, stirring periodically to prevent the amaranth from sticking to the bottom of the pan.
3. Stir in the remaining ingredients and continue to cook for 1 to 2 minutes more until cooked through. Bon appétit!

Freekeh Bowl With Dried Figs

Servings: 2
Cooking Time: 35 Minutes
Ingredients:
- 1/2 cup freekeh, soaked for 30 minutes, drained
- 1 1/3 cups almond milk
- 1/4 teaspoon sea salt
- 1/4 teaspoon ground cloves
- 1/4 teaspoon ground cinnamon
- 4 tablespoons agave syrup
- 2 ounces dried figs, chopped

Directions:
1. Place the freekeh, milk, sea salt, ground cloves and cinnamon in a saucepan. Bring to a boil over medium-high heat.
2. Immediately turn the heat to a simmer for 30 to 35 minutes, stirring occasionally to promote even cooking.
3. Stir in the agave syrup and figs. Ladle the porridge into individual bowls and serve. Bon appétit!

Freekeh Salad With Za'atar

Servings: 4
Cooking Time: 35 Minutes
Ingredients:
- 1 cup freekeh
- 2 ½ cups water
- 1 cup grape tomatoes, halved
- 2 bell peppers, seeded and sliced
- 1 habanero pepper, seeded and sliced
- 1 onion, thinly sliced
- 2 tablespoons fresh cilantro, chopped
- 2 tablespoons fresh parsley, chopped
- 2 ounces green olives, pitted and sliced
- 1/4 cup extra-virgin olive oil
- 2 tablespoons lemon juice
- 1 teaspoon deli mustard
- 1 teaspoon za'atar
- Sea salt and ground black pepper, to taste

Directions:
1. Place the freekeh and water in a saucepan. Bring to a boil over medium-high heat.
2. Immediately turn the heat to a simmer for 30 to 35 minutes, stirring occasionally to promote even cooking. Let it cool completely.
3. Toss the cooked freekeh with the remaining ingredients. Toss to combine well.
4. Bon appétit!

Teff Salad With Avocado And Beans

Servings: 2
Cooking Time: 20 Minutes
Ingredients:
- 2 cups water
- 1/2 cup teff grain
- 1 teaspoon fresh lemon juice
- 3 tablespoons vegan mayonnaise
- 1 teaspoon deli mustard
- 1 small avocado, pitted, peeled and sliced
- 1 small red onion, thinly sliced
- 1 small Persian cucumber, sliced
- 1/2 cup canned kidney beans, drained
- 2 cups baby spinach

Directions:
1. In a deep saucepan, bring the water to a boil over high heat. Add in the teff grain and turn the heat to a simmer.
2. Continue to cook, covered, for about 20 minutes or until tender. Let it cool completely.
3. Add in the remaining ingredients and toss to combine. Serve at room temperature. Bon appétit!

Hot Anasazi Bean Salad

Servings: 5
Cooking Time: 1 Hour
Ingredients:
- 2 cups Anasazi beans, soaked overnight, drained and rinsed
- 6 cups water
- 1 poblano pepper, chopped
- 1 onion, chopped
- 1 cup cherry tomatoes, halved
- 2 cups mixed greens, ton into pieces
- Dressing:
- 1 teaspoon garlic, chopped
- 1/2 cup extra-virgin olive oil
- 1 tablespoon lemon juice
- 2 tablespoons red wine vinegar
- 1 tablespoon stone-ground mustard
- 1 tablespoon soy sauce
- 1/2 teaspoon dried oregano
- 1/2 teaspoon dried basil
- Sea salt and ground black pepper, to taste

Directions:
1. In a saucepan, bring the Anasazi beans and water to a boil. Once boiling, turn the heat to a simmer and let it cook for about 1 hour or until tender.
2. Drain the cooked beans and place them in a salad bowl; add in the other salad ingredients.
3. Then, in a small mixing bowl, whisk all the dressing ingredients until well blended. Dress your salad and toss to combine. Serve at room temperature and enjoy!

Harissa Bulgur Bowl

Servings: 4
Cooking Time: 25 Minutes
Ingredients:
- 1 cup bulgur wheat
- 1 ½ cups vegetable broth
- 2 cups sweet corn kernels, thawed
- 1 cup canned kidney beans, drained
- 1 red onion, thinly sliced
- 1 garlic clove, minced
- Sea salt and ground black pepper, to taste
- 1/4 cup harissa paste
- 1 tablespoon lemon juice
- 1 tablespoon white vinegar
- 1/4 cup extra-virgin olive oil
- 1/4 cup fresh parsley leaves, roughly chopped

Directions:
1. In a deep saucepan, bring the bulgur wheat and vegetable broth to a simmer; let it cook, covered, for 12 to 13 minutes.
2. Let it stand for 5 to 10 minutes and fluff your bulgur with a fork.
3. Add the remaining ingredients to the cooked bulgur wheat; serve warm or at room temperature. Bon appétit!

Bulgur Muffins With Raisins

Servings: 6
Cooking Time: 20 Minutes
Ingredients:
- 1 cup bulgur, cooked
- 4 tablespoons coconut oil, melted
- 1 teaspoon baking powder
- 1 teaspoon baking soda

- 2 tablespoons flax egg
- 1 ¼ cups all-purpose flour
- 1/2 cup coconut flour
- 1 cup coconut milk
- 4 tablespoons brown sugar
- 1/2 cup raisins, packed

Directions:

1. Start by preheating your oven to 420 degrees F. Spritz a muffin tin with a nonstick cooking oil.
2. Thoroughly combine all the dry ingredients. Add in the cooked bulgur.
3. In another bowl, whisk all the wet ingredients; add the wet mixture to the bulgur mixture; fold in the raisins.
4. Mix until everything is well combined, but not overmixed; spoon the batter into the prepared muffin.
5. Now, bake your muffins for about 16 minutes or until a tester comes out dry and clean. Bon appétit!

Quick Everyday Chili

Servings: 5
Cooking Time: 35 Minutes
Ingredients:

- 2 tablespoons olive oil
- 1 large onion, chopped
- 1 celery with leaves, trimmed and diced
- 1 carrot, trimmed and diced
- 1 sweet potato, peeled and diced
- 3 cloves garlic, minced
- 1 jalapeno pepper, minced
- 1 teaspoon cayenne pepper
- 1 teaspoon coriander seeds
- 1 teaspoon fennel seeds
- 1 teaspoon paprika
- 2 cups stewed tomatoes, crushed
- 2 tablespoons tomato ketchup
- 2 teaspoons vegan bouillon granules
- 1 cup water
- 1 cup cream of onion soup
- 2 pounds canned pinto beans, drained
- 1 lime, sliced

Directions:

1. In a heavy-bottomed pot, heat the olive oil over medium heat. Once hot, sauté the onion, celery, carrot and sweet potato for about 4 minutes.
2. Sauté the garlic and jalapeno pepper for about 1 minute or so.
3. Add in the spices, tomatoes, ketchup, vegan bouillon granules, water, cream of onion soup and canned beans. Let it simmer, stirring occasionally, for about 30 minutes or until cooked through.
4. Serve garnished with the slices of lime. Bon appétit!

Oat Porridge With Almonds

Servings: 2
Cooking Time: 20 Minutes
Ingredients:

- 1 cup water
- 2 cups almond milk, divided

- 1 cup rolled oats
- 2 tablespoons coconut sugar
- 1/2 vanilla essence
- 1/4 teaspoon cardamom
- 1/2 cup almonds, chopped
- 1 banana, sliced

Directions:

1. In a deep saucepan, bring the water and milk to a rapid boil. Add in the oats, cover the saucepan and turn the heat to medium.
2. Add in the coconut sugar, vanilla and cardamom. Continue to cook for about 12 minutes, stirring periodically.
3. Spoon the mixture into serving bowls; top with almonds and banana. Bon appétit!

Wok-fried Spiced Snow Pea

Servings: 4
Cooking Time: 10 Minutes
Ingredients:

- 2 tablespoons sesame oil
- 1 onion, chopped
- 1 carrot, trimmed and chopped
- 1 teaspoon ginger-garlic paste
- 1 pound snow peas
- Szechuan pepper, to taste
- 1 teaspoon Sriracha sauce
- 2 tablespoons soy sauce
- 1 tablespoon rice vinegar

Directions:

1. Heat the sesame oil in a wok until sizzling. Now, stir-fry the onion and carrot for 2 minutes or until crisp-tender.
2. Add in the ginger-garlic paste and continue to cook for 30 seconds more.
3. Add in the snow peas and stir-fry over high heat for about 3 minutes until lightly charred.
4. Then, stir in the pepper, Sriracha, soy sauce and rice vinegar and stir-fry for 1 minute more. Serve immediately and enjoy!

Coconut Quinoa Pudding

Servings: 3
Cooking Time: 20 Minutes
Ingredients:

- 1 cup water
- 1 cup coconut milk
- 1 cup quinoa
- A pinch of kosher salt
- A pinch of ground allspice
- 1/2 teaspoon cinnamon
- 1/2 teaspoon vanilla extract
- 4 tablespoons agave syrup
- 1/2 cup coconut flakes

Directions:

1. Place the water, coconut milk, quinoa, salt, ground allspice, cinnamon and vanilla extract in a saucepan.
2. Bring it to a boil over medium-high heat. Turn the heat to a simmer and let it cook for about 20 minutes; fluff with a fork and add in the agave syrup.

3. Divide between three serving bowls and garnish with coconut flakes. Bon appétit!

Red Kidney Bean Salad

Servings: 6
Cooking Time: 1 Hour
Ingredients:
- 3/4 pound red kidney beans, soaked overnight
- 2 bell peppers, chopped
- 1 carrot, trimmed and grated
- 3 ounces frozen or canned corn kernels, drained
- 3 heaping tablespoons scallions, chopped
- 2 cloves garlic, minced
- 1 red chile pepper, sliced
- 1/2 cup extra-virgin olive oil
- 2 tablespoons apple cider vinegar
- 2 tablespoons fresh lemon juice
- Sea salt and ground black pepper, to taste
- 2 tablespoons fresh cilantro, chopped
- 2 tablespoons fresh parsley, chopped
- 2 tablespoons fresh basil, chopped

Directions:
1. Cover the soaked beans with a fresh change of cold water and bring to a boil. Let it boil for about 10 minutes. Turn the heat to a simmer and continue to cook for 50 to 55 minutes or until tender.
2. Allow your beans to cool completely, then, transfer them to a salad bowl.
3. Add in the remaining ingredients and toss to combine well. Bon appétit!

Colorful Risotto With Vegetables

Servings: 5
Cooking Time: 35 Minutes
Ingredients:
- 2 tablespoons sesame oil
- 1 onion, chopped
- 2 bell peppers, chopped
- 1 parsnip, trimmed and chopped
- 1 carrot, trimmed and chopped
- 1 cup broccoli florets
- 2 garlic cloves, finely chopped
- 1/2 teaspoon ground cumin
- 2 cups brown rice
- Sea salt and black pepper, to taste
- 1/2 teaspoon ground turmeric
- 2 tablespoons fresh cilantro, finely chopped

Directions:
1. Heat the sesame oil in a saucepan over medium-high heat.
2. Once hot, cook the onion, peppers, parsnip, carrot and broccoli for about 3 minutes until aromatic.
3. Add in the garlic and ground cumin; continue to cook for 30 seconds more until aromatic.
4. Place the brown rice in a saucepan and cover with cold water by 2 inches. Bring to a boil. Turn the heat to a simmer and continue to cook for about 30 minutes or until tender.

5. Stir the rice into the vegetable mixture; season with salt, black pepper and ground turmeric; garnish with fresh cilantro and serve immediately. Bon appétit!

Sunday Three-bean Soup

Servings: 6
Cooking Time: 20 Minutes
Ingredients:
- 2 tablespoons olive oil
- 1 large shallot, chopped
- 2 carrots, diced
- 2 celery stalks, diced
- 1 red bell pepper, seeded and diced
- 2 sweet potatoes, peeled and diced
- 1 tablespoon ginger-garlic paste
- 1 bay laurel
- 1 cup tomatoes, pureed
- 5 cups vegetable broth
- 1/2 teaspoon red pepper flakes, crushed
- Sea salt and ground black pepper, to taste
- 1 canned white beans, drained
- 1 canned red kidney beans, drained
- 1 canned garbanzo beans, drained

Directions:
1. In a heavy-bottomed pot, heat the olive oil over medium-high heat. Now, sauté the shallot, carrots, celery, peppers and sweet potatoes for about 4 minutes until your vegetables have softened.
2. Add in the ginger-garlic paste and bay laurel and continue sautéing an additional 30 seconds or until fragrant.
3. Add in the tomatoes, broth, red pepper, salt and black pepper. Afterwards, add in the canned beans and turn the heat to a simmer.
4. Let it cook, partially covered, for 10 minutes more or until everything is thoroughly cooked. Bon appétit!

Easy Red Lentil Salad

Servings: 3
Cooking Time: 20 Minutes
Ingredients:
- 1/2 cup red lentils, soaked overnight and drained
- 1 ½ cups water
- 1 sprig rosemary
- 1 bay leaf
- 1 cup grape tomatoes, halved
- 1 cucumber, thinly sliced
- 1 bell pepper, thinly sliced
- 1 clove garlic, minced
- 1 onion, thinly sliced
- 2 tablespoons fresh lime juice
- 4 tablespoons olive oil
- Sea salt and ground black pepper, to taste

Directions:
1. Add the red lentils, water, rosemary and bay leaf to a saucepan and bring to a boil over high heat. Then, turn the heat to a simmer and continue to cook for 20 minutes or until tender.

2. Place the lentils in a salad bowl and let them cool completely.
3. Add in the remaining ingredients and toss to combine well. Serve at room temperature or well-chilled.
4. Bon appétit!

Easy Sweet Maize Meal Porridge

Servings: 2
Cooking Time: 15 Minutes
Ingredients:
- 2 cups water
- 1/2 cup maize meal
- 1/4 teaspoon ground allspice
- 1/4 teaspoon salt
- 2 tablespoons brown sugar
- 2 tablespoons almond butter

Directions:
1. In a saucepan, bring the water to a boil; then, gradually add in the maize meal and turn the heat to a simmer.
2. Add in the ground allspice and salt. Let it cook for 10 minutes.
3. Add in the brown sugar and almond butter and gently stir to combine. Bon appétit!

Chickpea Garden Vegetable Medley

Servings: 4
Cooking Time: 30 Minutes
Ingredients:
- 2 tablespoons olive oil
- 1 onion, finely chopped
- 1 bell pepper, chopped
- 1 fennel bulb, chopped
- 3 cloves garlic, minced
- 2 ripe tomatoes, pureed
- 2 tablespoons fresh parsley, roughly chopped
- 2 tablespoons fresh basil, roughly chopped
- 2 tablespoons fresh coriander, roughly chopped
- 2 cups vegetable broth
- 14 ounces canned chickpeas, drained
- Kosher salt and ground black pepper, to taste
- 1/2 teaspoon cayenne pepper
- 1 teaspoon paprika
- 1 avocado, peeled and sliced

Directions:
1. In a heavy-bottomed pot, heat the olive oil over medium heat. Once hot, sauté the onion, bell pepper and fennel bulb for about 4 minutes.
2. Sauté the garlic for about 1 minute or until aromatic.
3. Add in the tomatoes, fresh herbs, broth, chickpeas, salt, black pepper, cayenne pepper and paprika. Let it simmer, stirring occasionally, for about 20 minutes or until cooked through.
4. Taste and adjust the seasonings. Serve garnished with the slices of the fresh avocado. Bon appétit!

Chinese-style Soybean Salad

Servings: 4
Cooking Time: 10 Minutes

Ingredients:
- 1 can soybeans, drained
- 1 cup arugula
- 1 cup baby spinach
- 1 cup green cabbage, shredded
- 1 onion, thinly sliced
- 1/2 teaspoon garlic, minced
- 1 teaspoon ginger, minced
- 1/2 teaspoon deli mustard
- 2 tablespoons soy sauce
- 1 tablespoon rice vinegar
- 1 tablespoon lime juice
- 2 tablespoons tahini
- 1 teaspoon agave syrup

Directions:
1. In a salad bowl, place the soybeans, arugula, spinach, cabbage and onion; toss to combine.
2. In a small mixing dish, whisk the remaining ingredients for the dressing.
3. Dress your salad and serve immediately. Bon appétit!

Lentil And Tomato Dip

Servings: 8
Cooking Time: 10 Minutes
Ingredients:
- 16 ounces lentils, boiled and drained
- 4 tablespoons sun-dried tomatoes, chopped
- 1 cup tomato paste
- 4 tablespoons tahini
- 1 teaspoon stone-ground mustard
- 1 teaspoon ground cumin
- 1/4 teaspoon ground bay leaf
- 1 teaspoon red pepper flakes
- Sea salt and ground black pepper, to taste

Directions:
1. Blitz all the ingredients in your blender or food processor until your desired consistency is reached.
2. Place in your refrigerator until ready to serve.
3. Serve with toasted pita wedges or vegetable sticks. Enjoy!

Holiday Mini Cornbread Puddings

Servings: 8
Cooking Time: 30 Minutes
Ingredients:
- 1 cup all-purpose flour
- 1 cup yellow cornmeal
- 1 teaspoon baking powder
- 1 teaspoon baking soda
- 1 teaspoon sea salt
- 2 tablespoons brown sugar
- 1/2 teaspoon ground allspice
- 1 cup soy yogurt
- 1/4 cup vegan butter, melted
- 1 teaspoon apple cider vinegar
- 1 red bell pepper, seeded and chopped
- 1 green bell pepper, seeded and chopped

- 1 cup marinated mushrooms, chopped
- 2 small pickled cucumbers, chopped
- 1 tablespoon fresh basil, chopped
- 1 tablespoon fresh cilantro, chopped
- 1 tablespoon fresh chives, chopped

Directions:

1. Start by preheating your oven to 420 degrees F. Now, spritz a muffin tin with a nonstick cooking spray.
2. In a mixing bowl, thoroughly combine the flour, cornmeal, baking soda, baking powder, salt, sugar and ground allspice.
3. Gradually add in the yogurt, vegan butter and apple cider vinegar, whisking constantly to avoid lumps. Fold in the vegetables and herbs.
4. Scrape the batter into the prepared muffin tin. Bake your muffins for about 25 minutes or until a toothpick inserted in the middle comes out dry and clean.
5. Transfer them to a wire rack to rest for 5 minutes before unmolding and serving. Bon appétit!

Bread Pudding With Raisins

Servings: 4
Cooking Time: 1 Hour
Ingredients:

- 4 cups day-old bread, cubed
- 1 cup brown sugar
- 4 cups coconut milk
- 1/2 teaspoon vanilla extract
- 1 teaspoon ground cinnamon
- 2 tablespoons rum
- 1/2 cup raisins

Directions:

1. Start by preheating your oven to 360 degrees F. Lightly oil a casserole dish with a nonstick cooking spray.
2. Place the cubed bread in the prepared casserole dish.
3. In a mixing bowl, thoroughly combine the sugar, milk, vanilla, cinnamon, rum and raisins. Pour the custard evenly over the bread cubes.
4. Let it soak for about 15 minutes.
5. Bake in the preheated oven for about 45 minutes or until the top is golden and set. Bon appétit!

Green Lentil Stew With Collard Greens

Servings: 5
Cooking Time: 30 Minutes
Ingredients:

- 2 tablespoons olive oil
- 1 onion, chopped
- 2 sweet potatoes, peeled and diced
- 1 bell pepper, chopped
- 2 carrots, chopped
- 1 parsnip, chopped
- 1 celery, chopped
- 2 cloves garlic
- 1 ½ cups green lentils
- 1 tablespoon Italian herb mix
- 1 cup tomato sauce
- 5 cups vegetable broth

- 1 cup frozen corn
- 1 cup collard greens, torn into pieces

Directions:

1. In a Dutch oven, heat the olive oil until sizzling. Now, sauté the onion, sweet potatoes, bell pepper, carrots, parsnip and celery until they've softened.
2. Add in the garlic and continue sautéing an additional 30 seconds.
3. Now, add in the green lentils, Italian herb mix, tomato sauce and vegetable broth; let it simmer for about 20 minutes until everything is thoroughly cooked.
4. Add in the frozen corn and collard greens; cover and let it simmer for 5 minutes more. Bon appétit!

Ginger Brown Rice

Servings: 4
Cooking Time: 30 Minutes
Ingredients:

- 1 ½ cups brown rice, rinsed
- 2 tablespoons olive oil
- 1 teaspoon garlic, minced
- 1 piece ginger, peeled and minced
- 1/2 teaspoon cumin seeds
- Sea salt and ground black pepper, to taste

Directions:

1. Place the brown rice in a saucepan and cover with cold water by 2 inches. Bring to a boil.
2. Turn the heat to a simmer and continue to cook for about 30 minutes or until tender.
3. In a sauté pan, heat the olive oil over medium-high heat. Once hot, cook the garlic, ginger and cumin seeds until aromatic.
4. Stir the garlic/ginger mixture into the hot rice; season with salt and pepper and serve immediately. Bon appétit!

Classic Snow Pea Salad

Servings: 4
Cooking Time: 10 Minutes
Ingredients:

- 14 ounce frozen snow peas
- 1 red onion, thinly sliced
- 1 garlic clove, minced
- 1 red bell pepper, seeded and sliced
- 1 green bell pepper, seeded and sliced
- 4 tablespoons olive oil
- 2 tablespoons rice vinegar
- 1/4 teaspoon dried dill weed
- 1/4 teaspoon dried oregano
- 1 teaspoon dried basil
- 1 teaspoon red pepper flakes
- Sea salt and ground black pepper, to taste

Directions:

1. Place the snow peas in steamer; place it in a saucepan over boiling water; steam the snow peas for about 5 minutes or until crisp-tender.
2. Transfer the peas to a salad bowl.
3. Toss them with the remaining ingredients and serve at room temperature or well-chilled. Bon appétit!

Mom's Famous Chili

Servings: 5
Cooking Time: 1 Hour 30 Minutes
Ingredients:
- 1 pound red black beans, soaked overnight and drained
- 3 tablespoons olive oil
- 1 large red onion, diced
- 2 bell peppers, diced
- 1 poblano pepper, minced
- 1 large carrot, trimmed and diced
- 2 cloves garlic, minced
- 2 bay leaves
- 1 teaspoon mixed peppercorns
- Kosher salt and cayenne pepper, to taste
- 1 tablespoon paprika
- 2 ripe tomatoes, pureed
- 2 tablespoons tomato ketchup
- 3 cups vegetable broth

Directions:
1. Cover the soaked beans with a fresh change of cold water and bring to a boil. Let it boil for about 10 minutes. Turn the heat to a simmer and continue to cook for 50 to 55 minutes or until tender.
2. In a heavy-bottomed pot, heat the olive oil over medium heat. Once hot, sauté the onion, peppers and carrot.
3. Sauté the garlic for about 30 seconds or until aromatic.
4. Add in the remaining ingredients along with the cooked beans. Let it simmer, stirring periodically, for 25 to 30 minutes or until cooked through.
5. Discard the bay leaves, ladle into individual bowls and serve hot!

Easy And Hearty Shakshuka

Servings: 4
Cooking Time: 50 Minutes
Ingredients:
- 2 tablespoons olive oil
- 1 onion, chopped
- 2 bell peppers, chopped
- 1 poblano pepper, chopped
- 2 cloves garlic, minced
- 2 tomatoes, pureed
- Sea salt and black pepper, to taste
- 1 teaspoon dried basil
- 1 teaspoon red pepper flakes
- 1 teaspoon paprika
- 2 bay leaves
- 1 cup chickpeas, soaked overnight, rinsed and drained
- 3 cups vegetable broth
- 2 tablespoons fresh cilantro, roughly chopped

Directions:
1. Heat the olive oil in a saucepan over medium heat. Once hot, cook the onion, peppers and garlic for about 4 minutes, until tender and aromatic.
2. Add in the pureed tomato tomatoes, sea salt, black pepper, basil, red pepper, paprika and bay leaves.

3. Turn the heat to a simmer and add in the chickpeas and vegetable broth. Cook for 45 minutes or until tender.
4. Taste and adjust seasonings. Spoon your shakshuka into individual bowls and serve garnished with the fresh cilantro. Bon appétit!

Decadent Bread Pudding With Apricots

Servings: 4
Cooking Time: 1 Hour
Ingredients:
- 4 cups day-old ciabatta bread, cubed
- 4 tablespoons coconut oil, melted
- 2 cups coconut milk
- 1/2 cup coconut sugar
- 4 tablespoons applesauce
- 1/4 teaspoon ground cloves
- 1/2 teaspoon ground cinnamon
- 1 teaspoon vanilla extract
- 1/3 cup dried apricots, diced

Directions:
1. Start by preheating your oven to 360 degrees F. Lightly oil a casserole dish with a nonstick cooking spray.
2. Place the cubed bread in the prepared casserole dish.
3. In a mixing bowl, thoroughly combine the coconut oil, milk, coconut sugar, applesauce, ground cloves, ground cinnamon and vanilla. Pour the custard evenly over the bread cubes; fold in the apricots.
4. Press with a wide spatula and let it soak for about 15 minutes.
5. Bake in the preheated oven for about 45 minutes or until the top is golden and set. Bon appétit!

Middle Eastern Za'atar Hummus

Servings: 8
Cooking Time: 10 Minutes
Ingredients:
- 10 ounces chickpeas, boiled and drained
- 1/4 cup tahini
- 2 tablespoons extra-virgin olive oil
- 2 tablespoons sun-dried tomatoes, chopped
- 1 lemon, freshly squeezed
- 2 garlic cloves, minced
- Kosher salt and ground black pepper, to taste
- 1/2 teaspoon smoked paprika
- 1 teaspoon Za'atar

Directions:
1. Blitz all the ingredients in your food processor until creamy and uniform.
2. Place in your refrigerator until ready to serve.
3. Bon appétit!

Sweet Cornbread Muffins

Servings: 8
Cooking Time: 30 Minutes
Ingredients:
- 1 cup all-purpose flour
- 1 cup yellow cornmeal
- 1 teaspoon baking powder

- 1 teaspoon baking soda
- 1 teaspoon kosher salt
- 1/2 cup sugar
- 1/2 teaspoon ground cinnamon
- 1 1/2 cups almond milk
- 1/2 cup vegan butter, melted
- 2 tablespoons applesauce

Directions:

1. Start by preheating your oven to 420 degrees F. Now, spritz a muffin tin with a nonstick cooking spray.
2. In a mixing bowl, thoroughly combine the flour, cornmeal, baking soda, baking powder, salt, sugar and cinnamon.
3. Gradually add in the milk, butter and applesauce, whisking constantly to avoid lumps.
4. Scrape the batter into the prepared muffin tin. Bake your muffins for about 25 minutes or until a tester inserted in the middle comes out dry and clean.
5. Transfer them to a wire rack to rest for 5 minutes before unmolding and serving. Bon appétit!

Chocolate Rye Porridge

Servings: 4
Cooking Time: 10 Minutes
Ingredients:
- 2 cups rye flakes
- 2 ½ cups almond milk
- 2 ounces dried prunes, chopped
- 2 ounces dark chocolate chunks

Directions:

1. Add the rye flakes and almond milk to a deep saucepan; bring to a boil over medium-high. Turn the heat to a simmer and let it cook for 5 to 6 minutes.
2. Remove from the heat. Fold in the chopped prunes and chocolate chunks, gently stir to combine.
3. Ladle into serving bowls and serve warm.
4. Bon appétit!

Quinoa Porridge With Dried Figs

Servings: 3
Cooking Time: 25 Minutes
Ingredients:
- 1 cup white quinoa, rinsed
- 2 cups almond milk
- 4 tablespoons brown sugar
- A pinch of salt
- 1/4 teaspoon grated nutmeg
- 1/2 teaspoon ground cinnamon
- 1/2 teaspoon vanilla extract
- 1/2 cup dried figs, chopped

Directions:

1. Place the quinoa, almond milk, sugar, salt, nutmeg, cinnamon and vanilla extract in a saucepan.
2. Bring it to a boil over medium-high heat. Turn the heat to a simmer and let it cook for about 20 minutes; fluff with a fork.
3. Divide between three serving bowls and garnish with dried figs. Bon appétit!

Beluga Lentil And Vegetable Mélange

Servings: 5
Cooking Time: 25 Minutes
Ingredients:
- 3 tablespoons olive oil
- 1 onion, minced
- 2 bell peppers, seeded and chopped
- 1 carrot, trimmed and chopped
- 1 parsnip, trimmed and chopped
- 1 teaspoon ginger, minced
- 2 cloves garlic, minced
- Sea salt and ground black pepper, to taste
- 1 large-sized zucchini, diced
- 1 cup tomato sauce
- 1 cup vegetable broth
- 1 ½ cups beluga lentils, soaked overnight and drained
- 2 cups Swiss chard

Directions:

1. In a Dutch oven, heat the olive oil until sizzling. Now, sauté the onion, bell pepper, carrot and parsnip, until they've softened.
2. Add in the ginger and garlic and continue sautéing an additional 30 seconds.
3. Now, add in the salt, black pepper, zucchini, tomato sauce, vegetable broth and lentils; let it simmer for about 20 minutes until everything is thoroughly cooked.
4. Add in the Swiss chard; cover and let it simmer for 5 minutes more. Bon appétit!

Barley With Portobello Mushrooms And Chard

Servings: 4
Cooking Time: 35 Minutes
Ingredients:
- 4 tablespoons olive oil
- 1 onion, chopped
- 3 cloves garlic, minced
- 12 ounces Portobello mushrooms, sliced
- 4 cups vegetable broth
- 1 cup pearl barley
- 1/2 cup dry white wine
- Sea salt and ground black pepper, to taste
- 1 teaspoon dried oregano
- 1 teaspoon dried thyme
- 4 cups Swiss chard, torn into pieces

Directions:

1. Heat the olive oil in a saucepan over medium-high heat. Once hot, cook the onion for about 3 minutes until just tender.
2. Add in the garlic and mushrooms and continue to sauté for 2 minutes or until aromatic.
3. Add in the vegetable broth, barley, wine, salt, black pepper, oregano and thyme; cover and continue to simmer for about 25 minutes.
4. Add in the Swiss chard and continue to cook for 5 to 6 minutes more until it wilts. Bon appétit!

Polenta With Mushrooms And Chickpeas

Servings: 4
Cooking Time: 25 Minutes
Ingredients:
- 3 cups vegetable broth
- 1 cup yellow cornmeal
- 2 tablespoons olive oil
- 1 onion, chopped
- 1 bell pepper, seeded and sliced
- 1 pound Cremini mushrooms, sliced
- 2 garlic cloves, minced
- 1/2 cup dry white wine
- 1/2 cup vegetable broth
- Kosher salt and freshly ground black pepper, to taste
- 1 teaspoon paprika
- 1 cup canned chickpeas, drained

Directions:
1. In a medium saucepan, bring the vegetable broth to a boil over medium-high heat. Now, add in the cornmeal, whisking continuously to prevent lumps.
2. Reduce the heat to a simmer. Continue to simmer, whisking periodically, for about 18 minutes, until the mixture has thickened.
3. Meanwhile, heat the olive oil in a saucepan over a moderately high heat. Cook the onion and pepper for about 3 minutes or until just tender and fragrant.
4. Add in the mushrooms and garlic; continue to sauté, gradually adding the wine and broth, for 4 more minutes or until cooked through. Season with salt, black pepper and paprika. Stir in the chickpeas.
5. Spoon the mushroom mixture over your polenta and serve warm. Bon appétit!

Beluga Lentil Salad With Herbs

Servings: 4
Cooking Time: 20 Minutes
Ingredients:
- 1 cup red lentils
- 3 cups water
- 1 cup grape tomatoes, halved
- 1 green bell pepper, seeded and diced
- 1 red bell pepper, seeded and diced
- 1 red chili pepper, seeded and diced
- 1 cucumber, sliced
- 4 tablespoons shallots, chopped
- 2 tablespoons fresh parsley, roughly chopped
- 2 tablespoons fresh cilantro, roughly chopped
- 2 tablespoons fresh chives, roughly chopped
- 2 tablespoons fresh basil, roughly chopped
- 1/4 cup olive oil
- 1/2 teaspoon cumin seeds
- 1/2 teaspoon ginger, minced
- 1/2 teaspoon garlic, minced
- 1 teaspoon agave syrup
- 2 tablespoons fresh lemon juice
- 1 teaspoon lemon zest
- Sea salt and ground black pepper, to taste
- 2 ounces black olives, pitted and halved

Directions:
1. Add the brown lentils and water to a saucepan and bring to a boil over high heat. Then, turn the heat to a simmer and continue to cook for 20 minutes or until tender.
2. Place the lentils in a salad bowl.
3. Add in the vegetables and herbs and toss to combine well. In a mixing bowl, whisk the oil, cumin seeds, ginger, garlic, agave syrup, lemon juice, lemon zest, salt and black pepper.
4. Dress your salad, garnish with olives and serve at room temperature. Bon appétit!

Indian Dal Makhani

Servings: 6
Cooking Time: 20 Minutes
Ingredients:
- 3 tablespoons sesame oil
- 1 large onion, chopped
- 1 bell pepper, seeded and chopped
- 2 garlic cloves, minced
- 1 tablespoon ginger, grated
- 2 green chilies, seeded and chopped
- 1 teaspoon cumin seeds
- 1 bay laurel
- 1 teaspoon turmeric powder
- 1/4 teaspoon red peppers
- 1/4 teaspoon ground allspice
- 1/2 teaspoon garam masala
- 1 cup tomato sauce
- 4 cups vegetable broth
- 1 ½ cups black lentils, soaked overnight and drained
- 4-5 curry leaves, for garnish

Directions:
1. In a saucepan, heat the sesame oil over medium-high heat; now, sauté the onion and bell pepper for 3 minutes more until they've softened.
2. Add in the garlic, ginger, green chilies, cumin seeds and bay laurel; continue to sauté, stirring frequently, for 1 minute or until fragrant.
3. Stir in the remaining ingredients, except for the curry leaves. Now, turn the heat to a simmer. Continue to cook for 15 minutes more or until thoroughly cooked.
4. Garnish with curry leaves and serve hot!

Colorful Spelt Salad

Servings: 4
Cooking Time: 50 Minutes
Ingredients:
- 3 ½ cups water
- 1 cup dry spelt
- 1 cup canned kidney beans, drained
- 1 bell pepper, seeded and diced
- 2 medium tomatoes, diced
- 2 tablespoons basil, chopped
- 2 tablespoons parsley, chopped
- 2 tablespoons mint, chopped

- 1/4 cup extra-virgin olive oil
- 1 teaspoon deli mustard
- 1 tablespoon fresh lime juice
- 1 tablespoon white vinegar
- Sea salt and cayenne pepper, to taste

Directions:

1. Bring the water to a boil over medium-high heat. Now, add in the spelt, turn the heat to a simmer and continue to cook for approximately 50 minutes, until the spelt is tender. Drain and allow it to cool completely.

2. Toss the spelt with the remaining ingredients; toss to combine well and place the salad in your refrigerator until ready to serve.

3. Bon appétit!

Grandma's Pilau With Garden Vegetables

Servings: 4
Cooking Time: 45 Minutes
Ingredients:

- 2 tablespoons olive oil
- 1 onion, chopped
- 1 carrot, trimmed and grated
- 1 parsnip, trimmed and grated
- 1 celery with leaves, chopped
- 1 teaspoon garlic, chopped
- 1 cup brown rice
- 2 cups vegetable broth
- 2 tablespoons fresh parsley, chopped
- 2 tablespoons finely basil, chopped

Directions:

1. Heat the olive oil in a saucepan over medium-high heat.

2. Once hot, cook the onion, carrot, parsnip and celery for about 3 minutes until just tender. Add in the garlic and continue to sauté for 1 minute or so until aromatic.

3. In a lightly oiled casserole dish, place the rice, flowed by the sautéed vegetables and broth.

4. Bake, covered, at 375 degrees F for about 40 minutes, stirring after 20 minutes.

5. Garnish with fresh parsley and basil and serve warm. Bon appétit!

Mexican-style Bean Bowl

Servings: 6
Cooking Time: 1 Hour
Ingredients:

- 1 pound red beans, soaked overnight and drained
- 1 cup canned corn kernels, drained
- 2 roasted bell peppers, sliced
- 1 chili pepper, finely chopped
- 1 cup cherry tomatoes, halved
- 1 red onion, chopped
- 1/4 cup fresh cilantro, chopped
- 1/4 cup fresh parsley, chopped
- 1 teaspoon Mexican oregano
- 1/4 cup red wine vinegar
- 2 tablespoons fresh lemon juice

- 1/3 cup extra-virgin olive oil
- Sea salt and ground black, to taste
- 1 avocado, peeled, pitted and sliced

Directions:

1. Cover the soaked beans with a fresh change of cold water and bring to a boil. Let it boil for about 10 minutes. Turn the heat to a simmer and continue to cook for 50 to 55 minutes or until tender.

2. Allow your beans to cool completely, then, transfer them to a salad bowl.

3. Add in the remaining ingredients and toss to combine well. Serve at room temperature.

4. Bon appétit!

Classic Italian Minestrone

Servings: 5
Cooking Time: 30 Minutes
Ingredients:

- 2 tablespoons olive oil
- 1 large onion, diced
- 2 carrots, sliced
- 4 cloves garlic, minced
- 1 cup elbow pasta
- 5 cups vegetable broth
- 1 can white beans, drained
- 1 large zucchini, diced
- 1 can tomatoes, crushed
- 1 tablespoon fresh oregano leaves, chopped
- 1 tablespoon fresh basil leaves, chopped
- 1 tablespoon fresh Italian parsley, chopped

Directions:

1. In a Dutch oven, heat the olive oil until sizzling. Now, sauté the onion and carrots until they've softened.

2. Add in the garlic, uncooked pasta and broth; let it simmer for about 15 minutes.

3. Stir in the beans, zucchini, tomatoes and herbs. Continue to cook, covered, for about 10 minutes until everything is thoroughly cooked.

4. Garnish with some extra herbs, if desired. Bon appétit!

Sweet Pea Salad With Tofu

Servings: 4
Cooking Time: 10 Minutes
Ingredients:

- 16 ounces sweet peas
- 4 tablespoons shallots, chopped
- 1 Persian cucumber, diced
- 4 tablespoons extra-virgin olive oil
- 1 tablespoon fresh lemon juice
- 1 teaspoon Dijon mustard
- 1 teaspoon garlic, minced
- 1 teaspoon fresh dill, chopped
- 2 tablespoons fresh parsley, chopped
- 6 ounces tofu, pressed and cubed

Directions:

1. Cook the green peas in a pot of a lightly salted water for 5 to 6 minutes. Let it cool completely.

2. Add the peas to a salad bowl; add in the shallot, cucumber, olive oil, lemon juice, mustard, garlic, dill and parsley.
3. Gently toss to combine and top with the cubed tofu. Serve at room temperature or place in your refrigerator until ready to serve. Bon appétit!

Easy Homemade Falafel

Servings: 6
Cooking Time: 20 Minutes
Ingredients:
- 1 ½ cups dried chickpeas, soaked overnight and drained
- 1 medium onion
- 3 garlic cloves
- 2 tablespoons fresh parsley leaves
- 2 tablespoons fresh basil leaves
- 1 teaspoon fresh mint leaves
- Sea salt and ground black pepper, to taste
- 1/2 teaspoon paprika
- 1/2 teaspoon ground bay leaf
- 1 teaspoon cumin
- 6 tablespoons all-purpose flour
- 1 teaspoon baking powder
- 4 tablespoons olive oil

Directions:
1. Place the chickpeas, onion, garlic, parsley, basil, mint and spices in the bowl of your food processor.
2. Pulse until well blended. Add in the flour and baking powder and stir to combine well. Roll the mixture into equal balls.
3. Heat the olive oil in a frying pan over medium-high heat.
4. Fry your falafel until golden brown. Serve with flatbread and vegetables, if desired. Enjoy!

Homemade Pea Burgers

Servings: 4
Cooking Time: 15 Minutes
Ingredients:
- 1 pound green peas, frozen and thawed
- 1/2 cup chickpea flour
- 1/2 cup plain flour
- 1/2 cup breadcrumbs
- 1 teaspoon baking powder
- 2 flax eggs
- 1 teaspoon paprika
- 1/2 teaspoon dried basil
- 1/2 teaspoon dried oregano
- Sea salt and ground black pepper, to taste
- 4 tablespoons olive oil
- 4 hamburger buns

Directions:
1. In a mixing bowl, thoroughly combine the green peas, flour, breadcrumbs, baking powder, flax eggs, paprika, basil, oregano, salt and black pepper.
2. Shape the mixture into four patties.
3. Then, heat the olive oil in a frying pan over a moderately high heat. Fry the patties for about 8 minutes, turning them over once or twice.

4. Serve on burger buns and enjoy!

Red Kidney Bean Patties

Servings: 4
Cooking Time: 15 Minutes
Ingredients:
- 12 ounces canned or boiled red kidney beans, drained
- 1/3 cup old-fashioned oats
- 1/4 cup all-purpose flour
- 1 teaspoon baking powder
- 1 small shallot, chopped
- 2 cloves garlic, minced
- Sea salt and ground black pepper, to taste
- 1 teaspoon paprika
- 1/2 teaspoon chili powder
- 1/2 teaspoon ground bay leaf
- 1/2 teaspoon ground cumin
- 1 chia egg
- 4 tablespoon olive oil

Directions:
1. Place the beans in a mixing bowl and mash them with a fork.
2. Thoroughly combine the beans, oats, flour, baking powder, shallot, garlic, salt, black pepper, paprika, chili powder, ground bay leaf, cumin and chia egg.
3. Shape the mixture into four patties.
4. Then, heat the olive oil in a frying pan over a moderately high heat. Fry the patties for about 8 minutes, turning them over once or twice.
5. Serve with your favorite toppings. Bon appétit!

Mom's Millet Muffins

Servings: 8
Cooking Time: 20 Minutes
Ingredients:
- 2 cup whole-wheat flour
- 1/2 cup millet
- 2 teaspoons baking powder
- 1/2 teaspoon salt
- 1 cup coconut milk
- 1/2 cup coconut oil, melted
- 1/2 cup agave nectar
- 1/2 teaspoon ground cinnamon
- 1/4 teaspoon ground cloves
- A pinch of grated nutmeg
- 1/2 cup dried apricots, chopped

Directions:
1. Begin by preheating your oven to 400 degrees F. Lightly oil a muffin tin with a nonstick oil.
2. In a mixing bowl, mix all dry ingredients. In a separate bowl, mix the wet ingredients. Stir the milk mixture into the flour mixture; mix just until evenly moist and do not overmix your batter.
3. Fold in the apricots and scrape the batter into the prepared muffin cups.
4. Bake the muffins in the preheated oven for about 15 minutes, or until a tester inserted in the center of your muffin comes out dry and clean.

5. Let it stand for 10 minutes on a wire rack before unmolding and serving. Enjoy!

Rye Porridge With Blueberry Topping

Servings: 3
Cooking Time: 15 Minutes
Ingredients:
- 1 cup rye flakes
- 1 cup water
- 1 cup coconut milk
- 1 cup fresh blueberries
- 1 tablespoon coconut oil
- 6 dates, pitted

Directions:
1. Add the rye flakes, water and coconut milk to a deep saucepan; bring to a boil over medium-high. Turn the heat to a simmer and let it cook for 5 to 6 minutes.
2. In a blender or food processor, puree the blueberries with the coconut oil and dates.
3. Ladle into three bowls and garnish with the blueberry topping.
4. Bon appétit!

Cornmeal Porridge With Maple Syrup

Servings: 4
Cooking Time: 20 Minutes
Ingredients:
- 2 cups water
- 2 cups almond milk
- 1 cinnamon stick
- 1 vanilla bean
- 1 cup yellow cornmeal
- 1/2 cup maple syrup

Directions:
1. In a saucepan, bring the water and almond milk to a boil. Add in the cinnamon stick and vanilla bean.
2. Gradually add in the cornmeal, stirring continuously; turn the heat to a simmer. Let it simmer for about 15 minutes.
3. Drizzle the maple syrup over the porridge and serve warm. Enjoy!

Greek-style Chickpea Bowl

Servings: 4
Cooking Time: 45 Minutes
Ingredients:
- 2 cups dry chickpeas, soaked overnight and drained
- 1 bay leaf
- 1 thyme sprig
- 1/2 teaspoon ground cumin
- Sea salt and cayenne pepper, to taste
- 2 cups baby spinach
- 1 cucumber, sliced
- 1 bell pepper, sliced
- 1 cup cherry tomatoes, halved
- 1/2 cup green olives, pitted and sliced
- 6 tablespoons olive oil
- 2 tablespoons lemon juice
- 1 teaspoon deli mustard

- 1 teaspoon dried basil
- 1 teaspoon dried oregano
- 4 pita bread, cut into wedges

Directions:
1. Place the chickpeas, bay leaf and thyme sprig in a stockpot; cover the chickpeas with water by 2 inches. Bring it to a boil.
2. Immediately turn the heat to a simmer and continue to cook for about 40 minutes or until tender.
3. Transfer your chickpeas to a salad bowl. Add in the cumin, salt, cayenne pepper, spinach, cucumber, pepper, tomatoes and olives; toss to combine well.
4. Then, in a mixing bowl, whisk 4 tablespoons of the olive oil, lemon juice and mustard. Dress the salad and place it in your refrigerator until ready to serve.
5. Heat the remaining 2 tablespoons of the olive oil in a nonstick skillet. Toast the pita bread with the basil and oregano. Top the chickpea salad with the toasted pita wedges and serve. Bon appétit!

Old-fashioned Lentil And Vegetable Stew

Servings: 5
Cooking Time: 25 Minutes
Ingredients:
- 3 tablespoons olive oil
- 1 large onion, chopped
- 1 carrot, chopped
- 1 bell pepper, diced
- 1 habanero pepper, chopped
- 3 cloves garlic, minced
- Kosher salt and black pepper, to taste
- 1 teaspoon ground cumin
- 1 teaspoon smoked paprika
- 1 can tomatoes, crushed
- 2 tablespoons tomato ketchup
- 4 cups vegetable broth
- 3/4 pound dry red lentils, soaked overnight and drained
- 1 avocado, sliced

Directions:
1. In a heavy-bottomed pot, heat the olive oil over medium heat. Once hot, sauté the onion, carrot and peppers for about 4 minutes.
2. Sauté the garlic for about 1 minute or so.
3. Add in the spices, tomatoes, ketchup, broth and canned lentils. Let it simmer, stirring occasionally, for about 20 minutes or until cooked through.
4. Serve garnished with the slices of avocado. Bon appétit!

Traditional Portuguese Papas

Servings: 4
Cooking Time: 35 Minutes
Ingredients:
- 4 cups water
- 2 cups rice milk
- 1 cup grits
- 1/4 teaspoon grated nutmeg
- 1/4 teaspoon kosher salt

- 4 tablespoon vegan butter
- 1/4 cup maple syrup

Directions:

1. Bring the water and milk to a boil over a moderately high heat.
2. Stir in the grits, nutmeg and salt. Turn the heat to a simmer, cover and continue to cook, for about 30 minutes or until cooked through.
3. Stir in the vegan butter and maple syrup. Bon appétit!

One-pot Italian Rice With Broccoli

Servings: 4
Cooking Time: 30 Minutes

Ingredients:

- 2 tablespoons olive oil
- 1 shallot, chopped
- 1 teaspoon ginger, minced
- 1 teaspoon garlic, minced
- 1/2 pound broccoli florets
- 1 cup Arborio rice
- 4 cups roasted vegetable broth

Directions:

1. In a medium-sized pot, heat the olive oil over a moderately high flame. Add in the shallot and cook for about 3 minutes or until tender and translucent.
2. Then, add in the ginger and garlic and continue to cook for 30 seconds more. Add in the broccoli and rice and continue to cook for 4 minutes more.
3. Pour the vegetable broth into the saucepan and bring to a boil; immediately turn the heat to a gentle simmer.
4. Cook for about 20 minutes or until all the liquid has absorbed. Taste and adjust the seasonings. Bon appétit!

Teff Porridge With Dried Figs

Servings: 4
Cooking Time: 25 Minutes

Ingredients:

- 1 cup whole-grain teff
- 1 cup water
- 2 cups coconut milk
- 2 tablespoons coconut oil
- 1/2 teaspoon ground cardamom
- 1/4 teaspoon ground cinnamon
- 4 tablespoons agave syrup
- 7-8 dried figs, chopped

Directions:

1. Bring the whole-grain teff, water and coconut milk to a boil.
2. Turn the heat to a simmer and add in the coconut oil, cardamom and cinnamon.
3. Let it cook for 20 minutes or until the grain has softened and the porridge has thickened. Stir in the agave syrup and stir to combine well.
4. Top each serving bowl with chopped figs and serve warm. Bon appétit!

Powerful Teff Bowl With Tahini Sauce

Servings: 4
Cooking Time: 20 Minutes

Ingredients:

- 3 cups water
- 1 cup teff
- 2 garlic cloves, pressed
- 4 tablespoons tahini
- 2 tablespoons tamari sauce
- 2 tablespoons white vinegar
- 1 teaspoon agave nectar
- 1 teaspoon deli mustard
- 1 teaspoon Italian herb mix
- 1 cup canned chickpeas, drained
- 2 cups mixed greens
- 1 cup grape tomatoes, halved
- 1 Italian peppers, seeded and diced

Directions:

1. In a deep saucepan, bring the water to a boil over high heat. Add in the teff grain and turn the heat to a simmer.
2. Continue to cook, covered, for about 20 minutes or until tender. Let it cool completely and transfer to a salad bowl.
3. In the meantime, mix the garlic, tahini, tamari sauce, vinegar, agave nectar, mustard and Italian herb mix; whisk until everything is well incorporated.
4. Add the canned chickpeas, mixed greens, tomatoes and peppers to the salad bowl; toss to combine. Dress the salad and toss again. Serve at room temperature. Bon appétit!

Millet Porridge With Sultanas

Servings: 3
Cooking Time: 25 Minutes

Ingredients:

- 1 cup water
- 1 cup coconut milk
- 1 cup millet, rinsed
- 1/4 teaspoon grated nutmeg
- 1/4 teaspoon ground cinnamon
- 1 teaspoon vanilla paste
- 1/4 teaspoon kosher salt
- 2 tablespoons agave syrup
- 4 tablespoons sultana raisins

Directions:

1. Place the water, milk, millet, nutmeg, cinnamon, vanilla and salt in a saucepan; bring to a boil.
2. Turn the heat to a simmer and let it cook for about 20 minutes; fluff the millet with a fork and spoon into individual bowls.
3. Serve with agave syrup and sultanas. Bon appétit!

Chipotle Cilantro Rice

Servings: 4
Cooking Time: 25 Minutes

Ingredients:

- 4 tablespoons olive oil
- 1 chipotle pepper, seeded and chopped
- 1 cup jasmine rice
- 1 ½ cups vegetable broth
- 1/4 cup fresh cilantro, chopped
- Sea salt and cayenne pepper, to taste

Directions:

1. In a saucepan, heat the olive oil over a moderately high flame. Add in the pepper and rice and cook for about 3 minutes or until aromatic.
2. Pour the vegetable broth into the saucepan and bring to a boil; immediately turn the heat to a gentle simmer.
3. Cook for about 18 minutes or until all the liquid has absorbed. Fluff the rice with a fork, add in the cilantro, salt and cayenne pepper; stir to combine well. Bon appétit!

Polenta Toasts With Balsamic Onions

Servings: 5
Cooking Time: 25 Minutes
Ingredients:
- 3 cups vegetable broth
- 1 cup yellow cornmeal
- 4 tablespoons vegan butter, divided
- 2 tablespoons olive oil
- 2 large onions, sliced
- Sea salt and ground black pepper, to taste
- 1 thyme sprig, chopped
- 1 tablespoon balsamic vinegar

Directions:
1. In a medium saucepan, bring the vegetable broth to a boil over medium-high heat. Now, add in the cornmeal, whisking continuously to prevent lumps.
2. Reduce the heat to a simmer. Continue to simmer, whisking periodically, for about 18 minutes, until the mixture has thickened. Stir the vegan butter into the cooked polenta.
3. Spoon the cooked polenta into a lightly greased square baking dish. Cover with the plastic wrap and chill for about 2 hours or until firm.
4. Meanwhile, heat the olive oil in a nonstick skillet over a moderately high heat. Cook the onions for about 3 minutes or until just tender and fragrant.
5. Stir in the salt, black pepper, thyme and balsamic vinegar and continue to sauté for 1 minute or so; remove from the heat.
6. Cut your polenta into squares. Spritz a nonstick skillet with a cooking spray. Fry the polenta squares for about 5 minutes per side or until golden brown.
7. Top each polenta toast with the balsamic onion and serve. Bon appétit!

Country Cornbread With Spinach

Servings: 8
Cooking Time: 50 Minutes
Ingredients:
- 1 tablespoon flaxseed meal
- 1 cup all-purpose flour
- 1 cup yellow cornmeal
- 1/2 teaspoon baking soda
- 1/2 teaspoon baking powder
- 1 teaspoon kosher salt
- 1 teaspoon brown sugar
- A pinch of grated nutmeg
- 1 ¼ cups oat milk, unsweetened
- 1 teaspoon white vinegar
- 1/2 cup olive oil

- 2 cups spinach, torn into pieces
Directions:
1. Start by preheating your oven to 420 degrees F. Now, spritz a baking pan with a nonstick cooking spray.
2. To make the flax eggs, mix flaxseed meal with 3 tablespoons of the water. Stir and let it sit for about 15 minutes.
3. In a mixing bowl, thoroughly combine the flour, cornmeal, baking soda, baking powder, salt, sugar and grated nutmeg.
4. Gradually add in the flax egg, oat milk, vinegar and olive oil, whisking constantly to avoid lumps. Afterwards, fold in the spinach.
5. Scrape the batter into the prepared baking pan. Bake your cornbread for about 25 minutes or until a tester inserted in the middle comes out dry and clean.
6. Let it stand for about 10 minutes before slicing and serving. Bon appétit!

Hot And Spicy Anasazi Bean Soup

Servings: 5
Cooking Time: 1 Hour 10 Minutes
Ingredients:
- 2 cups Anasazi beans, soaked overnight, drained and rinsed
- 8 cups water
- 2 bay leaves
- 3 tablespoons olive oil
- 2 medium onions, chopped
- 2 bell peppers, chopped
- 1 habanero pepper, chopped
- 3 cloves garlic, pressed or minced
- Sea salt and ground black pepper, to taste

Directions:
1. In a soup pot, bring the Anasazi beans and water to a boil. Once boiling, turn the heat to a simmer. Add in the bay leaves and let it cook for about 1 hour or until tender.
2. Meanwhile, in a heavy-bottomed pot, heat the olive oil over medium-high heat. Now, sauté the onion, peppers and garlic for about 4 minutes until tender.
3. Add the sautéed mixture to the cooked beans. Season with salt and black pepper.
4. Continue to simmer, stirring periodically, for 10 minutes more or until everything is cooked through. Bon appétit!

White Bean Stuffed Tomatoes

Servings: 3
Cooking Time: 10 Minutes
Ingredients:
- 3 medium tomatoes, cut a thin slice off the top and remove pulp
- 1 carrot, grated
- 1 red onion, chopped
- 1 garlic clove, peeled
- 1/2 teaspoon dried basil
- 1/2 teaspoon dried oregano
- 1 teaspoon dried rosemary
- 3 tablespoons olive oil
- 3 ounces canned white beans, drained

- 3 ounces sweet corn kernels, thawed
- 1/2 cup tortilla chips, crushed

Directions:
1. Place your tomatoes on a serving platter.
2. In a mixing bowl, stir the remaining ingredients for the stuffing until everything is well combined.
3. Fill the avocados and serve immediately. Bon appétit!

Chickpea Stuffed Avocados

Servings: 4
Cooking Time: 10 Minutes
Ingredients:
- 2 avocados, pitted and sliced in half
- 1/2 lemon, freshly squeezed
- 4 tablespoons scallions, chopped
- 1 garlic clove, minced
- 1 medium tomato, chopped
- 1 bell pepper, seeded and chopped
- 1 red chili pepper, seeded and chopped
- 2 ounces chickpeas, boiled or cabbed, drained
- Kosher salt and ground black pepper, to taste

Directions:
1. Place your avocados on a serving platter. Drizzle the lemon juice over each avocado.
2. In a mixing bowl, gently stir the remaining ingredients for the stuffing until well incorporated.
3. Fill the avocados with the prepared mixture and serve immediately. Bon appétit!

Winter Black-eyed Pea Soup

Servings: 5
Cooking Time: 1 Hour 5 Minutes
Ingredients:
- 2 tablespoons olive oil
- 1 onion, chopped
- 1 carrot, chopped
- 1 parsnip, chopped
- 1 cup fennel bulbs, chopped
- 2 cloves garlic, minced
- 2 cups dried black-eyed peas, soaked overnight
- 5 cups vegetable broth
- Kosher salt and freshly ground black pepper, to season

Directions:
1. In a Dutch oven, heat the olive oil over medium-high heat. Once hot, sauté the onion, carrot, parsnip and fennel for 3 minutes or until just tender.
2. Add in the garlic and continue to sauté for 30 seconds or until aromatic.
3. Add in the peas, vegetable broth, salt and black pepper. Continue to cook, partially covered, for 1 hour more or until cooked through.
4. Bon appétit!

Overnight Oatmeal With Prunes

Servings: 2
Cooking Time: 5 Minutes
Ingredients:
- 1 cup hemp milk

- 1 tablespoon flax seed, ground
- 2/3 cup rolled oats
- 2 ounces prunes, sliced
- 2 tablespoons agave syrup
- A pinch of salt
- 1/2 teaspoon ground cinnamon

Directions:
1. Divide the ingredients, except for the prunes, between two mason jars.
2. Cover and shake to combine well. Let them sit overnight in your refrigerator.
3. Garnish with sliced prunes just before serving. Enjoy!

Mediterranean-style Rice

Servings: 4
Cooking Time: 20 Minutes
Ingredients:
- 3 tablespoons vegan butter, at room temperature
- 4 tablespoons scallions, chopped
- 2 cloves garlic, minced
- 1 bay leaf
- 1 thyme sprig, chopped
- 1 rosemary sprig, chopped
- 1 ½ cups white rice
- 2 cups vegetable broth
- 1 large tomato, pureed
- Sea salt and ground black pepper, to taste
- 2 ounces Kalamata olives, pitted and sliced

Directions:
1. In a saucepan, melt the vegan butter over a moderately high flame. Cook the scallions for about 2 minutes or until tender.
2. Add in the garlic, bay leaf, thyme and rosemary and continue to sauté for about 1 minute or until aromatic.
3. Add in the rice, broth and pureed tomato. Bring to a boil; immediately turn the heat to a gentle simmer.
4. Cook for about 15 minutes or until all the liquid has absorbed. Fluff the rice with a fork, season with salt and pepper and garnish with olives; serve immediately.
5. Bon appétit!

Red Kidney Bean Pâté

Servings: 8
Cooking Time: 10 Minutes
Ingredients:
- 2 tablespoons olive oil
- 1 onion, chopped
- 1 bell pepper, chopped
- 2 cloves garlic, minced
- 2 cups red kidney beans, boiled and drained
- 1/4 cup olive oil
- 1 teaspoon stone-ground mustard
- 2 tablespoons fresh parsley, chopped
- 2 tablespoons fresh basil, chopped
- Sea salt and ground black pepper, to taste

Directions:

1. In a saucepan, heat the olive oil over medium-high heat. Now, cook the onion, pepper and garlic until just tender or about 3 minutes.

2. Add the sautéed mixture to your blender; add in the remaining ingredients. Puree the ingredients in your blender or food processor until smooth and creamy.

3. Bon appétit!

Aromatic Rice Pudding With Dried Figs

Servings: 4
Cooking Time: 45 Minutes
Ingredients:
- 2 cups water
- 1 cup medium-grain white rice
- 3 ½ cups coconut milk
- 1/2 cup coconut sugar
- 1 cinnamon stick
- 1 vanilla bean
- 1/2 cup dried figs, chopped
- 4 tablespoons coconut, shredded

Directions:
1. In a saucepan, bring the water to a boil over medium-high heat. Immediately turn the heat to a simmer, add in the rice and let it cook for about 20 minutes.

2. Add in the milk, sugar and spices and continue to cook for 20 minutes more, stirring constantly to prevent the rice from sticking to the pan.

3. Top with dried figs and coconut; serve your pudding warm or at room temperature. Bon appétit!

Pinto Bean Soup With Herbs

Servings: 5
Cooking Time: 1 Hour 35 Minutes
Ingredients:
- 2 cups pinto beans, soaked overnight and drained
- 3 tablespoons olive oil
- 1 large onion, chopped
- 1 celery with leaves, chopped
- 1 bell pepper, seeded and chopped
- 1 red chili pepper, seeded and chopped
- 1 teaspoon garlic, minced
- 1 teaspoon dried thyme
- 1 teaspoon dried marjoram
- 1 teaspoon dried oregano
- 1 cup tomato, pureed
- 4 cups vegetable broth
- Sea salt and ground black pepper, to taste
- 1 bay leaf

Directions:
1. Cover the soaked beans with a fresh change of cold water and bring to a boil. Let it boil for about 10 minutes. Turn the heat to a simmer and continue to cook for 50 to 55 minutes or until tender.

2. In a heavy-bottomed pot, heat the olive oil over medium heat. Once hot, sauté the onion, celery and peppers for about 3 minutes.

3. Sauté the garlic and herbs for approximately 3 minutes or until fragrant.

4. Add in the vegetable broth, salt, black pepper, bay leaf and cooked beans. Let it simmer, stirring periodically, for about 25 minutes or until cooked through. Bon appétit!

Red Rice And Vegetable Stir-fry

Servings: 4
Cooking Time: 55 Minutes
Ingredients:
- 1 cup cream of celery soup
- 1/2 cup water
- 1 cup red rice
- 2 tablespoons vegan butter
- 1 small leek, chopped
- 1 cup green cabbage, chopped
- 2 bell peppers, sliced
- 3 cloves garlic, minced
- 4 tablespoons rice wine
- Sea salt and ground black pepper, to season
- 2 tablespoons soy sauce

Directions:
1. Bring the soup and water to a boil over medium-high heat. Turn the heat to a simmer.

2. Cook the brown rice for about 45 minutes or until all the liquid has been absorbed.

3. In a saucepan, melt the vegan butter over a moderately high heat. Once hot, cook the leek, cabbage and peppers for about 3 minutes until they've softened.

4. Add in the garlic and continue to sauté an additional 30 seconds. Add a splash of wine to deglaze the pan.

5. Add in the salt, black pepper and the reserved rice. Stir fry for about 5 minutes or until cooked through; add in the soy sauce and stir again to combine. Serve immediately.

Everyday Savory Grits

Servings: 4
Cooking Time: 35 Minutes
Ingredients:
- 2 tablespoons vegan butter
- 1 sweet onion, chopped
- 1 teaspoon garlic, minced
- 4 cups water
- 1 cup stone-ground grits
- Sea salt and cayenne pepper, to taste

Directions:
1. In a saucepan, melt the vegan butter over medium-high heat. Once hot, cook the onion for about 3 minutes or until tender.

2. Add in the garlic and continue to sauté for 30 seconds more or until aromatic; reserve.

3. Bring the water to a boil over a moderately high heat. Stir in the grits, salt and pepper. Turn the heat to a simmer, cover and continue to cook, for about 30 minutes or until cooked through.

4. Stir in the sautéed mixture and serve warm. Bon appétit!

Last-minute Baked Rice

Servings: 4
Cooking Time: 35 Minutes
Ingredients:
- 2 cups boiling vegetable broth
- 2 tablespoons olive oil
- 1 cup white rice
- 3 cups vegetable broth
- 4 scallion stalks, chopped
- 1 celery stalk, chopped
- 2 garlic cloves, minced

Directions:
1. Start by preheating your oven to 350 degrees F.
2. In a lightly oiled baking dish, thoroughly combine all ingredients until well combined.
3. Bake in the preheated oven for about 35 minutes or until all the liquid has been absorbed. Serve hot!

Black Bean Soup

Servings: 4
Cooking Time: 1 Hour 50 Minutes
Ingredients:
- 2 cups black beans, soaked overnight and drained
- 1 thyme sprig
- 2 tablespoons coconut oil
- 2 onions, chopped
- 1 celery rib, chopped
- 1 carrot, peeled and chopped
- 1 Italian pepper, seeded and chopped
- 1 chili pepper, seeded and chopped
- 4 garlic cloves, pressed or minced
- Sea salt and freshly ground black pepper, to taste
- 1/2 teaspoon ground cumin
- 1/4 teaspoon ground bay leaf
- 1/4 teaspoon ground allspice
- 1/2 teaspoon dried basil
- 4 cups vegetable broth
- 1/4 cup fresh cilantro, chopped
- 2 ounces tortilla chips

Directions:
1. In a soup pot, bring the beans and 6 cups of water to a boil. Once boiling, turn the heat to a simmer. Add in the thyme sprig and let it cook for about 1 hour 30 minutes or until tender.
2. Meanwhile, in a heavy-bottomed pot, heat the oil over medium-high heat. Now, sauté the onion, celery, carrot and peppers for about 4 minutes until tender.
3. Then, sauté the garlic for about 1 minute or until fragrant.
4. Add the sautéed mixture to the cooked beans. Then, add in the salt, black pepper, cumin, ground bay leaf, ground allspice, dried basil and vegetable broth.
5. Continue to simmer, stirring periodically, for 15 minutes longer or until everything is cooked through.
6. Garnish with fresh cilantro and tortilla chips. Bon appétit!

Black Bean And Spinach Stew

Servings: 4
Cooking Time: 1 Hour 35 Minutes
Ingredients:
- 2 cups black beans, soaked overnight and drained
- 2 tablespoons olive oil
- 1 onion, peeled, halved
- 1 jalapeno pepper, sliced
- 2 peppers, seeded and sliced
- 1 cup button mushrooms, sliced
- 2 garlic cloves, chopped
- 2 cups vegetable broth
- 1 teaspoon paprika
- Kosher salt and ground black pepper, to taste
- 1 bay leaf
- 2 cups spinach, torn into pieces

Directions:
1. Cover the soaked beans with a fresh change of cold water and bring to a boil. Let it boil for about 10 minutes. Turn the heat to a simmer and continue to cook for 50 to 55 minutes or until tender.
2. In a heavy-bottomed pot, heat the olive oil over medium heat. Once hot, sauté the onion and peppers for about 3 minutes.
3. Sauté the garlic and mushrooms for approximately 3 minutes or until the mushrooms release the liquid and the garlic is fragrant.
4. Add in the vegetable broth, paprika, salt, black pepper, bay leaf and cooked beans. Let it simmer, stirring periodically, for about 25 minutes or until cooked through.
5. Afterwards, add in the spinach and let it simmer, covered, for about 5 minutes. Bon appétit!

One-pot Winter Chili With Tofu

Servings: 4
Cooking Time: 1 Hour 30 Minutes
Ingredients:
- 3/4 pound cannellini beans, soaked overnight and drained
- 3 tablespoons olive oil
- 1 large onion, diced
- 1 cup turnip, chopped
- 1 carrot, chopped
- 1 bell pepper, sliced
- 1 sweet potato, chopped
- 3 cloves garlic, minced
- 2 ripe tomatoes, pureed
- 3 tablespoons tomato paste
- 2 cups vegetable broth
- 2 bay leaves
- 1 tablespoon red chili powder
- 1 tablespoon brown sugar
- Sea salt and cayenne pepper, to taste
- 12 ounces silken tofu, cubed

Directions:
1. Cover the soaked beans with a fresh change of cold water and bring to a boil. Let it boil for about 10 minutes.

Turn the heat to a simmer and continue to cook for 50 to 55 minutes or until tender.

2. In a heavy-bottomed pot, heat the olive oil over medium heat. Once hot, sauté the onion, turnip, carrot, bell pepper and sweet potato.

3. Sauté the garlic for about 1 minute or so.

4. Add in the tomatoes, tomato paste, vegetable broth, bay leaves, red chili powder, brown sugar, salt, cayenne pepper and cooked beans. Let it simmer, stirring periodically, for 25 to 30 minutes or until cooked through.

5. Serve garnished with the silken tofu. Bon appétit!

Split Pea And Potato Soup

Servings: 5
Cooking Time: 1 Hour 5 Minutes
Ingredients:
- 2 tablespoons olive oil
- 1 large onion, chopped
- 2 medium carrots, chopped
- 2 medium potatoes, diced
- 1 teaspoon garlic, minced
- 2 cups split peas, soaked overnight and drained
- 5 cups vegetable broth
- 2 tablespoons fresh cilantro, chopped

Directions:
1. In a Dutch oven, heat the olive oil over medium-high heat. Once hot, sauté the onion, carrot and potatoes for 4 minutes, stirring periodically to ensure even cooking.

2. Add in the garlic and continue to sauté for 30 seconds or until aromatic.

3. Add in the peas and vegetable broth. Continue to cook, partially covered, for 1 hour more or until cooked through.

4. Bon appétit!

Black-eyed Pea Salad (ñebbe)

Servings: 5
Cooking Time: 1 Hour
Ingredients:
- 2 cups dried black-eyed peas, soaked overnight and drained
- 2 tablespoons basil leaves, chopped
- 2 tablespoons parsley leaves, chopped
- 1 shallot, chopped
- 1 cucumber, sliced
- 2 bell peppers, seeded and diced
- 1 Scotch bonnet chili pepper, seeded and finely chopped
- 1 cup cherry tomatoes, quartered
- Sea salt and ground black pepper, to taste
- 2 tablespoons fresh lime juice
- 1 tablespoon apple cider vinegar
- 1/4 cup extra-virgin olive oil
- 1 avocado, peeled, pitted and sliced

Directions:
1. Cover the black-eyed peas with water by 2 inches and bring to a gentle boil. Let it boil for about 15 minutes.

2. Then, turn the heat to a simmer for about 45 minutes. Let it cool completely.

3. Place the black-eyed peas in a salad bowl. Add in the basil, parsley, shallot, cucumber, bell peppers, cherry tomatoes, salt and black pepper.

4. In a mixing bowl, whisk the lime juice, vinegar and olive oil.

5. Dress the salad, garnish with fresh avocado and serve immediately. Bon appétit!

Mediterranean-style Chickpea Salad

Servings: 4
Cooking Time: 40 Minutes
Ingredients:
- 2 cups chickpeas, soaked overnight and drained
- 1 Persian cucumber, sliced
- 1 cup cherry tomatoes, halved
- 1 red bell peppers, seeded and sliced
- 1 green bell pepper, seeded and sliced
- 1 teaspoon deli mustard
- 1 teaspoon coriander seeds
- 1 teaspoon jalapeno pepper, minced
- 1 tablespoon fresh lemon juice
- 1 tablespoon balsamic vinegar
- 1/4 cup extra-virgin olive oil
- Sea salt and ground black pepper, to taste
- 2 tablespoons fresh cilantro, chopped
- 2 tablespoons Kalamata olives, pitted and sliced

Directions:
1. Place the chickpeas in a stockpot; cover the chickpeas with water by 2 inches. Bring it to a boil.

2. Immediately turn the heat to a simmer and continue to cook for about 40 minutes or until tender.

3. Transfer your chickpeas to a salad bowl. Add in the remaining ingredients and toss to combine well. Bon appétit!

Traditional Tuscan Bean Stew (ribollita)

Servings: 5
Cooking Time: 25 Minutes
Ingredients:
- 3 tablespoons olive oil
- 1 medium leek, chopped
- 1 celery with leaves, chopped
- 1 zucchini, diced
- 1 Italian pepper, sliced
- 3 garlic cloves, crushed
- 2 bay leaves
- Kosher salt and ground black pepper, to taste
- 1 teaspoon cayenne pepper
- 1 can tomatoes, crushed
- 2 cups vegetable broth
- 2 cans Great Northern beans, drained
- 2 cups Lacinato kale, torn into pieces
- 1 cup crostini

Directions:
1. In a heavy-bottomed pot, heat the olive oil over medium heat. Once hot, sauté the leek, celery, zucchini and pepper for about 4 minutes.

2. Sauté the garlic and bay leaves for about 1 minute or so.

3. Add in the spices, tomatoes, broth and canned beans. Let it simmer, stirring occasionally, for about 15 minutes or until cooked through.
4. Add in the Lacinato kale and continue simmering, stirring occasionally, for 4 minutes.
5. Serve garnished with crostini. Bon appétit!

Asian Green Peas Stir-fry

Servings: 4
Cooking Time: 10 Minutes
Ingredients:
- 2 tablespoons peanut oil
- 4 garlic cloves, pressed
- 4 tablespoons scallions
- 1/2 teaspoon dried dill
- 1 pound green peas, fresh or thawed
- 1/4 teaspoon red pepper, flakes
- 1/2 teaspoon Five-spice powder
- 2 tablespoons soy sauce
- 2 tablespoons pine nuts, chopped

Directions:
1. Heat the peanut oil in a wok until sizzling. Now, stir-fry the garlic and scallions for 2 minutes or until crisp-tender.
2. Add in the dried dill and continue to cook for 30 seconds more or until fragrant.
3. Add in the green peas and stir-fry over high heat for about 3 minutes until lightly charred. Then, stir in the red pepper, Five-spice powder and soy sauce; stir-fry for 1 minute more.
4. Garnish with chopped pine nuts and enjoy.

Anasazi Bean And Vegetable Stew

Servings: 3
Cooking Time: 1 Hour
Ingredients:
- 1 cup Anasazi beans, soaked overnight and drained
- 3 cups roasted vegetable broth
- 1 bay laurel
- 1 thyme sprig, chopped
- 1 rosemary sprig, chopped
- 3 tablespoons olive oil
- 1 large onion, chopped
- 2 celery stalks, chopped
- 2 carrots, chopped
- 2 bell peppers, seeded and chopped
- 1 green chili pepper, seeded and chopped
- 2 garlic cloves, minced
- Sea salt and ground black pepper, to taste
- 1 teaspoon cayenne pepper
- 1 teaspoon paprika

Directions:
1. In a saucepan, bring the Anasazi beans and broth to a boil. Once boiling, turn the heat to a simmer. Add in the bay laurel, thyme and rosemary; let it cook for about 50 minutes or until tender.
2. Meanwhile, in a heavy-bottomed pot, heat the olive oil over medium-high heat. Now, sauté the onion, celery, carrots and peppers for about 4 minutes until tender.

3. Add in the garlic and continue to sauté for 30 seconds more or until aromatic.
4. Add the sautéed mixture to the cooked beans. Season with salt, black pepper, cayenne pepper and paprika.
5. Continue to simmer, stirring periodically, for 10 minutes more or until everything is cooked through. Bon appétit!

Brown Rice With Vegetables And Tofu

Servings: 4
Cooking Time: 45 Minutes
Ingredients:
- 4 teaspoons sesame seeds
- 2 spring garlic stalks, minced
- 1 cup spring onions, chopped
- 1 carrot, trimmed and sliced
- 1 celery rib, sliced
- 1/4 cup dry white wine
- 10 ounces tofu, cubed
- 1 ½ cups long-grain brown rice, rinsed thoroughly
- 2 tablespoons soy sauce
- 2 tablespoons tahini
- 1 tablespoon lemon juice

Directions:
1. In a wok or large saucepan, heat 2 teaspoons of the sesame oil over medium-high heat. Now, cook the garlic, onion, carrot and celery for about 3 minutes, stirring periodically to ensure even cooking.
2. Add the wine to deglaze the pan and push the vegetables to one side of the wok. Add in the remaining sesame oil and fry the tofu for 8 minutes, stirring occasionally.
3. Bring 2 ½ cups of water to a boil over medium-high heat. Bring to a simmer and cook the rice for about 30 minutes or until it is tender; fluff the rice and stir it with the soy sauce and tahini.
4. Stir the vegetables and tofu into the hot rice; add a few drizzles of the fresh lemon juice and serve warm. Bon appétit!

Aromatic Millet Bowl

Servings: 3
Cooking Time: 20 Minutes
Ingredients:
- 1 cup water
- 1 ½ cups coconut milk
- 1 cup millet, rinsed and drained
- 1/4 teaspoon crystallized ginger
- 1/4 teaspoon ground cinnamon
- A pinch of grated nutmeg
- A pinch of Himalayan salt
- 2 tablespoons maple syrup

Directions:
1. Place the water, milk, millet, crystallized ginger cinnamon, nutmeg and salt in a saucepan; bring to a boil.
2. Turn the heat to a simmer and let it cook for about 20 minutes; fluff the millet with a fork and spoon into individual bowls.
3. Serve with maple syrup. Bon appétit!

Chapter 5. Soups, Stews & Salads

Mediterranean Vegetable Stew

Servings:4
Cooking Time:30 Minutes
Ingredients:
- 2 tbsp olive oil
- 1 onions, chopped
- 2 carrots, chopped
- ½ tsp ground cumin
- ½ tsp ground ginger
- ½ tsp paprika
- ½ tsp saffron
- 1 can diced tomatoes
- ½ head broccoli, cut into florets
- 2 cups winter squash, chopped
- 1 russet potato, cubed
- 1 ½ cups vegetable broth
- 1 can chickpeas, drained
- 1 tsp lemon zest
- Salt and black pepper to taste
- ½ cup pitted green olives
- 1 tbsp minced cilantro for garnish
- ½ cup toasted slivered almonds

Directions:
1. Heat the oil in a pot over medium heat. Place onions and carrots and sauté for 5 minutes. Add in cumin, ginger, paprika, salt, pepper, and saffron and cook for 30 seconds. Stir in tomatoes, broccoli, squash, potato, chickpeas, and broth. Bring to a boil, then lower the heat and simmer for 20 minutes. Add in olives and lemon zest and simmer for 2-3 minutes. Garnish with cilantro and almonds to serve.

Lime Lentil Soup

Servings:2
Cooking Time:35 Minutes
Ingredients:
- 1 tsp olive oil
- 1 onion, chopped
- 6 garlic cloves, minced
- 1 tsp chili powder
- ½ tsp ground cinnamon
- Salt to taste
- 1 cup yellow lentils
- 1 cup canned crushed tomatoes
- 2 cups water
- 1 celery stalk, chopped
- 2 cups chopped collard greens

Directions:
1. Heat oil in a pot over medium heat. Place onion and garlic and cook for 5 minutes. Stir in chili powder, celery, cinnamon, and salt. Pour in lentils, tomatoes and juices, and water. Bring to a boil, then lower the heat and simmer for 15 minutes. Stir in collard greens. Cook for an additional 5 minutes. Serve.

Rotini & Tomato Soup

Servings:4
Cooking Time:25 Minutes
Ingredients:
- 1 tbsp olive oil
- 1 medium onion, chopped
- 1 celery rib, minced
- 3 garlic cloves, minced
- 1 can crushed tomatoes
- 3 cups chopped fresh ripe tomatoes
- 2 tbsp tomato paste
- 3 cups vegetable broth
- 2 bay leaves
- 1 cup plain unsweetened soy milk
- ½ cup whole-wheat rotini pasta
- 2 tbsp chopped fresh basil

Directions:
1. Heat oil in a pot and sauté onion, celery, and garlic for 5 minutes. Add in tomatoes, tomato paste, broth, sugar, and bay leaves. Bring to a boil and add the rotini. Cook for 10 minutes. Discard bay leaves. Garnish with the basil and serve.

Spicy Winter Farro Soup

Servings: 4
Cooking Time: 30 Minutes
Ingredients:
- 2 tablespoons olive oil
- 1 medium-sized leek, chopped
- 1 medium-sized turnip, sliced
- 2 Italian peppers, seeded and chopped
- 1 jalapeno pepper, minced
- 2 potatoes, peeled and diced
- 4 cups vegetable broth
- 1 cup farro, rinsed
- 1/2 teaspoon granulated garlic
- 1/2 teaspoon turmeric powder
- 1 bay laurel
- 2 cups spinach, turn into pieces

Directions:
1. In a heavy-bottomed pot, heat the olive oil over a moderate heat. Now, sauté the leek, turnip, peppers and potatoes for about 5 minutes until they are crisp-tender.
2. Add in the vegetable broth, farro, granulated garlic, turmeric and bay laurel; bring it to a boil.
3. Immediately turn the heat to a simmer. Let it cook for about 25 minutes or until farro and potatoes have softened.
4. Add in the spinach and remove the pot from the heat; let the spinach sit in the residual heat until it wilts. Bon appétit!

Creamy Golden Veggie Soup

Servings: 4
Cooking Time: 45 Minutes
Ingredients:

- 2 tablespoons avocado oil
- 1 yellow onion, chopped
- 2 Yukon Gold potatoes, peeled and diced
- 2 pounds butternut squash, peeled, seeded and diced
- 1 parsnip, trimmed and sliced
- 1 teaspoon ginger-garlic paste
- 1 teaspoon turmeric powder
- 1 teaspoon fennel seeds
- 1/2 teaspoon chili powder
- 1/2 teaspoon pumpkin pie spice
- Kosher salt and ground black pepper, to taste
- 3 cups vegetable stock
- 1 cup full-fat coconut milk
- 2 tablespoons pepitas

Directions:

1. In a heavy-bottomed pot, heat the oil over medium-high heat. Now, sauté the onion, potatoes, butternut squash and parsnip for about 10 minutes, stirring periodically to ensure even cooking.
2. Add in the ginger-garlic paste and continue sautéing for 1 minute or until aromatic.
3. Then, stir in the turmeric powder, fennel seeds, chili powder, pumpkin pie spice, salt, black pepper and vegetable stock; bring to a boil. Immediately reduce the heat to a simmer and let it cook for about 25 minutes.
4. Puree the soup using an immersion blender until creamy and uniform.
5. Return the pureed mixture to the pot. Fold in the coconut milk and continue to simmer until heated through or about 5 minutes longer.
6. Ladle into individual bowls and serve garnished with pepitas. Bon appétit!

Basil Coconut Soup

Servings:4
Cooking Time:15 Minutes
Ingredients:

- 2 tbsp coconut oil
- 1 ½ cups vegetable broth
- 2 garlic cloves, minced
- 1 onion, chopped
- 1 tbsp minced fresh ginger
- 1 cup green bell peppers, sliced
- 1 can coconut milk
- Juice of ½ lime
- 2 tbsp chopped basil
- 1 tbsp chopped cilantro
- 4 Lime wedges

Directions:

1. Warm the coconut oil in a pot over medium heat. Place in onion, garlic, and ginger and sauté for 3 minutes. Add in bell peppers and broth. Bring to a boil, then lower the heat and simmer. Stir in coconut milk, lime juice, and chopped cilantro. Simmer for 5 minutes. Serve garnished with basil and lime.

Vegetable Chili

Servings:4
Cooking Time:30 Minutes
Ingredients:

- 1 onion, chopped
- 1 cup vegetable broth
- 2 garlic cloves, minced
- 1 potato, cubed
- 1 carrot, chopped
- 2 tsp olive oil
- 1 can tomatoes
- 1 tbsp tomato paste
- 1 can chickpeas
- 1 tsp chili powder
- Salt and black pepper to taste
- ¼ cup parsley leaves, chopped

Directions:

1. Heat oil in a pot over medium heat. Place in onion and garlic and sauté for 3 minutes. Add in potato, carrot, tomatoes, broth, tomato paste, chickpeas, and chili; season. Simmer for 20 minutes. Serve garnished with parsley.

Pumpkin Soup With Apples

Servings:4
Cooking Time:25 Minutes
Ingredients:

- 1 tsp olive oil
- 1 onion, chopped
- 1-inch piece fresh ginger, diced
- 1 apple, cored and chopped
- 1 tsp curry powder
- ½ tsp pumpkin pie spice
- ½ tsp smoked paprika
- ¼ tsp red pepper flakes
- 3 cups canned pumpkin purée
- Salt and black pepper to taste
- ½ cup almond milk
- 4 tbsp nutritional yeast

Directions:

1. Warm the olive oil in a pot over medium heat. Place in the onion, ginger, and apple and cook for 5 minutes. Add in curry powder, pumpkin pie spice, paprika, and pepper flakes. Stir in 4 cups water, pumpkin, salt, and pepper. Cook for 10 minutes. Puree with an immersion blender until smooth. Pour in milk and nutritional yeast.

Asparagus And Chickpea Salad

Servings: 5
Cooking Time: 10 Minutes
Ingredients:

- 1 ¼ pounds asparagus, trimmed and cut into bite-sized pieces
- 5 ounces canned chickpeas, drained and rinsed
- 1 chipotle pepper, seeded and chopped
- 1 Italian pepper, seeded and chopped

- 1/4 cup fresh basil leaves, chopped
- 1/4 cup fresh parsley leaves, chopped
- 2 tablespoons fresh mint leaves
- 2 tablespoons fresh chives, chopped
- 1 teaspoon garlic, minced
- 1/4 cup extra-virgin olive oil
- 1 tablespoon balsamic vinegar
- 1 tablespoon fresh lime juice
- 2 tablespoons soy sauce
- 1/4 teaspoon ground allspice
- 1/4 teaspoon ground cumin
- Sea salt and freshly cracked peppercorns, to taste

Directions:
1. Bring a large pot of salted water with the asparagus to a boil; let it cook for 2 minutes; drain and rinse.
2. Transfer the asparagus to a salad bowl.
3. Toss the asparagus with the chickpeas, peppers, herbs, garlic, olive oil, vinegar, lime juice, soy sauce and spices.
4. Toss to combine and serve immediately. Bon appétit!

Indian Chana Chaat Salad

Servings: 4
Cooking Time: 45 Minutes
Ingredients:
- 1 pound dry chickpeas, soaked overnight
- 2 San Marzano tomatoes, diced
- 1 Persian cucumber, sliced
- 1 onion, chopped
- 1 bell pepper, seeded and thinly sliced
- 1 green chili, seeded and thinly sliced
- 2 handfuls baby spinach
- 1/2 teaspoon Kashmiri chili powder
- 4 curry leaves, chopped
- 1 tablespoon chaat masala
- 2 tablespoons fresh lemon juice, or to taste
- 4 tablespoons olive oil
- 1 teaspoon agave syrup
- 1/2 teaspoon mustard seeds
- 1/2 teaspoon coriander seeds
- 2 tablespoons sesame seeds, lightly toasted
- 2 tablespoons fresh cilantro, roughly chopped

Directions:
1. Drain the chickpeas and transfer them to a large saucepan. Cover the chickpeas with water by 2 inches and bring it to a boil.
2. Immediately turn the heat to a simmer and continue to cook for approximately 40 minutes.
3. Toss the chickpeas with the tomatoes, cucumber, onion, peppers, spinach, chili powder, curry leaves and chaat masala.
4. In a small mixing dish, thoroughly combine the lemon juice, olive oil, agave syrup, mustard seeds and coriander seeds.
5. Garnish with sesame seeds and fresh cilantro. Bon appétit!

Pumpkin & Garbanzo Chili With Kale

Servings:6
Cooking Time:60 Minutes
Ingredients:
- ¾ cup dried garbanzo beans, soaked
- 1 can crushed tomatoes
- 2 cups chopped pumpkin
- 6 cups water
- 2 tbsp chili powder
- 1 tsp onion powder
- ½ tsp garlic powder
- 3 cups kale, chopped
- ½ tsp salt

Directions:
1. In a saucepan over medium heat, add garbanzo, tomatoes, pumpkin, 2 cups water, salt, chili, onion, and garlic powders. Bring to a boil. Reduce the heat and simmer for 50 minutes. Stir in kale and cook for 5 minutes until the kale wilts. Serve.

Greek-style Roasted Pepper Salad

Servings: 2
Cooking Time: 10 Minutes
Ingredients:
- 2 red bell peppers
- 2 yellow bell peppers
- 2 garlic cloves, pressed
- 4 teaspoons extra-virgin olive oil
- 1 tablespoon capers, rinsed and drained
- 2 tablespoons red wine vinegar
- Seas salt and ground pepper, to taste
- 1 teaspoon fresh dill weed, chopped
- 1 teaspoon fresh oregano, chopped
- 1/4 cup Kalamata olives, pitted and sliced

Directions:
1. Broil the peppers on a parchment-lined baking sheet for about 10 minutes, rotating the pan halfway through the cooking time, until they are charred on all sides.
2. Then, cover the peppers with a plastic wrap to steam. Discard the skin, seeds and cores.
3. Slice the peppers into strips and place them in a salad bowl. Add in the remaining ingredients and toss to combine well.
4. Place in your refrigerator until ready to serve. Bon appétit!

Traditional French Onion Soup

Servings: 4
Cooking Time: 1 Hour 30 Minutes
Ingredients:
- 2 tablespoons olive oil
- 2 large yellow onions, thinly sliced
- 2 thyme sprigs, chopped
- 2 rosemary sprigs, chopped
- 2 teaspoons balsamic vinegar
- 4 cups vegetable stock
- Sea salt and ground black pepper, to taste

Directions:

1. In a or Dutch oven, heat the olive oil over a moderate heat. Now, cook the onions with thyme, rosemary and 1 teaspoon of the sea salt for about 2 minutes.
2. Now, turn the heat to medium-low and continue cooking until the onions caramelize or about 50 minutes.
3. Add in the balsamic vinegar and continue to cook for a further 15 more. Add in the stock, salt and black pepper and continue simmering for 20 to 25 minutes.
4. Serve with toasted bread and enjoy!

Mexican-style Chili Soup

Servings: 4
Cooking Time: 1 Hour 15 Minutes
Ingredients:
- 2 cups dry red beans, soaked overnight and drained
- 2 tablespoons olive oil
- 1 medium-sized leek, chopped
- 2 red bell peppers, chopped
- 1 chipotle chili pepper, chopped
- 2 cloves garlic, chopped
- 4 cups vegetable broth
- 1 bay laurel
- 1/2 teaspoon fennel seeds
- 1/2 teaspoon mustard seeds
- 1/2 teaspoon cumin seeds
- Kosher salt and ground black pepper, to taste
- 1/2 cup salsa
- 3 heaping tablespoons fresh cilantro, chopped
- 2 ounces tortilla chips

Directions:
1. Place the soaked beans in a soup pot; cover with a fresh change of the water and bring to a boil over medium-high heat. Let it boil for about 10 minutes.
2. Next, turn the heat to a simmer and continue to cook for 45 minutes; reserve.
3. In the same pot, heat the olive over medium-high heat. Now, sauté the leek and peppers for approximately 3 minutes or until the vegetables have softened.
4. Add in the chipotle chili pepper and garlic and continue to sauté for 1 minute or until aromatic.
5. Then, add in the vegetable broth, bay laurel, fennel seeds, mustard seeds, cumin seeds, salt and black pepper and bring to a boil. Immediately reduce the heat to a simmer and let it cook for 10 minutes.
6. Fold in the reserved beans and continue to simmer for about 10 minutes longer until everything is thoroughly heated.
7. Ladle into individual bowls and serve with salsa, cilantro and tortilla chips. Bon appétit!

Potato Soup With Kale

Servings:4
Cooking Time:45 Minutes
Ingredients:
- 2 tbsp olive oil
- 1 onion, chopped
- 1 ½ lb potatoes, chopped
- 4 cups vegetable broth
- ⅓ cup plant butter
- ¼ tsp ground cayenne pepper
- ⅛ tsp ground nutmeg
- Salt and black pepper to taste
- 4 cups kale

Directions:
1. Heat the oil in a pot over medium heat. Place in the onion and sauté for 5 minutes. Pour in potatoes and broth and cook for 20 minutes. Stir in butter, cayenne pepper, nutmeg, salt, and pepper. Add in kale and cook 5 minutes until wilted. Serve.

Spinach, Rice & Bean Soup

Servings:6
Cooking Time:45 Minutes
Ingredients:
- 6 cups baby spinach
- 2 tbsp olive oil
- 1 onion, chopped
- 2 garlic cloves, minced
- 1 can black-eyed peas
- 6 cups vegetable broth
- Salt and black pepper to taste
- ½ cup brown rice
- Tabasco sauce, for serving

Directions:
1. Heat oil in a pot over medium heat. Place the onion and garlic and sauté for 3 minutes. Pour in broth and season with salt and pepper. Bring to a boil, then lower the heat and stir in rice. Simmer for 15 minutes. Stir in peas and spinach and cook for another 5 minutes. Serve topped with Tabasco sauce.

Pressure Cooker Green Onion & Potato Soup

Servings:5
Cooking Time:25 Minutes
Ingredients:
- 3 green onions, chopped
- 4 garlic cloves, minced
- 1 tbsp olive oil
- 6 russet potatoes, chopped
- ½ can coconut milk
- 5 cups vegetable broth
- Salt and black pepper to taste

Directions:
1. Set your IP to Sauté. Place in green onions, garlic, and olive oil. Cook for 3 minutes until softened. Add in potatoes, coconut milk, broth, and salt. Lock the lid in place, set time to 6 minutes on High. Once ready, perform a natural pressure release for 10 minutes. Allow cooling for a few minutes. Using an immersion blender, blitz the soup until smooth. Serve.

Chicago-style Vegetable Stew

Servings:4
Cooking Time:35 Minutes
Ingredients:
- 2 tbsp olive oils
- 3 shallots, chopped
- 1 carrot, sliced
- ½ cup dry white wine
- 3 new potatoes, cubed
- 1 red bell pepper, chopped
- 1 ½ cups vegetable broth
- 2 zucchini, sliced
- 1 yellow summer squash, sliced
- 1 lb plum tomatoes, chopped
- 2 Salt and black pepper to taste
- 3 cups fresh corn kernels
- 1 cup green beans
- ¼ cup fresh basil
- ¼ cup chopped fresh parsley

Directions:
1. Heat oil in a pot over medium heat. Place shallots and carrot and cook for 5 minutes. Pour in white wine, potatoes, bell pepper, and broth. Bring to a boil, lower the heat, and simmer for 5 minutes. Stir in zucchini, yellow squash and tomatoes. Sprinkle with salt and pepper. Simmer for 20 more minutes. Put in corn, green peas, basil, and parsley. Simmer an additional 5 minutes. Serve hot.

Carrot & Mushroom Broth

Servings:6
Cooking Time:1 Hour 15 Minutes
Ingredients:
- 5 dried porcini mushrooms, soaked and liquid reserved
- 1 tbsp olive oil
- 1 onion, unpeeled and quartered
- 1 medium carrot, coarsely chopped
- 1 celery rib with leaves, chopped
- 8 oz Cremini mushrooms, chopped
- 1 onion, chopped
- ½ cup chopped fresh parsley
- Salt and black pepper to taste
- 5 cups water

Directions:
1. Warm the oil in a pot over medium heat. Place in onion, carrot, celery, and cremini mushrooms. Cook for 5 minutes until softened. Add in the dried mushrooms and reserved liquid, onion, salt, and water. Bring to a boil and simmer for 1 hour.
2. Let cool for a few minutes, then pour over a strainer into a pot. Divide between glass mason jars and allow cooling completely. Seal and store in the fridge for up to 5 days or 1 month in the freezer.

Traditional Ukrainian Borscht

Servings: 4
Cooking Time: 40 Minutes
Ingredients:
- 2 tablespoons sesame oil
- 1 red onion, chopped
- 2 carrots, trimmed and sliced
- 2 large beets, peeled and sliced
- 2 large potatoes, peeled and diced
- 4 cups vegetable stock
- 2 garlic cloves, minced
- 1/2 teaspoon caraway seeds
- 1/2 teaspoon celery seeds
- 1/2 teaspoon fennel seeds
- 1 pound red cabbage, shredded
- 1/2 teaspoon mixed peppercorns, freshly cracked
- Kosher salt, to taste
- 2 bay leaves
- 2 tablespoons wine vinegar

Directions:
1. In a Dutch oven, heat the sesame oil over a moderate flame. Once hot, sauté the onions until tender and translucent, about 6 minutes.
2. Add in the carrots, beets and potatoes and continue to sauté an additional 10 minutes, adding the vegetable stock periodically.
3. Next, stir in the garlic, caraway seeds, celery seeds, fennel seeds and continue sautéing for another 30 seconds.
4. Add in the cabbage, mixed peppercorns, salt and bay leaves. Add in the remaining stock and bring to boil.
5. Immediately turn the heat to a simmer and continue to cook for 20 to 23 minutes longer until the vegetables have softened.
6. Ladle into individual bowls and drizzle wine vinegar over it. Serve and enjoy!

Fennel & Parsnip Bisque

Servings:6
Cooking Time:30 Minutes
Ingredients:
- 1 tbsp olive oil
- 2 green onions, chopped
- ½ fennel bulb, sliced
- 2 large carrots, shredded
- 2 parsnips, shredded
- 1 potato, chopped
- 2 garlic cloves, minced
- ½ tsp dried thyme
- ¼ tsp dried marjoram
- 6 cups vegetable broth
- 1 cup plain unsweetened soy milk
- 1 tbsp minced fresh parsley

Directions:
1. Heat the oil in a pot over medium heat. Place in green onions, fennel, carrots, parsnips, potato, and garlic. Sauté for 5 minutes until softened. Add in thyme, marjoram, and broth. Bring to a boil, lower the heat, and simmer for 20 minutes. Transfer to a blender and pulse the soup until smooth. Return to the pot and mix in soy milk. Top with parsley to serve.

Tangy Bean Tomato Soup

Servings:5
Cooking Time:30 Minutes
Ingredients:
- 2 tsp olive oil
- 1 onion, chopped
- 2 garlic cloves, minced
- 1 cup mushrooms, chopped
- Sea salt to taste
- 1 tbsp dried basil
- ½ tbsp dried oregano
- 1 can diced tomatoes
- 1 can kidney beans, drained
- 5 cups water
- 2 cups chopped mustard greens

Directions:
1. Heat the oil in a pot over medium heat. Place in the onion, garlic, mushrooms, and salt and cook for 5 minutes. Stir in basil and oregano, tomatoes, and beans. Pour in water and stir. Simmer for 20 minutes and add in mustard greens; cook for 5 minutes until greens soften. Serve immediately.

Winter Quinoa Salad With Pickles

Servings: 4
Cooking Time: 20 Minutes
Ingredients:
- 1 cup quinoa
- 4 garlic cloves, minced
- 2 pickled cucumber, chopped
- 10 ounces canned red peppers, chopped
- 1/2 cup green olives, pitted and sliced
- 2 cups green cabbages, shredded
- 2 cups Iceberg lettuce, torn into pieces
- 4 pickled chilies, chopped
- 4 tablespoons olive oil
- 1 tablespoon lemon juice
- 1 teaspoon lemon zest
- 1/2 teaspoon dried marjoram
- Sea salt and ground black pepper, to taste
- 1/4 cup fresh chives, coarsely chopped

Directions:
1. Place two cups of water and the quinoa in a pot and bring it to a boil. Immediately turn the heat to a simmer.
2. Let it simmer for about 13 minutes until the quinoa has absorbed all of the water; fluff the quinoa with a fork and let it cool completely. Then, transfer the quinoa to a salad bowl.
3. Add the garlic, pickled cucumber, peppers, olives, cabbage, lettuce and pickled chilies to the salad bowl and toss to combine.
4. In a small mixing bowl, make the dressing by whisking the remaining ingredients. Dress the salad, toss to combine well and serve immediately. Bon appétit!

Rosemary Tomato Soup With Parmesan Croutons

Servings:6
Cooking Time:1 Hour 25 Minutes

Ingredients:
- 3 tbsp flax seed powder
- 1 ¼ cups almond flour
- 2 tsp baking powder
- 5 tbsp psyllium husk powder
- 2 tsp plain vinegar
- 3 oz plant butter
- 2 oz grated plant-based Parmesan
- 2 lb fresh ripe tomatoes
- 4 cloves garlic, peeled only
- 1 small white onion, diced
- 1 small red bell pepper, diced
- 3 tbsp olive oil
- 1 cup coconut cream
- ½ tsp dried rosemary
- ½ tsp dried oregano
- 2 tbsp chopped fresh basil
- Salt and black pepper to taste
- Basil leaves to garnish

Directions:
1. In a medium bowl, mix the flax seed powder with 9 tbsp of water and set aside to soak for 5 minutes. Preheat oven to 350 F and line a baking sheet with parchment paper.
2. In another bowl, combine almond flour, baking powder, psyllium husk powder, and salt. When the vegan "flax egg" is ready, mix in 1 ¼ cups boiling water and plain vinegar. Add in the flour mixture and whisk for 30 seconds. Form 8 flat pieces out of the dough. Place the flattened dough on the baking sheet while leaving enough room between each to allow rising.
3. Bake for 40 minutes. Remove the croutons to cool and break them into halves. Mix the plant butter with plant-based Parmesan cheese and spread the mixture in the inner parts of the croutons. Increase the oven's temperature to 450 F and bake the croutons further for 5 minutes or until golden brown and crispier.
4. In a baking pan, add tomatoes, garlic, onion, red bell pepper, and drizzle with olive oil. Roast in the oven for 25 minutes and after broil for 3 to 4 minutes until some of the tomatoes are slightly charred. Transfer to a blender and add coconut cream, rosemary, oregano, basil, salt, and black pepper. Puree until smooth and creamy. Pour the soup into serving bowls, drop some croutons on top, garnish with basil leaves, and serve.

Cannellini Bean Soup With Kale

Servings: 5
Cooking Time: 25 Minutes
Ingredients:
- 1 tablespoon olive oil
- 1/2 teaspoon ginger, minced
- 1/2 teaspoon cumin seeds
- 1 red onion, chopped
- 1 carrot, trimmed and chopped
- 1 parsnip, trimmed and chopped
- 2 garlic cloves, minced
- 5 cups vegetable broth
- 12 ounces Cannellini beans, drained

- 2 cups kale, torn into pieces
- Sea salt and ground black pepper, to taste

Directions:

1. In a heavy-bottomed pot, heat the olive over medium-high heat. Now, sauté the ginger and cumin for 1 minute or so.

2. Now, add in the onion, carrot and parsnip; continue sautéing an additional 3 minutes or until the vegetables are just tender.

3. Add in the garlic and continue to sauté for 1 minute or until aromatic.

4. Then, pour in the vegetable broth and bring to a boil. Immediately reduce the heat to a simmer and let it cook for 10 minutes.

5. Fold in the Cannellini beans and kale; continue to simmer until the kale wilts and everything is thoroughly heated. Season with salt and pepper to taste.

6. Ladle into individual bowls and serve hot. Bon appétit!

Sunday Soup

Servings:5
Cooking Time:45 Minutes

Ingredients:

- 2 tbsp vegetable oil
- 1 onion, chopped
- 1 carrot, chopped
- 2 garlic cloves, minced
- 3 small new potatoes, sliced
- 1 zucchini, sliced
- 1 yellow summer squash, sliced
- 2 ripe tomatoes, diced
- Salt and black pepper to taste
- 5 cups vegetable broth
- 2 cups chopped kale
- ¼ cup fresh basil leaves, chopped

Directions:

1. Heat oil in a pot over medium heat. Place onion, carrot, and garlic and cook covered for 5 minutes. Add in potatoes, zucchini, yellow squash, tomatoes, salt, and pepper. Cook for 5 minutes. Stir in broth and bring to a boil. Lower the heat and simmer for 30 minutes. Stir in kale and basil. Serve in bowls.

Sudanese Veggie Stew

Servings:6
Cooking Time:30 Minutes

Ingredients:

- 3 potatoes, cubed
- 3 tbsp olive oil
- 2 carrots, sliced
- 4 shallots, chopped
- 2 garlic cloves, minced
- 1 tbsp ground turmeric
- 1 tsp ground ginger
- 1 ½ cups vegetable broth
- 4 cups shredded spinach

Directions:

1. Cook the potatoes in salted water over medium heat, about 15 minutes. Drain and reserve. Heat the oil in a saucepan over medium heat. Place in carrots and shallots and cook for 5 minutes. Stir in garlic, turmeric, ginger, and salt. Cook for 1 minute more. Add in cooked potatoes and broth. Bring to a boil, then lower the heat. Stir in the spinach and cook for another 3 minutes until wilted.

Mom's Cauliflower Coleslaw

Servings: 4
Cooking Time: 10 Minutes

Ingredients:

- 2 cups small cauliflower florets, frozen and thawed
- 2 cups red cabbage, shredded
- 1 cup carrots, trimmed and shredded
- 1 medium onion, chopped
- 1/2 cup vegan mayonnaise
- 4 tablespoons coconut yogurt, unsweetened
- 1 tablespoon yellow mustard
- 1 tablespoon fresh lemon juice
- 1/2 teaspoon cayenne pepper
- Sea salt and ground black pepper, to taste

Directions:

1. In a salad bowl, toss the vegetables until well combined.

2. In a small mixing bowl, thoroughly combine the remaining ingredients. Add the mayo dressing to the vegetables and toss to combine well.

3. Place the coleslaw in your refrigerator until ready to serve. Bon appétit!

Quinoa And Black Bean Salad

Servings: 4
Cooking Time: 15 Minutes

Ingredients:

- 2 cups water
- 1 cup quinoa, rinsed
- 16 ounces canned black beans, drained
- 2 Roma tomatoes, sliced
- 1 red onion, thinly sliced
- 1 cucumber, seeded and chopped
- 2 cloves garlic, pressed or minced
- 2 Italian peppers, seeded and sliced
- 2 tablespoons fresh parsley, chopped
- 2 tablespoons fresh cilantro, chopped
- 1/4 cup olive oil
- 1 lemon, freshly squeezed
- 1 tablespoon apple cider vinegar
- 1/2 teaspoon dried dill weed
- 1/2 teaspoon dried oregano
- Sea salt and ground black pepper, to taste

Directions:

1. Place the water and quinoa in a saucepan and bring it to a rolling boil. Immediately turn the heat to a simmer.

2. Let it simmer for about 13 minutes until the quinoa has absorbed all of the water; fluff the quinoa with a fork and let it cool completely. Then, transfer the quinoa to a salad bowl.

3. Add the remaining ingredients to the salad bowl and toss to combine well. Bon appétit!

Moroccan Bean Stew

Servings:4
Cooking Time:40 Minutes
Ingredients:
- 3 cups cooked red kidney beans
- 2 tbsp olive oil
- 1 yellow onion, chopped
- 2 carrots, sliced
- 3 garlic cloves, minced
- 1 tsp grated fresh ginger
- ½ tsp ground cumin
- 1 tsp ras el hanout
- 2 russet potatoes, chopped
- 1 can crushed tomatoes
- 1 can diced green chiles, drained
- 1 ½ cups vegetable broth
- Salt and black pepper to taste
- 3 cups eggplants, chopped
- ⅓ cup chopped roasted peanuts

Directions:
1. Heat the oil in a pot over medium heat. Place the onion, garlic, ginger, and carrots and sauté for 5 minutes until tender. Stir in cumin, ras el hanout, potatoes, beans, tomatoes, chiles, and broth. Season with salt and pepper. Bring to a boil, then lower the heat and simmer for 20 minutes. Add in eggplants and cook for 10 minutes. Serve garnished with peanuts.

Green Bean & Zucchini Velouté

Servings:6
Cooking Time:30 Minutes
Ingredients:
- 3 tbsp olive oil
- 1 onion, chopped
- 1 garlic clove, minced
- 2 cups green beans
- 4 cups vegetable broth
- 3 medium zucchini, sliced
- ½ tsp dried marjoram
- ½ cup plain almond milk
- 2 tbsp minced jarred pimiento

Directions:
1. Heat oil in a pot and sauté onion and garlic for 5 minutes. Add in green beans and broth. Cook for 10 minutes. Stir in zucchini and cook for 10 minutes. Transfer to a food processor and pulse until smooth. Return to the pot and mix in almond milk; cook until hot. Serve topped with pimiento.

Authentic Italian Panzanella Salad

Servings: 3
Cooking Time: 35 Minutes
Ingredients:
- 3 cups artisan bread, broken into 1-inch cubes
- 3/4 pound asparagus, trimmed and cut into bite-sized pieces
- 4 tablespoons extra-virgin olive oil
- 1 red onion, chopped
- 2 tablespoons fresh lime juice
- 1 teaspoon deli mustard
- 2 medium heirloom tomatoes, diced
- 2 cups arugula
- 2 cups baby spinach
- 2 Italian peppers, seeded and sliced
- Sea salt and ground black pepper, to taste

Directions:
1. Arrange the bread cubes on a parchment-lined baking sheet. Bake in the preheated oven at 310 degrees F for about 20 minutes, rotating the baking sheet twice during the baking time; reserve.
2. Turn the oven to 420 degrees F and toss the asparagus with 1 tablespoon of olive oil. Roast the asparagus for about 15 minutes or until crisp-tender.
3. Toss the remaining ingredients in a salad bowl; top with the roasted asparagus and toasted bread.
4. Bon appétit!

Classic Roasted Pepper Salad

Servings: 3
Cooking Time: 15 Minutes
Ingredients:
- 6 bell peppers
- 3 tablespoons extra-virgin olive oil
- 3 teaspoons red wine vinegar
- 3 garlic cloves, finely chopped
- 2 tablespoons fresh parsley, chopped
- Sea salt and freshly cracked black pepper, to taste
- 1/2 teaspoon red pepper flakes
- 6 tablespoons pine nuts, roughly chopped

Directions:
1. Broil the peppers on a parchment-lined baking sheet for about 10 minutes, rotating the pan halfway through the cooking time, until they are charred on all sides.
2. Then, cover the peppers with a plastic wrap to steam. Discard the skin, seeds and cores.
3. Slice the peppers into strips and toss them with the remaining ingredients. Place in your refrigerator until ready to serve. Bon appétit!

Classic Lentil Soup With Swiss Chard

Servings: 5
Cooking Time: 25 Minutes
Ingredients:
- 2 tablespoons olive oil
- 1 white onion, chopped
- 1 teaspoon garlic, minced
- 2 large carrots, chopped
- 1 parsnip, chopped
- 2 stalks celery, chopped
- 2 bay leaves
- 1/2 teaspoon dried thyme
- 1/4 teaspoon ground cumin
- 5 cups roasted vegetable broth
- 1 ¼ cups brown lentils, soaked overnight and rinsed
- 2 cups Swiss chard, torn into pieces

Directions:

1. In a heavy-bottomed pot, heat the olive oil over a moderate heat. Now, sauté the vegetables along with the spices for about 3 minutes until they are just tender.

2. Add in the vegetable broth and lentils, bringing it to a boil. Immediately turn the heat to a simmer and add in the bay leaves. Let it cook for about 15 minutes or until lentils are tender.

3. Add in the Swiss chard, cover and let it simmer for 5 minutes more or until the chard wilts.

4. Serve in individual bowls and enjoy!

Bell Pepper & Mushroom Soup

Servings:6
Cooking Time:45 Minutes
Ingredients:
- 3 tbsp olive oil
- 1 onion, chopped
- 1 large carrot, chopped
- 1 lb mixed bell peppers, chopped
- 1 cup cremini mushrooms, quartered
- 1 cup white mushrooms, quartered
- 6 cups vegetable broth
- ¼ cup chopped fresh parsley
- 1 tsp minced fresh thyme
- Salt and black pepper to taste

Directions:
1. Heat the oil in a pot over medium heat. Place onion, carrot, and celery and cook for 5 minutes. Add in bell peppers and broth and stir. Bring to a boil, lower the heat, and simmer for 20 minutes. Adjust the seasoning with salt and black pepper. Serve in soup bowls topped with parsley and thyme.

Asian-style Bean Soup

Servings:4
Cooking Time:55 Minutes
Ingredients:
- 1 cup canned cannellini beans
- 2 tsp curry powder
- 2 tsp olive oil
- 1 red onion, diced
- 1 tbsp minced fresh ginger
- 2 cubed sweet potatoes
- 1 cup sliced zucchini
- Salt and black pepper to taste
- 4 cups vegetable stock
- 1 bunch spinach, chopped
- Toasted sesame seeds

Directions:
1. Mix the beans with 1 tsp of curry powder until well combined. Warm the oil in a pot over medium heat. Place the onion and ginger and cook for 5 minutes until soft. Add in sweet potatoes and cook for 10 minutes. Put in zucchini and cook for 5 minutes. Season with the remaining curry, pepper, and salt.

2. Pour in the stock and bring to a boil. Lower the heat and simmer for 25 minutes. Stir in beans and spinach. Cook until

the spinach wilts and remove from the heat. Garnish with sesame seeds to serve.

Greek-style Pinto Bean And Tomato Soup

Servings: 4
Cooking Time: 30 Minutes
Ingredients:
- 2 tablespoons olive oil
- 1 carrot, chopped
- 1 parsnip, chopped
- 1 red onion, chopped
- 1 chili pepper, minced
- 2 garlic cloves, minced
- 3 cups vegetable broth
- 1 cup canned tomatoes, crushed
- 1/2 teaspoon cumin
- Sea salt and ground black pepper, to taste
- 1 teaspoon cayenne pepper
- 1 teaspoon Greek herb mix
- 20 ounces canned pinto beans
- 12 ounces canned corn, drained
- 2 tablespoons fresh cilantro, chopped
- 2 tablespoons fresh parsley, chopped
- 2 tablespoons Kalamata olives, pitted and sliced

Directions:
1. In a heavy-bottomed pot, heat the olive over medium-high heat. Now, sauté the carrot, parsnip and onion for approximately 3 minutes or until the vegetables are just tender.

2. Add in the chili pepper and garlic and continue to sauté for 1 minute or until aromatic.

3. Then, add in the vegetable broth, canned tomatoes, cumin, salt, black pepper, cayenne pepper and Greek herb mix and bring to a boil. Immediately reduce the heat to a simmer and let it cook for 10 minutes.

4. Fold in the beans and corn and continue simmering for about 10 minutes longer until everything is thoroughly heated. Taste and adjust the seasonings.

5. Ladle into individual bowls and garnish with cilantro, parsley and olives. Bon appétit!

Caribbean Lentil Stew

Servings:4
Cooking Time:50 Minutes
Ingredients:
- 2 tbsp olive oil
- 1 onion, chopped
- 1 carrot, sliced
- 2 garlic cloves, minced
- 1 sweet potato, chopped
- ¼ tsp crushed red pepper
- 1 cup red lentils, rinsed
- 1 can diced tomatoes
- 1 tsp hot curry powder
- 1 tsp chopped thyme
- ¼ tsp ground allspice

- Salt and black pepper to taste
- 1 cup water
- 1 can coconut milk

Directions:

1. Warm oil in a pot and sauté onion and carrot for 5 minutes, stirring occasionally until softened. Add in garlic, sweet potato, and crushed red pepper. Put in red lentils, tomatoes, curry powder, allspice, salt, and black pepper, stir to combine. Pour in water and simmer for 30 minutes until the vegetables are tender. Stir in coconut milk and simmer for 10 minutes. Serve hot topped with thyme.

Creamy Rutabaga Soup

Servings: 4
Cooking Time: 35 Minutes

Ingredients:

- 2 tablespoons olive oil
- 1 onion, chopped
- 1/2 pound rutabaga, peeled and chopped
- 1/2 pound sweet potatoes, peeled and chopped
- 1/2 cup carrots, chopped
- 1/2 cup parsnip, chopped
- 1 teaspoon ginger-garlic paste
- 3 cups vegetable broth
- Salt and ground black pepper, to taste
- 1/4 teaspoon dried dill
- 1/2 teaspoon dried oregano
- 1 teaspoon dried basil
- 1 teaspoon dried parsley flakes
- 1 teaspoon paprika
- 1/2 cup raw cashews, soaked
- 1 cup water, divided
- 1 tablespoon lemon juice
- 2 tablespoons fresh cilantro, chopped

Directions:

1. In a heavy-bottomed pot, heat the olive oil over medium-high heat. Now, sauté the onion, rutabaga, sweet potatoes, carrot and parsnip for about 5 minutes, stirring periodically.
2. Add in the ginger-garlic paste and continue sautéing for 1 minute or until fragrant.
3. Then, stir in the vegetable broth, salt, black pepper, dried dill, oregano, basil, parsley and paprika; bring to a boil. Immediately reduce the heat to a simmer and let it cook for about 20 to 22 minutes.
4. Puree the soup using an immersion blender until creamy and uniform.
5. Drain the cashews and add them to the bowl of your blender or food processor; add in the water, lemon juice and salt to taste. Blend into a cream.
6. Return the pureed mixture to the pot. Fold in the cashew cream and continue simmering until heated through or about 5 minutes longer.
7. Ladle into serving bowls and serve garnished with the fresh cilantro. Bon appétit!

Celery & Potato Rice Soup

Servings:6
Cooking Time:40 Minutes

Ingredients:

- 3 tbsp olive oil
- 1 onion, chopped
- 1 medium carrot, chopped
- 1 celery stalk, chopped
- 1 lb potatoes, chopped
- ½ cup long-grain brown rice
- 1 can crushed tomatoes
- 2 cups tomato juice
- 2 bay leaves
- ½ tsp ground cumin
- Salt and black pepper to taste
- 1 tbsp minced fresh parsley

Directions:

1. Heat oil in a pot and sauté onion, carrot, and celery for 10 minutes. Add in potatoes, rice, tomatoes, tomato juices, bay leaves, cumin, 6 cups water, salt, and pepper. Bring to a boil, then lower the heat and simmer uncovered for 20 minutes. Discard the bay leaves. Scatter with parsley. Serve immediately.

Mushroom Rice Soup

Servings:6
Cooking Time:30 Minutes

Ingredients:

- 3 tbsp olive oil
- 1 onion, chopped
- 1 carrot, chopped
- 1 celery stalk, chopped
- 1 cup wild mushrooms, sliced
- ½ cup brown rice
- 7 cups vegetable broth
- 1 tsp dried dill weed
- Salt and black pepper to taste

Directions:

1. Heat the oil in a pot over medium heat. Place in onion, carrot, and celery and sauté for 5 minutes. Add in mushrooms, rice, broth, dill weed, salt, and pepper. Bring to a boil, then lower the heat and simmer uncovered for 20 minutes. Serve.

Fennel & Corn Chowder

Servings:4
Cooking Time:30 Minutes

Ingredients:

- 2 tbsp olive oil
- 1 onion, chopped
- 1 cup chopped fennel bulb
- 2 carrots, chopped
- 1 cup mushrooms, chopped
- ¼ cup whole-wheat flour
- 4 cups vegetable stock
- 2 cups canned corn
- 2 cups cubed red potatoes
- 1 cup almond milk
- ½ tsp chili paste

- Sea salt and black pepper to taste

Directions:

1. Heat the oil in a pot over medium heat. Place in onion, fennel, carrots, and mushrooms. Sauté for 5 minutes until tender. Stir in flour. Pour in vegetable stock. Lower the heat. Add in corn, potatoes, almond milk, and chili paste. Simmer for 20 minutes. Sprinkle with salt and pepper. Serve immediately.

Arugula Coconut Soup

Servings:4
Cooking Time:30 Minutes

Ingredients:

- 1 tsp coconut oil
- 1 onion, diced
- 2 cups green beans
- 4 cups water
- 1 cup arugula, chopped
- 1 tbsp fresh mint, chopped
- Sea salt and black pepper to taste
- ¾ cup coconut milk

Directions:

1. Place a pot over medium heat and heat the coconut oil. Add in the onion and sauté for 5 minutes. Pour in green beans and water. Bring to a boil, lower the heat and stir in arugula, mint, salt, and pepper. Simmer for 10 minutes. Stir in coconut milk. Transfer to a food processor and blitz the soup until smooth. Serve.

Butternut Squash Coconut Cream Soup

Servings:5
Cooking Time:30 Minutes

Ingredients:

- 1 butternut squash, cubed
- 1 red bell pepper, chopped
- 1 large onion, chopped
- 3 garlic cloves, minced
- 4 cups vegetable broth
- 1 cup coconut cream

Directions:

1. Place the squash, bell pepper, onion, garlic, and broth in a pot. Bring to a boil. Lower the heat and simmer for 20 minutes. Stir in coconut cream, salt, and pepper. Transfer to a food processor purée the soup until smooth. Serve warm.

Easy Garbanzo Soup

Servings:4
Cooking Time:25 Minutes

Ingredients:

- 2 tbsp olive oil
- 1 onion, chopped
- 1 green bell pepper, diced
- 1 carrot, peeled and diced
- 4 garlic cloves, minced
- 1 can garbanzo beans
- 1 cup spinach, chopped
- 4 cups vegetable stock
- ¼ tsp ground cumin

- Sea salt to taste
- ¼ cup chopped cilantro

Directions:

1. Heat the oil in a pot over medium heat. Place in onion, garlic, bell pepper, and carrot and sauté for 5 minutes until tender. Stir in garbanzo beans, spinach, vegetable stock, cumin, and salt. Cook for 10 minutes. Mash the garbanzo using a potato masher, leaving some chunks. Top with cilantro and serve.

Daikon & Sweet Potato Soup

Servings:6
Cooking Time:40 Minutes

Ingredients:

- 6 cups water
- 2 tsp olive oil
- 1 chopped onion
- 3 garlic cloves, minced
- 1 tbsp thyme
- 2 tsp paprika
- 2 cups peeled and chopped daikon
- 2 cups chopped sweet potatoes
- 2 cups peeled and chopped parsnips
- ½ tsp sea salt
- 1 cup fresh mint, chopped
- ½ avocado
- 2 tbsp balsamic vinegar
- 2 tbsp pumpkin seeds

Directions:

1. Heat the oil in a pot and place onion and garlic. Sauté for 3 minutes. Add in thyme, paprika, daikon, sweet potato, parsnips, water, and salt. Bring to a boil and cook for 30 minutes. Remove the soup to a food processor and add in balsamic vinegar; purée until smooth. Top with mint and pumpkin seeds to serve.

Pearl Barley & Vegetable Stew

Servings:6
Cooking Time:30 Minutes

Ingredients:

- 3 tbsp olive oil
- 1 onion, chopped
- 2 garlic cloves, minced
- 2 turnips, chopped
- 4 potatoes, chopped
- 1 cup pearl barley
- 1 can diced tomatoes
- 3 tsp dried mixed herbs
- Salt and black pepper to taste

Directions:

1. Warm oil in a pot over medium heat. Add onion and garlic and sauté for 3 minutes until fragrant. Stir in the turnips, potatoes, barley, tomatoes, 3 cups water, and herbs. Cook for 20 minutes. Serve.

Decadent Broccoli Salad

Servings: 4
Cooking Time: 10 Minutes
Ingredients:
- 2 pounds broccoli florets
- 1/4 cup sunflower seeds
- 1/4 cup pine nuts
- 1 shallot, chopped
- 2 garlic cloves, finely chopped
- 1 cup vegan mayonnaise
- 1 tablespoon balsamic vinegar
- 1 tablespoon fresh lime juice
- 1 teaspoon mustard
- Sea salt and freshly ground black pepper, to taste
- 1/2 cup pomegranate seeds

Directions:
1. In a saucepan, bring about 1/4 inch of water to a boil. Add in the broccoli florets. Cover and steam the broccoli until crisp-tender or about 5 minutes.
2. Let the broccoli florets cool completely and place them in a salad bowl.
3. Add in the sunflower seeds, pine nuts, shallot, garlic, mayo, balsamic vinegar, lime juice, mustard, salt and black pepper. Toss to combine well.
4. Garnish with pomegranate seeds and serve well-chilled. Bon appétit!

Roasted Wild Mushroom Soup

Servings: 3
Cooking Time: 55 Minutes
Ingredients:
- 3 tablespoons sesame oil
- 1 pound mixed wild mushrooms, sliced
- 1 white onion, chopped
- 3 cloves garlic, minced and divided
- 2 sprigs thyme, chopped
- 2 sprigs rosemary, chopped
- 1/4 cup flaxseed meal
- 1/4 cup dry white wine
- 3 cups vegetable broth
- 1/2 teaspoon red chili flakes
- Garlic salt and freshly ground black pepper, to seasoned

Directions:
1. Start by preheating your oven to 395 degrees F.
2. Place the mushrooms in a single layer onto a parchment-lined baking pan. Drizzle the mushrooms with 1 tablespoon of the sesame oil.
3. Roast the mushrooms in the preheated oven for about 25 minutes, or until tender.
4. Heat the remaining 2 tablespoons of the sesame oil in a stockpot over medium heat. Then, sauté the onion for about 3 minutes or until tender and translucent.
5. Then, add in the garlic, thyme and rosemary and continue to sauté for 1 minute or so until aromatic. Sprinkle flaxseed meal over everything.
6. Add in the remaining ingredients and continue to simmer for 10 to 15 minutes longer or until everything is cooked through.

7. Stir in the roasted mushrooms and continue simmering for a further 12 minutes. Ladle into soup bowls and serve hot. Enjoy!

Roasted Basil & Tomato Soup

Servings:4
Cooking Time:60 Minutes
Ingredients:
- 2 lb tomatoes, halved
- 2 tsp garlic powder
- 3 tbsp olive oil
- 1 tbsp balsamic vinegar
- Salt and black pepper to taste
- 4 shallots, chopped
- 2 cups vegetable broth
- ½ cup basil leaves, chopped

Directions:
1. Preheat oven to 450 F.
2. In a bowl, mix tomatoes, garlic, 2 tbsp of oil, vinegar, salt, and pepper. Arrange the tomatoes onto a baking dish. Sprinkle with some olive oil, garlic powder, balsamic vinegar, salt, and pepper. Bake for 30 minutes until the tomatoes get dark brown color. Take out from the oven; reserve.
3. Heat the remaining oil in a pot over medium heat. Place the shallots and cook for 3 minutes, stirring often. Add in roasted tomatoes and broth. Bring to a boil, then lower the heat and simmer for 10 minutes. Transfer to a food processor and blitz the soup until smooth. Serve topped with basil.

Rosemary White Bean Soup

Servings:4
Cooking Time:30 Minutes
Ingredients:
- 2 tsp olive oil
- 1 carrot, chopped
- 1 onion, chopped
- 2 garlic cloves, minced
- 1 tbsp rosemary, chopped
- 2 tbsp apple cider vinegar
- 1 cup dried white beans
- ¼ tsp salt
- 2 tbsp nutritional yeast

Directions:
1. Heat the oil in a pot over medium heat. Place carrots, onion, and garlic and cook for 5 minutes.
2. Pour in vinegar to deglaze the pot. Stir in 5 cups water and beans and bring to a boil. Lower the heat and simmer for 45 minutes until the beans are soft. Add in salt and nutritional yeast and stir. Serve topped with chopped rosemary.

Lime Pumpkin Soup

Servings:4
Cooking Time:30 Minutes
Ingredients:

- 2 tsp olive oil
- 3 cups pumpkin, chopped
- 1 onion, chopped
- 1 garlic clove, minced
- 2 cups water
- 1 can black-eyed peas
- 2 tbsp lime juice
- 1 tbsp pure date sugar
- 1 tsp paprika
- 1 tbsp red pepper flakes
- 3 cups shredded cabbage
- 1 cup mushrooms, chopped

Directions:
1. Warm the oil in a pot over medium heat. Place in pumpkin, onion, garlic, and salt. Cook for 5 minutes. Stir in water, peas, lime juice, sugar, paprika, and pepper flakes. Bring to a boil and cook for 15 minutes. Add in cabbage and mushrooms and cook for 5 minutes. Allow cooling before serving.

Turnip & Rutabaga Soup

Servings:5
Cooking Time:30 Minutes
Ingredients:

- 2 tbsp olive oil
- 1 onion, diced
- 3 garlic cloves, minced
- 1 carrot, chopped
- 1 rutabaga, chopped
- 1 turnip chopped
- 1 red potato, chopped
- 5 cups vegetable stock
- 2 tsp dried thyme

Directions:
1. Heat the oil in a pot over medium heat. Place the onion and garlic and sauté for 3 minutes until translucent. Stir in carrot, rutabaga, turnip, potato, vegetable stock, salt, pepper, and thyme. Simmer for 10 minutes. In a food processor, put the soup and blend until purée. Serve warm.

Spicy Potato Soup

Servings:6
Cooking Time:25 Minutes
Ingredients:

- 3 tbsp olive oil
- 1 onion, chopped
- 1 garlic clove, minced
- 1 tbsp hot powder
- 1 lb carrots, chopped
- 2 potatoes, chopped
- 6 cups vegetable broth
- Salt to taste
- 1 can coconut milk

- 1 tbsp minced fresh parsley
- Chopped roasted cashews

Directions:
1. Heat the oil in a pot over medium heat. Place in onion and garlic and cook for 3 minutes. Add in hot powder, cook for 30 seconds. Stir in carrots, potatoes, broth, and salt. Bring to a boil, lower the heat and simmer for 15 minutes.
2. With an immersion blender, blitz the soup until smooth. Sprinkle with salt and pepper. Mix in coconut milk and cook until hot. Garnish with parsley and chopped cashews to serve.

Classic Minestrone Soup

Servings:4
Cooking Time:20 Minutes
Ingredients:

- 2 tbsp olive oil
- 1 onion, chopped
- 1 carrot, chopped
- 1 stalk celery, chopped
- 2 garlic cloves, minced
- 4 cups vegetable stock
- 1 cup green peas
- ½ cup orzo
- 1 can chopped tomatoes
- 2 tsp Italian seasoning
- Sea salt and black pepper to taste

Directions:
1. Heat the oil in a pot over medium heat. Place in onion, garlic, carrot, and celery and sauté for 5 minutes until tender. Stir in vegetable stock, green peas, orzo, tomatoes, salt, pepper, and Italian seasoning. Cook for 10 minutes. Serve right away.

Rainbow Chickpea Salad

Servings: 4
Cooking Time: 30 Minutes
Ingredients:

- 16 ounces canned chickpeas, drained
- 1 medium avocado, sliced
- 1 bell pepper, seeded and sliced
- 1 large tomato, sliced
- 2 cucumber, diced
- 1 red onion, sliced
- 1/2 teaspoon garlic, minced
- 1/4 cup fresh parsley, chopped
- 1/4 cup olive oil
- 2 tablespoons apple cider vinegar
- 1/2 lime, freshly squeezed
- Sea salt and ground black pepper, to taste

Directions:
1. Toss all the ingredients in a salad bowl.
2. Place the salad in your refrigerator for about 1 hour before serving.
3. Bon appétit!

Coconut Cream Pumpkin Soup

Servings:4
Cooking Time:55 Minutes
Ingredients:

- 2 small red onions, cut into wedges
- 2 garlic cloves, skinned
- 10 oz pumpkin, cubed
- 10 oz butternut squash
- 2 tbsp olive oil
- 4 tbsp plant butter
- Juice of 1 lime
- ¾ cup tofu mayonnaise
- Toasted pumpkin seeds for garnish

Directions:
1. Preheat oven to 400 F.
2. Place onions, garlic, and pumpkin on a baking sheet and drizzle with olive oil. Season with salt and pepper. Roast for 30 minutes or until the vegetables are golden brown and fragrant. Remove the vegetables from the oven and transfer to a pot. Add 2 cups of water, bring the ingredients to boil over medium heat for 15 minutes. Turn the heat off. Add in plant butter and puree until smooth. Stir in lime juice and tofu mayonnaise. Spoon into serving bowls and garnish with pumpkin seeds to serve.

Sweet African Soup

Servings:4
Cooking Time:45 Minutes
Ingredients:

- 1 tbsp canola oil
- 1 onion, chopped
- 1 carrot, chopped
- 1 garlic clove, minced
- 3 Granny Smith apples, chopped
- 2 tbsp curry powder
- 2 tsp tomato paste
- 3 cups vegetable broth
- Salt to taste
- 1 cup soy milk
- 4 tsp sugar-free apricot preserves

Directions:
1. Heat the oil in a pot over medium heat. Place onion, carrot, and garlic and sauté for 5 minutes. Stir in apples and cook for 5 minutes, until the apples soften. Add in tomato paste, broth, and salt. Cook for 10 minutes. Blend the soup in a food processor until smooth. Transfer to a bowl and mix with soy milk. Close the lid and let chill in the fridge for 3 hours. Serve topped with apricot preserves.

Celery & Potato Soup

Servings:6
Cooking Time:55 Minutes
Ingredients:

- 2 tbsp olive oil
- 1 onion, chopped
- 1 carrot, chopped
- 1 celery stalk, chopped
- 2 garlic cloves, minced
- 1 golden beet, peeled and diced
- 1 yellow bell pepper, chopped
- 1 Yukon Gold potato, diced
- 6 cups vegetable broth
- 1 tsp dried thyme
- Salt and black pepper to taste
- 1 tbsp lemon juice

Directions:
1. Heat the oil in a pot over medium heat. Place the onion, carrot, celery, and garlic. Cook for 5 minutes or until softened. Stir in beet, bell pepper, and potato, cook uncovered for 1 minute. Pour in the broth and thyme. Season with salt and pepper. Cook for 45 minutes until the vegetables are tender. Serve sprinkled with lemon juice.

Garlicky Broccoli Soup

Servings:6
Cooking Time:35 Minutes
Ingredients:

- 2 tbsp olive oil
- 3 spring onions, chopped
- 6 cups vegetable broth
- 3 potatoes, chopped
- 2 cups broccoli florets, chopped
- 2 garlic cloves, minced
- 1 cup plain unsweetened soy milk
- Salt and black pepper to taste
- 1 tbsp minced chives

Directions:
1. Heat the oil in a pot over medium heat. Place in spring onions and garlic and sauté for 5 minutes until translucent. Add in broth, potatoes, and broccoli. Bring to a boil, then lower the heat and simmer for 20 minutes. Mix in soy milk, salt, and pepper. Cook for 5 more minutes. Serve topped with chives.

Green Bean & Rice Soup

Servings:4
Cooking Time:50 Minutes
Ingredients:

- 2 tbsp olive oil
- 1 medium onion, minced
- 2 garlic cloves minced
- ½ cup brown rice
- 1 cup green beans, chopped
- 2 tbsp chopped parsley

Directions:
1. Heat oil in a pot over medium heat. Place in onion and garlic and sauté for 3 minutes. Add in rice, 4 cups water, salt, and pepper. Bring to a boil, lower the heat, and simmer for 15 minutes. Stir in beans and cook for 10 minutes. Top with parsley.

Butternut Squash Soup

Servings:4
Cooking Time:30 Minutes
Ingredients:
- 2 tbsp olive oil
- 1 onion, chopped
- ½ lb butternut squash, chopped
- 1 red bell pepper, chopped
- 4 cups vegetable broth
- Salt and black pepper to taste
- ½ cup plant butter
- ¼ cup toasted pumpkin seeds

Directions:
1. Heat oil in a pot over medium heat. Place in onion, squash, and bell pepper and sauté for 5 minutes until soft. Stir in broth, salt and pepper. Bring to a boil, then lower the heat and simmer for 20 minutes. Stir in butter and blend the soup using an immersion blender. Top with toasted seeds and serve.

Creamed Potato Soup With Herbs

Servings: 4
Cooking Time: 40 Minutes
Ingredients:
- 2 tablespoons olive oil
- 1 onion, chopped
- 1 celery stalk, chopped
- 4 large potatoes, peeled and chopped
- 2 garlic cloves, minced
- 1 teaspoon fresh basil, chopped
- 1 teaspoon fresh parsley, chopped
- 1 teaspoon fresh rosemary, chopped
- 1 bay laurel
- 1 teaspoon ground allspice
- 4 cups vegetable stock
- Salt and fresh ground black pepper, to taste
- 2 tablespoons fresh chives chopped

Directions:
1. In a heavy-bottomed pot, heat the olive oil over medium-high heat. Once hot, sauté the onion, celery and potatoes for about 5 minutes, stirring periodically.
2. Add in the garlic, basil, parsley, rosemary, bay laurel and allspice and continue sautéing for 1 minute or until fragrant.
3. Now, add in the vegetable stock, salt and black pepper and bring to a rapid boil. Immediately reduce the heat to a simmer and let it cook for about 30 minutes.
4. Puree the soup using an immersion blender until creamy and uniform.
5. Reheat your soup and serve with fresh chives. Bon appétit!

Mushroom, Chickpea & Eggplant Stew

Servings:4
Cooking Time:30 Minutes
Ingredients:
- 2 tbsp olive oil
- 1 onion, chopped
- 1 eggplant, chopped
- 2 medium carrots, sliced
- 1 red potato, chopped
- 1 cup mushrooms, sliced
- 2 garlic cloves, minced
- 1 cans chickpeas, drained
- 1 can diced tomatoes
- 1 tbsp minced parsley
- ½ tsp dried oregano
- ½ tsp dried basil
- 1 tbsp soy sauce
- ½ cup vegetable broth
- Salt and black pepper to taste

Directions:
1. Heat the oil in a pot over medium heat. Place in onion, garlic, eggplant, and carrots and sauté for 5 minutes. Lower the heat and stir in potato, mushrooms, chickpeas, tomatoes, oregano, basil, soy sauce, salt, pepper, and broth. Simmer for 15 minutes. Serve sprinkled with parsley.

Coconut & Tofu Soup

Servings:4
Cooking Time:30 Minutes
Ingredients:
- 1 tbsp canola oil
- 1 onion, chopped
- 2 tbsp minced fresh ginger
- 2 tbsp soy sauce
- 1 cup shiitake mushrooms, sliced
- 1 tbsp pure date sugar
- 1 tsp chili paste
- 2 cups light vegetable broth
- 8 oz extra-firm tofu, chopped
- 2 cans coconut milk
- 1 tbsp fresh lime juice
- 3 tbsp chopped fresh cilantro

Directions:
1. Heat the oil in a pot over medium heat. Place in onion and ginger and sauté for 3 minutes until softened. Add in soy sauce, mushrooms, sugar, and chili paste. Stir in broth. Bring to a boil, then lower the heat and simmer for 15 minutes. Strain the liquid and discard solids. Return the broth to the pot. Stir in tofu, coconut milk, and lime juice. Cook for 5 minutes. Garnish with cilantro and serve.

Turmeric Bean Soup

Servings:6
Cooking Time:50 Minutes
Ingredients:
- 3 tbsp olive oil
- 1 onion, chopped
- 2 carrots, chopped
- 1 sweet potato, chopped
- 1 yellow bell pepper, chopped
- 2 garlic cloves, minced
- 4 tomatoes, chopped
- 6 cups vegetable broth

- 1 bay leaf
- Salt to taste
- 1 tsp ground cayenne pepper
- 1 can white beans, drained
- ⅓ cup whole-wheat pasta
- ¼ tsp turmeric

Directions:

1. Heat the oil in a pot over medium heat. Place onion, carrots, sweet potato, bell pepper, and garlic. Cook for 5 minutes. Add in tomatoes, broth, bay leaf, salt, and cayenne pepper. Stir and bring to a boil. Lower the heat and simmer for 10 minutes. Put in white beans and simmer for 15 more minutes.

2. Cook the pasta in a pot with boiling salted water and turmeric for 8-10 minutes, until pasta is al dente. Strain and transfer to the soup. Discard the bay leaf. Spoon into a bowl and serve.

Hot Lentil Soup With Zucchini

Servings:4
Cooking Time:30 Minutes
Ingredients:

- 2 tbsp olive oil
- 1 onion, chopped
- 1 zucchini, chopped
- 1 garlic clove, minced
- 1 tbsp hot paprika
- 1 can crushed tomatoes
- 1 cup red lentils, rinsed
- 4 cups vegetable broth
- 3 cups chopped Swiss chard

Directions:

1. Heat the oil in a pot over medium heat. Place in onion, zucchini, and garlic and sauté for 5 minutes until tender. Add in paprika, tomatoes, lentils, broth, salt, and pepper. Bring to a boil, then lower the heat and simmer for 15 minutes, stirring often. Add in the Swiss chard and cook for another 3-5 minutes. Serve immediately.

The Best Cauliflower Salad Ever

Servings: 4
Cooking Time: 10 Minutes
Ingredients:

- 1 ½ pounds cauliflower florets
- 1/4 cup extra-virgin olive oil
- 1 teaspoon garlic, minced
- 1 teaspoon lemon zest
- 2 tablespoons lemon juice
- Sea salt and ground black pepper, to taste
- 1/4 teaspoon dried dill
- 1/2 teaspoon dried oregano
- 1 teaspoon dried mint
- 10 ounces canned chickpeas, drained
- 1/4 cup fresh cilantro, chopped

Directions:

1. In a saucepan, bring about 1/4 inch of water to a boil. Add in the cauliflower florets. Cover and steam the cauliflower until crisp-tender or about 4 minutes.

2. Let the cauliflower florets cool completely and place them in a salad bowl.

3. Add the remaining ingredients, except for the cilantro, to the salad bowl and toss to combine well. Garnish with fresh cilantro leaves and serve well-chilled.

4. Bon appétit!

Fall Medley Stew

Servings:4
Cooking Time:65 Minutes
Ingredients:

- 2 tbsp olive oil
- 8 oz seitan, cubed
- 1 leek, chopped
- 2 garlic cloves, minced
- 1 russet potato, chopped
- 1 carrot, chopped
- 1 parsnip, chopped
- 1 cup butternut squash, cubed
- 1 head savoy cabbage, chopped
- 1 can diced tomatoes
- 1 can white beans
- 2 cups vegetable broth
- ½ cup dry white wine
- ½ tsp dried thyme
- ½ cup crumbled angel hair pasta

Directions:

1. Heat oil in a pot over medium heat. Place in seitan and cook for 3 minutes. Sprinkle with salt and pepper. Add in leek and garlic and cook for another 3 minutes. Stir in potato, carrot, parsnip, and squash, cook for 10 minutes. Add in cabbage, tomatoes, white beans, broth, wine, thyme, salt, and pepper. Bring to a boil, lower the heat and simmer for 15 minutes. Put in pasta and cook for 5 minutes.

Chili Cannellini Bean Stew

Servings:4
Cooking Time:40 Minutes
Ingredients:

- 2 tbsp olive oil
- 1 onion, chopped
- 2 potatoes, chopped
- 2 cans cannellini beans
- 1 can crushed tomatoes
- 1 can mild chopped green chilies
- 2 tbsp tamarind paste
- ¼ cup pure agave syrup
- 1 cup vegetable broth
- 2 tbsp chili powder
- 1 tsp ground coriander
- ½ tsp ground cumin
- Salt and black pepper to taste
- 1 cup frozen peas, thawed

Directions:

1. Heat the oil in a pot over medium heat. Place in the onion and sauté for 3 minutes until translucent. Stir in potatoes, beans, tomatoes, and chilies. Cook for 5 minutes more. In a bowl, whisk the tamarind paste with agave syrup

and broth. Pour the mixture into the pot. Stir in chili powder, coriander, cumin, salt, and pepper. Bring to a boil, then lower the heat and simmer for 20 minutes until the potatoes are tender. Add in peas and cook for another 5 minutes. Serve warm.

Hearty Winter Quinoa Soup

Servings: 4
Cooking Time: 25 Minutes
Ingredients:
- 2 tablespoons olive oil
- 1 onion, chopped
- 2 carrots, peeled and chopped
- 1 parsnip, chopped
- 1 celery stalk, chopped
- 1 cup yellow squash, chopped
- 4 garlic cloves, pressed or minced
- 4 cups roasted vegetable broth
- 2 medium tomatoes, crushed
- 1 cup quinoa
- Sea salt and ground black pepper, to taste
- 1 bay laurel
- 2 cup Swiss chard, tough ribs removed and torn into pieces
- 2 tablespoons Italian parsley, chopped

Directions:
1. In a heavy-bottomed pot, heat the olive over medium-high heat. Now, sauté the onion, carrot, parsnip, celery and yellow squash for about 3 minutes or until the vegetables are just tender.
2. Add in the garlic and continue to sauté for 1 minute or until aromatic.
3. Then, stir in the vegetable broth, tomatoes, quinoa, salt, pepper and bay laurel; bring to a boil. Immediately reduce the heat to a simmer and let it cook for 13 minutes.
4. Fold in the Swiss chard; continue to simmer until the chard wilts.
5. Ladle into individual bowls and serve garnished with the fresh parsley. Bon appétit!

Winter Bean Soup

Servings: 4
Cooking Time: 25 Minutes
Ingredients:
- 1 tablespoon olive oil
- 2 tablespoons shallots, chopped
- 1 carrot, chopped
- 1 parsnip, chopped
- 1 celery stalk, chopped
- 1 teaspoon fresh garlic, minced
- 4 cups vegetable broth
- 2 bay leaves
- 1 rosemary sprig, chopped
- 16 ounces canned navy beans
- Flaky sea salt and ground black pepper, to taste

Directions:
1. In a heavy-bottomed pot, heat the olive over medium-high heat. Now, sauté the shallots, carrot, parsnip and celery

for approximately 3 minutes or until the vegetables are just tender.
2. Add in the garlic and continue to sauté for 1 minute or until aromatic.
3. Then, add in the vegetable broth, bay leaves and rosemary and bring to a boil. Immediately reduce the heat to a simmer and let it cook for 10 minutes.
4. Fold in the navy beans and continue to simmer for about 5 minutes longer until everything is thoroughly heated. Season with salt and black pepper to taste.
5. Ladle into individual bowls, discard the bay leaves and serve hot. Bon appétit!

Cabbage Soup With Garlic Crostini

Servings: 4
Cooking Time: 1 Hour
Ingredients:
- Soup:
- 2 tablespoons olive oil
- 1 medium leek, chopped
- 1 cup turnip, chopped
- 1 parsnip, chopped
- 1 carrot, chopped
- 2 cups cabbage, shredded
- 2 garlic cloves, finely chopped
- 4 cups vegetable broth
- 2 bay leaves
- Sea salt and ground black pepper, to taste
- 1/4 teaspoon cumin seeds
- 1/2 teaspoon mustard seeds
- 1 teaspoon dried basil
- 2 tomatoes, pureed
- Crostini:
- 8 slices of baguette
- 2 heads garlic
- 4 tablespoons extra-virgin olive oil

Directions:
1. In a soup pot, heat 2 tablespoons of the olive over medium-high heat. Now, sauté the leek, turnip, parsnip and carrot for about 4 minutes or until the vegetables are crisp-tender.
2. Add in the garlic and cabbage and continue to sauté for 1 minute or until aromatic.
3. Then, stir in the vegetable broth, bay leaves, salt, black pepper, cumin seeds, mustard seeds, dried basil and pureed tomatoes; bring to a boil. Immediately reduce the heat to a simmer and let it cook for about 20 minutes.
4. Meanwhile, preheat your oven to 375 degrees F. Now, roast the garlic and baguette slices for about 15 minutes. Remove the crostini from the oven.
5. Continue baking the garlic for 45 minutes more or until very tender. Allow the garlic to cool.
6. Now, cut each head of the garlic using a sharp serrated knife in order to separate all the cloves.
7. Squeeze the roasted garlic cloves out of their skins. Mash the garlic pulp with 4 tablespoons of the extra-virgin olive oil.

8. Spread the roasted garlic mixture evenly on the tops of the crostini. Serve with the warm soup. Bon appétit!

Garden Pasta Salad

Servings: 4
Cooking Time: 10 Minutes
Ingredients:
- 12 ounces rotini pasta
- 1 small onion, thinly sliced
- 1 cup cherry tomatoes, halved
- 1 bell pepper, chopped
- 1 jalapeno pepper, chopped
- 1 tablespoon capers, drained
- 2 cups Iceberg lettuce, torn into pieces
- 2 tablespoons fresh parsley, chopped
- 2 tablespoons fresh cilantro, chopped
- 2 tablespoons fresh basil, chopped
- 1/4 cup olive oil
- 2 tablespoons apple cider vinegar
- 1 teaspoon garlic, pressed
- Kosher salt and ground black pepper, to taste
- 2 tablespoons nutritional yeast
- 2 tablespoons pine nuts, toasted and chopped

Directions:
1. Cook the pasta according to the package directions. Drain and rinse the pasta. Let it cool completely and then, transfer it to a salad bowl.
2. Then, add in the onion, tomatoes, peppers, capers, lettuce, parsley, cilantro and basil to the salad bowl.
3. Whisk the olive oil, vinegar, garlic, salt, black pepper and nutritional yeast. Dress your salad and top with toasted pine nuts. Bon appétit!

Habanero Bean Soup With Brown Rice

Servings:6
Cooking Time:40 Minutes
Ingredients:
- 2 tbsp olive oil
- 3 garlic cloves, minced
- 1 tbsp chili powder
- 1 tsp dried oregano
- 3 cans kidney beans
- 1 habanero pepper, chopped
- ¼ cup sun-dried tomatoes, chopped
- 6 cups vegetable broth
- Salt and black pepper to taste
- ½ cup brown rice
- 1 tbsp chopped cilantro

Directions:
1. Heat the oil in a pot over medium heat. Place in garlic and sauté for 1 minute. Add in chili powder, oregano, beans, habanero, tomatoes, broth, rice, salt, and pepper. Cook for 30 minutes.
2. Meanwhile, put the rice in a pot with boiling salted water and cook for 5 minutes. Spoon the soup in individual bowls and garnish with cilantro to serve.

Sicilian Eggplant And Pasta Salad

Servings: 4
Cooking Time: 15 Minutes
Ingredients:
- 1 tablespoon olive oil
- 1 pound eggplant, cut into rounds
- 4 tablespoons dry white wine
- 1 teaspoon Italian seasoning blend
- 12 ounces shell pasta
- 2 Roma tomatoes, diced
- 1 cup radicchio, sliced
- 1/2 cup olives, pitted and halved
- 4 tablespoons extra-virgin olive oil
- 2 tablespoons balsamic vinegar
- 1/2 teaspoon lemon zest
- Sea salt and ground black pepper, to taste

Directions:
1. Heat 2 tablespoons of the olive oil in a cast-iron skillet over a moderate flame. Once hot, fry the eggplant for about 10 minutes until browned on all sides.
2. Meanwhile, cook the pasta according to the package directions. Drain and rinse the pasta. Let it cool completely and then, transfer it to a salad bowl.
3. Then, add in the remaining ingredients, including the cooked eggplant; toss until well combined.
4. Taste and adjust the seasonings; serve at room temperature or well-chilled. Bon appétit!

Cream Of Carrot Soup

Servings: 4
Cooking Time: 30 Minutes
Ingredients:
- 2 tablespoons sesame oil
- 1 onion, chopped
- 1 ½ pounds carrots, trimmed and chopped
- 1 parsnip, chopped
- 2 garlic cloves, minced
- 1/2 teaspoon curry powder
- Sea salt and cayenne pepper, to taste
- 4 cups vegetable broth
- 1 cup full-fat coconut milk

Directions:
1. In a heavy-bottomed pot, heat the sesame oil over medium-high heat. Now, sauté the onion, carrots and parsnip for about 5 minutes, stirring periodically.
2. Add in the garlic and continue sautéing for 1 minute or until fragrant.
3. Then, stir in the curry powder, salt, cayenne pepper and vegetable broth; bring to a rapid boil. Immediately reduce the heat to a simmer and let it cook for 18 to 20 minutes.
4. Puree the soup using an immersion blender until creamy and uniform.
5. Return the pureed mixture to the pot. Fold in the coconut milk and continue to simmer until heated through or about 5 minutes longer.
6. Ladle into four bowls and serve hot. Bon appétit!

Tofu Goulash Soup

Servings:4
Cooking Time:25 Minutes
Ingredients:

- 1 ½ cups extra-firm tofu, crumbled
- 3 tbsp plant butter
- 1 white onion
- 2 garlic cloves
- 8 oz chopped butternut squash
- 1 red bell pepper
- 1 tbsp paprika powder
- ¼ tsp red chili flakes
- 1 tbsp dried basil
- ½ tbsp crushed cardamom seeds
- Salt and black pepper to taste
- 1 ½ cups crushed tomatoes
- 4 cups vegetable broth
- 1 ½ tsp red wine vinegar
- Chopped cilantro to serve

Directions:

1. Melt plant butter in a pot over medium heat and sauté onion and garlic for 3 minutes. Stir in tofu and cook for 3 minutes; add the butternut squash, bell pepper, paprika, red chili flakes, basil, cardamom seeds, salt, and pepper. Cook for 2 minutes. Pour in tomatoes and vegetable broth. Bring to a boil, reduce the heat and simmer for 10 minutes. Mix in red wine vinegar. Garnish with cilantro and serve.

French Green Bean Salad With Sesame And Mint

Servings: 5
Cooking Time: 10 Minutes
Ingredients:

- 1 ½ pounds French green beans, trimmed
- 1 white onion, thinly sliced
- 2 garlic cloves, minced
- Himalayan salt and ground black pepper, to taste
- 1/4 cup extra-virgin olive oil
- 2 tablespoons fresh lime juice
- 2 tablespoons tamari sauce
- 1 tablespoon mustard
- 2 tablespoons sesame seeds, lightly toasted
- 2 tablespoons fresh mint leaves, roughly chopped

Directions:

1. Boil the green beans in a large saucepan of salted water until they are just tender or about 2 minutes.
2. Drain and let the beans cool completely; then, transfer them to a salad bowl. Add in the onion, garlic, salt, black pepper, olive oil, lime juice, tamari sauce and mustard.
3. Top your salad with the sesame seeds and mint leaves.
4. Bon appétit!

Roasted Carrot Soup

Servings: 4
Cooking Time: 50 Minutes
Ingredients:

- 1 ½ pounds carrots

- 4 tablespoons olive oil
- 1 yellow onion, chopped
- 2 cloves garlic, minced
- 1/3 teaspoon ground cumin
- Sea salt and white pepper, to taste
- 1/2 teaspoon turmeric powder
- 4 cups vegetable stock
- 2 teaspoons lemon juice
- 2 tablespoons fresh cilantro, roughly chopped

Directions:

1. Start by preheating your oven to 400 degrees F. Place the carrots on a large parchment-lined baking sheet; toss the carrots with 2 tablespoons of the olive oil.
2. Roast the carrots for about 35 minutes or until they've softened.
3. In a heavy-bottomed pot, heat the remaining 2 tablespoons of the olive oil. Now, sauté the onion and garlic for about 3 minutes or until aromatic.
4. Add in the cumin, salt, pepper, turmeric, vegetable stock and roasted carrots. Continue to simmer for 12 minutes more.
5. Puree your soup with an immersion blender. Drizzle lemon juice over your soup and serve garnished with fresh cilantro leaves. Bon appétit!

Chili Gazpacho

Servings:4
Cooking Time:15 Minutes
Ingredients:

- 2 tbsp olive oil
- 2 cups water
- 1 red onion, chopped
- 6 tomatoes, chopped
- 1 red bell pepper, diced
- 2 garlic cloves, minced
- juice of 1 lemon
- 2 tbsp chopped fresh basil
- ½ tsp chili pepper

Directions:

1. In a food processor, place the olive oil, half of the onion, half of the tomato, half of the bell pepper, garlic, lemon juice, basil, and chili pepper. Season with salt and pepper. Blitz until smooth. Transfer to a bowl and add in the reserved onion, tomatoes, and bell pepper. Let chill in the fridge before serving.

Rice Noodle Soup With Beans

Servings:6
Cooking Time:10 Minutes
Ingredients:

- 2 carrots, chopped
- 2 celery stalks, chopped
- 6 cups vegetable broth
- 8 oz brown rice noodles
- 1 can pinto beans
- 1 tsp dried herbs

Directions:

1. Place a pot over medium heat and add in the carrots, celery, and vegetable broth. Bring to a boil. Add in noodles,

beans, dried herbs, salt, and pepper. Reduce the heat and simmer for 5 minutes. Serve.

Creamed Cavatappi And Cauliflower Salad

Servings: 4
Cooking Time: 15 Minutes
Ingredients:
- 12 ounces cavatappi pasta
- 1 cup cauliflower florets
- 1/2 cup vegan mayonnaise
- 1 tablespoon fresh lemon juice
- 1 onion, chopped
- 2 garlic cloves, finely chopped
- 1 teaspoon deli mustard
- 2 medium tomatoes, sliced
- 2 cups arugula, torn into pieces

Directions:
1. Bring a large pot of salted water to a boil. Now, cook the pasta and cauliflower florets for about 6 minutes.
2. Remove the cauliflower with a slotted spoon from the water. Continue to cook your pasta for a further 6 minutes until al dente.
3. Allow the pasta and cauliflower to cool completely; then, transfer them to a salad bowl.
4. Then, add in the remaining ingredients and toss until well combined.
5. Taste and adjust the seasonings; place the salad in your refrigerator until ready to use. Bon appétit!

Green Onion Corn & Bean Soup

Servings:4
Cooking Time:55 Minutes
Ingredients:
- 2 tbsp olive oil
- 1 red onion, chopped
- 1 red bell pepper, chopped
- 1 carrot, chopped
- 2 garlic cloves, minced
- 1 tsp ground cumin
- 1 tsp dried oregano
- 1 can diced tomatoes
- 1 can pinto beans
- 4 cups vegetable broth
- 2 cups corn kernels
- 1 tsp fresh lemon juice
- Salt and black pepper to taste
- 2 stalks green onions, chopped
- Tabasco sauce for garnish

Directions:
1. Heat the oil in a pot over medium heat. Place in onion, bell pepper, carrot, and garlic. Sauté for 5 minutes. Add in cumin, oregano, tomatoes, beans, salt, pepper, and broth. Bring to a boil, then lower the heat and simmer for 15 minutes.
2. In a food processor, transfer ⅓ of the soup and blend until smooth. Return to the pot and stir in the corn. Cook for

10 minutes. Drizzle with lemon juice before serving and garnish with green onions and hot sauce to serve.

Italian Nonna's Pizza Salad

Servings: 4
Cooking Time: 15 Minutes
Ingredients:
- 1 pound macaroni
- 1 cup marinated mushrooms, sliced
- 1 cup grape tomatoes, halved
- 4 tablespoons scallions, chopped
- 1 teaspoon garlic, minced
- 1 Italian pepper, sliced
- 1/4 cup extra-virgin olive oil
- 1/4 cup balsamic vinegar
- 1 teaspoon dried oregano
- 1 teaspoon dried basil
- 1/2 teaspoon dried rosemary
- Sea salt and cayenne pepper, to taste
- 1/2 cup black olives, sliced

Directions:
1. Cook the pasta according to the package directions. Drain and rinse the pasta. Let it cool completely and then, transfer it to a salad bowl.
2. Then, add in the remaining ingredients and toss until the macaroni are well coated.
3. Taste and adjust the seasonings; place the pizza salad in your refrigerator until ready to use. Bon appétit!

Autumn Squash Soup

Servings: 4
Cooking Time: 35 Minutes
Ingredients:
- 2 tablespoons olive oil
- 1 onion, chopped
- 1 large carrot, trimmed and chopped
- 1 bell pepper, chopped
- 2 pounds acorn squash, peeled, seeded and cubed
- 4 garlic cloves, pressed
- 1 teaspoon fresh ginger, peeled and minced
- 1 tablespoon fresh coriander, chopped
- 1 tablespoon fresh Italian parsley, chopped
- 1 teaspoon curry powder
- 1 tablespoon brown sugar
- 1/2 teaspoon chili powder
- Kosher salt and ground black pepper, to taste
- 1/2 teaspoon paprika
- 4 cups vegetable broth
- 1 cup full-fat coconut milk
- 1 lemon, cut into wedges
- 2 tablespoons fresh chervil, for garnish

Directions:
1. In a heavy-bottomed pot, heat the olive oil over medium-high heat. Now, sauté the onion, carrot, pepper and acorn squash for about 5 minutes, stirring periodically.
2. Add in the garlic, ginger, coriander and parsley and continue sautéing for 1 minute or until fragrant.

3. Then, stir in the curry powder, brown sugar, chili powder, salt, black pepper, paprika and vegetable broth; bring to a boil. Immediately reduce the heat to a simmer and let it cook for about 20 to 22 minutes.

4. Puree the soup using an immersion blender until creamy and uniform.

5. Return the pureed mixture to the pot. Fold in the coconut milk and continue to simmer until heated through or about 5 minutes longer.

6. Ladle into four bowls and serve garnished with lemon wedges and fresh chervil. Bon appétit!

Mediterranean-style Lentil Salad

Servings: 5
Cooking Time: 20 Minutes
Ingredients:
- 1 ½ cups red lentil, rinsed
- 1 teaspoon deli mustard
- 1/2 lemon, freshly squeezed
- 2 tablespoons tamari sauce
- 2 scallion stalks, chopped
- 1/4 cup extra-virgin olive oil
- 2 garlic cloves, minced
- 1 cup butterhead lettuce, torn into pieces
- 2 tablespoons fresh parsley, chopped
- 2 tablespoons fresh cilantro, chopped
- 1 teaspoon fresh basil
- 1 teaspoon fresh oregano
- 1 ½ cups cherry tomatoes, halved
- 3 ounces Kalamata olives, pitted and halved

Directions:
1. In a large-sized saucepan, bring 4 ½ cups of the water and the red lentils to a boil.

2. Immediately turn the heat to a simmer and continue to cook your lentils for about 15 minutes or until tender. Drain and let it cool completely.

3. Transfer the lentils to a salad bowl; toss the lentils with the remaining ingredients until well combined.

4. Serve chilled or at room temperature. Bon appétit!

Grandma's Creamy Soup

Servings: 4
Cooking Time: 40 Minutes
Ingredients:
- 2 tablespoons olive oil
- 1 shallot, chopped
- 4 large carrots, trimmed and sliced
- 4 large potatoes, peeled and sliced
- 2 garlic cloves, minced
- 1/2 teaspoon ground cumin
- 1/2 teaspoon mustard powder
- 1/2 teaspoon fennel seeds
- Kosher salt and cayenne pepper, to taste
- 3 ½ cups vegetable broth
- 1 cup coconut milk

Directions:

1. In a heavy-bottomed pot, heat the olive oil over medium-high heat. Once hot, sauté the shallot, carrots and potatoes for about 5 minutes, stirring periodically.

2. Add in the garlic and continue sautéing for 1 minute or until fragrant.

3. Then, stir in the ground cumin, mustard powder, fennel seeds, salt, cayenne pepper and vegetable broth; bring to a rapid boil. Immediately reduce the heat to a simmer and let it cook for about 30 minutes.

4. Puree the soup using an immersion blender until creamy and uniform.

5. Return the pureed soup to the pot. Fold in the coconut milk and continue to simmer until heated through or about 5 minutes longer.

6. Ladle into four bowls and serve hot. Bon appétit!

Ginger Broccoli Soup

Servings:4
Cooking Time:50 Minutes
Ingredients:
- 1 onion, chopped
- 1 tbsp minced peeled fresh ginger
- 2 tsp olive oil
- 2 carrots, chopped
- 1 head broccoli, chopped into florets
- 1 cup coconut milk
- 3 cups vegetable broth
- ½ tsp turmeric
- Salt and black pepper to taste

Directions:
1. In a pot over medium heat, place the onion, ginger, and olive oil, cook for 4 minutes. Add in carrots, broccoli, broth, turmeric, pepper, and salt. Bring to a boil and cook for 15 minutes. Transfer the soup to a food processor and blend until smooth. Stir in coconut milk and serve warm.

Mushroom & Bean Stew

Servings:4
Cooking Time:35 Minutes
Ingredients:
- 2 tbsp olive oil
- 1 onion, chopped
- 1 carrot, chopped
- 2 garlic cloves, minced
- 1 red bell pepper, chopped
- ½ cup capers
- 1 medium zucchini, chopped
- 1 can diced tomatoes
- 1 cup vegetable broth
- Salt and black pepper to taste
- 8 oz porcini mushrooms, sliced
- 3 cups fresh baby spinach
- 1 can cannellini beans,
- ½ tsp dried basil
- 2 tbsp minced fresh parsley

Directions:
1. Heat oil in a pot and sauté onion, carrot, garlic, mushrooms, and bell pepper for 5 minutes. Stir in capers,

zucchini, tomatoes, broth, salt, and pepper. Bring to a boil, then lower the heat and simmer for 20 minutes. Add in beans and basil. Simmer an additional 2-3 minutes. Serve topped with parsley.

Cabbage & Red Bean Chili

Servings:4
Cooking Time:35 Minutes
Ingredients:
- 2 tsp sesame oil
- 1 cup green onions, chopped
- 3 cloves garlic, minced
- 1 lb yellow squash, chopped
- 2 cups shredded napa cabbage
- 1 can red beans, drained
- 1 can diced tomatoes
- 2 cups vegetable broth
- 2 tbsp red miso paste
- 2 tbsp water
- 1 tbsp hot sauce
- 2 tsp tamari sauce

Directions:
1. Heat the sesame oil in a pot over medium heat. Place in green onion, garlic and yellow squash, and cook for 5 minutes. Stir in cabbage, beans, tomatoes, and broth. Bring to a boil, then lower the heat and simmer covered for 15 minutes.
2. Meanwhile, mix the miso paste with hot water in a bowl. Remove the pot from heat and stir in the miso, tamari, and hot sauces. Adjust the seasoning and serve.

Italian-style Cremini Mushrooms Soup

Servings: 3
Cooking Time: 15 Minutes
Ingredients:
- 3 tablespoons vegan butter
- 1 white onion, chopped
- 1 red bell pepper, chopped
- 1/2 teaspoon garlic, pressed
- 3 cups Cremini mushrooms, chopped
- 2 tablespoons almond flour
- 3 cups water
- 1 teaspoon Italian herb mix
- Sea salt and ground black pepper, to taste
- 1 heaping tablespoon fresh chives, roughly chopped

Directions:
1. In a stockpot, melt the vegan butter over medium-high heat. Once hot, sauté the onion and pepper for about 3 minutes until they have softened.
2. Add in the garlic and Cremini mushrooms and continue sautéing until the mushrooms have softened. Sprinkle almond meal over the mushrooms and continue to cook for 1 minute or so.
3. Add in the remaining ingredients. Let it simmer, covered and continue to cook for 5 to 6 minutes more until the liquid has thickened slightly.
4. Ladle into three soup bowls and garnish with fresh chives. Bon appétit!

Vegetable & Rice Soup

Servings:6
Cooking Time:40 Minutes
Ingredients:
- 3 tbsp olive oil
- 2 carrots, chopped
- 1 onion, chopped
- 1 celery stalk, chopped
- 2 garlic cloves, minced
- 2 cups chopped cabbage
- ½ red bell pepper, chopped
- 4 potatoes, unpeeled and quartered
- 6 cups vegetable broth
- ½ cup brown rice, rinsed
- ½ cup frozen green peas
- 2 tbsp chopped parsley

Directions:
1. Heat the oil in a pot over medium heat. Place carrots, onion, celery, and garlic. Cook for 5 minutes. Add in cabbage, bell pepper, potatoes, and broth. Bring to a boil, lower the heat, and add the brown rice, salt, and pepper. Simmer uncovered for 25 minutes until vegetables are tender. Stir in peas and cook for 5 minutes. Top with parsley and serve warm.

Cauliflower Dill Soup

Servings:4
Cooking Time:26 Minutes
Ingredients:
- 2 tbsp coconut oil
- ½ lb celery root, trimmed
- 1 garlic clove
- 1 medium white onion
- ¼ cup fresh dill, roughly chopped
- 1 tsp cumin powder
- ¼ tsp nutmeg powder
- 1 head cauliflower, cut into florets
- 3 ½ cups seasoned vegetable stock
- 5 oz plant butter
- Juice from 1 lemon
- ¼ cup coconut whipping cream

Directions:
1. Set a pot over medium heat, add the coconut oil and allow heating until no longer shimmering.
2. Add the celery root, garlic clove, and onion; sauté the vegetables until fragrant and soft, about 5 minutes. Stir in the dill, cumin, and nutmeg, and fry further for 1 minute. Mix in the cauliflower florets and vegetable stock. Bring the soup to a boil for 12 to 15 minutes or until the cauliflower is soft. Turn the heat off. Add the plant butter and lemon juice. Puree the ingredients with an immersion blender until smooth. Mix in coconut whipping cream and season the soup with salt and black pepper. Serve warm.

Medley Of Mushroom Soup

Servings:4
Cooking Time:40 Minutes
Ingredients:
- 4 oz unsalted plant butter
- 1 small onion, finely chopped
- 1 clove garlic, minced
- 5 oz button mushrooms, chopped
- 5 oz cremini mushrooms, chopped
- 5 oz shiitake mushrooms, chopped
- ½ lb celery root, chopped
- ½ tsp dried rosemary
- 1 vegetable stock cube, crushed
- 1 tbsp plain vinegar
- 1 cup coconut cream
- 4 – 6 leaves basil, chopped

Directions:
1. Place a saucepan over medium-high heat, add the plant butter to melt, then sauté the onion, garlic, mushrooms, and celery root in the butter until golden brown and fragrant, about 6 minutes. Fetch out some mushrooms and reserve for garnishing. Add the rosemary, 3 cups of water, stock cube, and vinegar. Stir the mixture and bring it to a boil for 6 minutes. After, reduce the heat and simmer the soup for 15 minutes or until the celery is soft.
2. Mix in the coconut cream and puree the ingredients using an immersion blender. Simmer for 2 minutes. Spoon the soup into serving bowls, garnish with the reserved mushrooms and basil. Serve.

Spanish Gazpacho

Servings:4
Cooking Time:15 Minutes
Ingredients:
- 3 tbsp olive oil
- 2 garlic cloves, crushed
- Salt and black pepper to taste
- 2 cucumbers
- 2 tsp lemon juice
- 2 lb ripe plum tomatoes, chopped
- 1 can crushed tomatoes
- 1 cup tomato juice
- 2 tbsp chopped dill

Directions:
1. Put the garlic, olive oil, and salt and pulse in a food processor until paste-like consistency forms. Add in 1 cucumber and lemon juice. Blitz until smooth. Put in tomatoes, tomato juice, salt, and pepper. Blend until smooth. Transfer to a bowl, close the lid and let chill in the fridge before serving.

Tomato Lentil Stew

Servings:4
Cooking Time:25 Minutes
Ingredients:
- 2 tsp olive oil
- 4 carrots, chopped
- 1 onion, chopped
- ½ green bell pepper, chopped
- 1 tbsp paprika
- 2 garlic cloves, sliced
- 4 cups vegetable broth
- 1 can crushed tomatoes
- 2 cans lentils, drained

Directions:
1. Heat the oil in a pot over medium heat. Place in carrots, onion, bell pepper, paprika, and garlic. Sauté for 5 minutes until tender. Stir in broth, tomatoes, and lentils. Bring to a boil, then lower the heat and simmer for 15 minutes. Sprinkle with salt and pepper. Serve warm.

Roasted Asparagus And Avocado Salad

Servings: 4
Cooking Time: 20 Minutes
Ingredients:
- 1 pound asparagus, trimmed, cut into bite-sized pieces
- 1 white onion, chopped
- 2 garlic cloves, minced
- 1 Roma tomato, sliced
- 1/4 cup olive oil
- 1/4 cup balsamic vinegar
- 1 tablespoon stone-ground mustard
- 2 tablespoons fresh parsley, chopped
- 1 tablespoon fresh cilantro, chopped
- 1 tablespoon fresh basil, chopped
- Sea salt and ground black pepper, to taste
- 1 small avocado, pitted and diced
- 1/2 cup pine nuts, roughly chopped

Directions:
1. Begin by preheating your oven to 420 degrees F.
2. Toss the asparagus with 1 tablespoon of the olive oil and arrange them on a parchment-lined roasting pan.
3. Bake for about 15 minutes, rotating the pan once or twice to promote even cooking. Let it cool completely and place in your salad bowl.
4. Toss the asparagus with the vegetables, olive oil, vinegar, mustard and herbs. Salt and pepper to taste.
5. Toss to combine and top with avocado and pine nuts. Bon appétit!

Brussels Sprouts & Tofu Soup

Servings:4
Cooking Time:40 Minutes
Ingredients:
- 7 oz firm tofu, cubed
- 2 tsp olive oil
- 1 cup sliced mushrooms
- 1 cup shredded Brussels sprouts
- 1 garlic clove, minced
- ½-inch piece fresh ginger, minced
- Salt to taste
- 2 tbsp apple cider vinegar
- 2 tbsp soy sauce
- 1 tsp pure date sugar
- ¼ tsp red pepper flakes

- 1 scallion, chopped

Directions:

1. Heat the oil in a skillet over medium heat. Place mushrooms, Brussels sprouts, garlic, ginger, and salt. Sauté for 7-8 minutes until the veggies are soft. Pour in 4 cups of water, vinegar, soy sauce, sugar, pepper flakes, and tofu. Bring to a boil, then lower the heat and simmer for 5-10 minutes. Top with scallions and serve.

Broccoli Fennel Soup

Servings:4
Cooking Time:25 Minutes
Ingredients:

- 1 fennel bulb, chopped
- 10 oz broccoli, cut into florets
- 3 cups vegetable stock
- Salt and black pepper to taste
- 1 garlic clove
- 1 cup cashew cream cheese
- 3 oz plant butter
- ½ cup chopped fresh oregano

Directions:

1. Put the fennel and broccoli into a pot, and cover with the vegetable stock. Bring the ingredients to a boil over medium heat until the vegetables are soft, about 10 minutes. Season the liquid with salt and black pepper, and drop in the garlic. Simmer the soup for 5 to 7 minutes and turn the heat off.

2. Pour the cream cheese, plant butter, and oregano into the soup; puree the ingredients with an immersion blender until completely smooth. Adjust the taste with salt and black pepper. Spoon the soup into serving bowls and serve.

Chapter 6. Sauces & Condiments

Classic Alfredo Sauce

Servings: 4
Cooking Time: 10 Minutes
Ingredients:

- 2 tablespoons olive oil
- 2 cloves garlic, minced
- 2 tablespoons rice flour
- 1 ½ cups rice milk, unsweetened
- Sea salt and ground black pepper, to taste
- 1/2 teaspoon red pepper flakes, crushed
- 4 tablespoons tahini
- 2 tablespoons nutritional yeast

Directions:

1. In a large saucepan, heat the olive oil over a moderate heat. Once hot, sauté the garlic for about 30 seconds or until fragrant.

2. Add in the rice flour and turn the heat to a simmer. Gradually add in the milk and continue to cook for a few minutes more, whisking constantly to avoid the lumps.

3. Add in the salt, black pepper, red pepper flakes, tahini and nutritional yeast.

4. Continue to cook on low until the sauce has thickened.

5. Store in an airtight container in your refrigerator for up to four days. Bon appétit!

Perfect Hollandaise Sauce

Servings: 6
Cooking Time: 15 Minutes
Ingredients:

- 1/2 cup cashews, soaked and drained
- 1 cup almond milk
- 2 tablespoons fresh lemon juice
- 3 tablespoons coconut oil
- 3 tablespoons nutritional yeast
- Sea salt and ground white pepper, to taste
- A pinch of grated nutmeg
- 1/2 teaspoon red pepper flakes, crushed

Directions:

1. Puree all the ingredients in a high-speed blender or food processor.

2. Then, heat the mixture in a small saucepan over low-medium heat; cook, stirring occasionally, until the sauce has reduced and thickened.

3. Bon appétit!

Easiest Vegan Mayo Ever

Servings: 6
Cooking Time: 15 Minutes
Ingredients:

- 1/2 cup olive oil, at room temperature
- 1/4 cup rice milk, unsweetened, at room temperature
- 1 teaspoon yellow mustard
- 1 tablespoon fresh lemon juice
- 1/3 teaspoon kosher salt

Directions:

1. Blend the milk, mustard, lemon juice and salt using your high-speed blender.

2. While the machine is going, gradually add in the olive oil and continue to blend at a low speed until the mixture has thickened.

3. Store in your refrigerator for about 6 days. Bon appétit!

Authentic Mediterranean Aïoli

Servings: 16
Cooking Time: 10 Minutes
Ingredients:
- 4 tablespoons aquafaba
- 1 teaspoon fresh lemon juice
- 1 teaspoon apple cider vinegar
- 1 teaspoon Dijon mustard
- 1 teaspoon garlic, crushed
- Coarse sea salt and ground white pepper, to taste
- 1 cup olive oil
- 1/4 teaspoon dried dill

Directions:
1. Place the aquafaba, lemon juice, vinegar, mustard, garlic, salt and pepper in the bowl of your food blender. Mix for 30 to 40 seconds.
2. Slowly and gradually, pour in the oil and continue to blend until the sauce has thickened.
3. Sprinkle dried dill over the top of your sauce. Store in your refrigerator until ready to serve.
4. Bon appétit!

Spinach And Pistachio Pesto

Servings: 10
Cooking Time: 10 Minutes
Ingredients:
- 2 cups baby spinach
- 1 teaspoon dried parsley flakes
- 1/2 teaspoon dried oregano
- 1/2 teaspoon dried savory
- 1/2 cup pistachio, hulled
- 2 cloves garlic, peeled
- 1/3 cup extra-virgin olive oil
- Kosher salt and ground black pepper, to taste
- 1/2 lemon, freshly squeezed

Directions:
1. In your food processor, place all ingredients, except for the oil. Process until well combined.
2. While the machine is running, gradually pour in the olive oil until the mixture comes together.
3. Serve with pasta or pita. Bon appétit!

Kale And Hemp Seed Pesto

Servings: 10
Cooking Time: 10 Minutes
Ingredients:
- 1/2 cup hemp seeds, hulled
- 1/2 cup raw cashews
- 2 cloves garlic, minced
- 1 cup fresh kale
- 1/2 cup fresh basil
- 1/2 cup fresh parsley
- 3 tablespoons nutritional yeast
- 1 tablespoon fresh lemon juice
- 1 teaspoon sherry vinegar
- Sea salt and ground black pepper, to taste
- 1/4 cup olive oil

Directions:
1. In your food processor, place all ingredients, except for the oil. Process until well combined.
2. While the machine is running, gradually pour in the olive oil until the sauce is uniform and creamy.
3. Serve with pasta, crackers or breadsticks. Bon appétit!

Cashew, Lime And Dill Sauce

Servings: 8
Cooking Time: 25 Minutes
Ingredients:
- 1 cup raw cashews
- 1/2 cup water
- 2 tablespoons dill
- 1 tablespoon lime juice
- Sea salt and red pepper, to taste

Directions:
1. Place all the ingredients in the bowl of your food processor or high-speed blender until smooth, uniform and creamy.
2. Season to taste and serve with crudités.

Dad's Homemade Ketchup

Servings: 12
Cooking Time: 30 Minutes
Ingredients:
- 2 tablespoons olive oil
- 1 onion, chopped
- 2 garlic cloves, chopped
- 1 teaspoon cayenne pepper
- 2 tablespoons tomato paste
- 30 ounces canned tomatoes, crushed
- 3 tablespoons brown sugar
- 1/4 cup apple cider vinegar
- Salt and fresh ground black pepper, to taste

Directions:
1. In a medium saucepan, heat the olive oil over a moderately high heat. Sauté the onions until tender and aromatic.
2. Add in the garlic and continue to sauté for 1 minute or until fragrant.
3. Add in the remaining ingredients and bring to a simmer. Continue to cook for about 25 minutes.
4. Process the mixture in your blender until smooth and uniform. Bon appétit!

Garlic Cilantro Dressing

Servings: 6
Cooking Time: 10 Minutes
Ingredients:
- 1/2 cup almonds
- 1/2 cup water
- 1 bunch cilantro
- 1 red chili pepper, chopped
- 2 cloves garlic, crushed
- 2 tablespoons fresh lime juice
- 1 teaspoon lime zest
- Sea salt and ground black pepper

- 5 tablespoons extra-virgin olive oil

Directions:

1. Place the almonds and water in your blender and mix until creamy and smooth.
2. Add in the cilantro, chili pepper, garlic, lime juice, lime zest, salt and black pepper; blitz until everything is well combined.
3. Then, gradually add in the olive oil and mix until smooth. Store in your refrigerator for up to 5 days.
4. Bon appétit!

Traditional Russian Chrain

Servings: 12
Cooking Time: 40 Minutes
Ingredients:

- 1 cup boiled water
- 6 ounces raw beets, peeled
- 1 tablespoon brown salt
- 9 ounces raw horseradish, peeled
- 1 tablespoon olive oil
- 1/2 cup apple cider vinegar

Directions:

1. In a heavy-bottomed saucepan, bring the water a boil. Then, cook the beets for about 35 minutes or until they have softened.
2. Remove the skins and transfer the beets to a food processor. Add in the remaining ingredients and blend until well combined.
3. Bon appétit!

Easy Homemade Pear Sauce

Servings: 8
Cooking Time: 30 Minutes
Ingredients:

- 2 pounds pears, peeled, cored and diced
- 1/4 cup water
- 1/4 cup brown sugar
- 1/2 teaspoon fresh ginger, minced
- 1/2 teaspoon ground cloves
- 1 teaspoon ground cinnamon
- 1 teaspoon fresh lime juice
- 1 teaspoon cider vinegar
- 1 teaspoon vanilla paste

Directions:

1. Add the apples, water and sugar to a heavy-bottomed pot and cook for about 20 minutes.
2. Then, mash the cooked pears with a potato masher. Add in the remaining ingredients.
3. Continue to simmer until the pear sauce has thickened to your desired consistency.
4. Bon appétit!

Sunflower Seed Pasta Sauce

Servings: 3
Cooking Time: 10 Minutes
Ingredients:

- 1/2 cup sunflower seeds, soaked overnight
- 1/2 cup almond milk, unsweetened
- 2 tablespoons lemon juice

- 1 teaspoon granulated garlic
- 1/4 teaspoon dried oregano
- 1/2 teaspoon dried basil
- 1 teaspoon dried dill
- Sea salt and ground black pepper, to taste

Directions:

1. Place all the ingredients in the bowl of your food processor or a high-speed blender.
2. Puree until the sauce is uniform and smooth.
3. Serve the sauce over the cooked pasta or vegetable noodles. Bon appétit!

French-style White Sauce

Servings: 6
Cooking Time: 10 Minutes
Ingredients:

- 3 tablespoons dairy-free butter
- 3 tablespoons rice flour
- 1 ½ cups rice milk
- A pinch of salt
- A pinch of grated nutmeg

Directions:

1. Melt the butter in a sauté pan over a moderate flame. Add in the flour and continue to cook, whisking continuously to avoid lumps.
2. Pour the milk and continue whisking for about 4 minutes until the sauce has thickened.
3. Add in the spices and stir to combine well. Bon appétit!

Turkish Biber Salçası

Servings: 16
Cooking Time: 1 Hour 25 Minutes
Ingredients:

- 4 sweet red peppers
- 4 red chili peppers
- Juice of 1/2 lemon juice
- 2 tablespoons olive oil
- 1 teaspoon sea salt
- 1/2 teaspoon freshly ground black pepper

Directions:

1. Place the peppers directly over a low gas flame; roast the peppers for about 8 minutes until they are charred on all sides.
2. Let the peppers steam in a plastic bag or covered bowl for about 30 minutes. Remove the blackened skin and core and transfer the flesh to your food processor
3. Blitz until a smooth paste forms.
4. Heat the prepared paste in a saucepan; add in the remaining ingredients and stir to combine well. Turn the heat to a simmer and let it cook, partially covered, for about 45 minutes or until the sauce has thickened.
5. Store in your refrigerator for up to 4 weeks. Bon appétit!

Mediterranean Herb Ketchup

Servings: 8
Cooking Time: 30 Minutes
Ingredients:
- 1 tablespoon olive oil
- 16 ounces tomato paste
- 3 tablespoons brown sugar
- 1 teaspoon kosher salt
- 1/4 teaspoon ground cloves
- 1/4 teaspoon ground allspice
- 1 teaspoon dried basil
- 1 teaspoon dried oregano
- 1 teaspoon dried rosemary
- 1 teaspoon garlic powder
- 1 teaspoon onion powder
- 1 teaspoon porcini powder
- 3 tablespoons apple cider vinegar
- 1/4 cup water

Directions:
1. In a medium saucepan, heat the olive oil until sizzling.
2. Add in the remaining ingredients and bring to a simmer. Continue to simmer for about 25 minutes.
3. Process the mixture in your blender until smooth and uniform. Bon appétit!

Tomato Sauce With Garlic And Herbs

Servings: 12
Cooking Time: 25 Minutes
Ingredients:
- 3 tablespoons olive oil
- 4 garlic cloves, minced
- 1 teaspoon dried parsley flakes
- 1 teaspoon dried rosemary
- 1 teaspoon dried basil
- Kosher salt and black pepper, to taste
- 1 teaspoon red pepper flakes, crushed
- 1 can tomatoes, crushed

Directions:
1. In a medium saucepan, heat the olive oil over a moderately high heat. Sauté the garlic for 1 minute or until aromatic.
2. Add in the herbs, spices and tomatoes and turn the heat to a simmer. Continue to simmer for about 22 minutes.
3. Bon appétit!

Mexican-style Chili Sauce

Servings: 5
Cooking Time: 5 Minutes
Ingredients:
- 10 ounces canned tomato sauce
- 2 tablespoons apple cider vinegar
- 2 tablespoons brown sugar
- 1 Mexican chili pepper, minced
- 1/2 teaspoon dried Mexican oregano
- 1/4 teaspoon ground allspices
- Sea salt and ground black pepper, to taste

Directions:

1. In a mixing bowl, thoroughly combine all the ingredients.
2. Store in a glass jar in your refrigerator.
3. Bon appétit!

Easy Raw Pasta Sauce

Servings: 4
Cooking Time: 10 Minutes
Ingredients:
- 1 pound ripe tomatoes, cored
- 1 small onion, peeled
- 1 small garlic clove, minced
- 1 tablespoon fresh parsley leaves
- 1 tablespoon fresh basil leaves
- 1 tablespoon fresh rosemary leaves
- 4 tablespoons extra-virgin olive oil
- Sea salt and ground black pepper, to taste

Directions:
1. Blend all the ingredients in your food processor or blender until well combined.
2. Serve with warm pasta or zoodles (zucchini noodles).
3. Bon appétit!

Ligurian Walnut Sauce

Servings: 4
Cooking Time: 30 Minutes
Ingredients:
- 1/2 cup almond milk
- 1 slice white bread, crusts removed
- 1 cup raw walnuts
- 1/2 teaspoon garlic powder
- 1 teaspoon onion powder
- 1 teaspoon smoked paprika
- 2 tablespoons olive oil
- 1 tablespoon basil, chopped
- 3 curry leaves
- Sea salt and ground black pepper, to taste

Directions:
1. Put the almond milk and bread in a bowl and let it soak well.
2. Transfer the soaked bread to the bowl of your food processor or high-speed blender; add in the remaining ingredients.
3. Process until smooth, uniform and creamy.
4. Serve with pasta or zucchini noodles. Bon appétit!

Country-style Mustard

Servings: 16
Cooking Time: 5 Minutes
Ingredients:
- 1/3 cup mustard seeds
- 1/2 cup wine vinegar
- 1 Medjool date, pitted
- 1 teaspoon olive oil
- 1/2 teaspoon Himalayan rock salt

Directions:
1. Soak the mustard seeds for at least 12 hours.

2. Then, mix all the ingredients in a high-speed blender until creamy and uniform.
3. Store in a glass jar in your refrigerator. Bon appétit!

Sophisticated Cashew Mayonnaise

Servings: 12
Cooking Time: 10 Minutes
Ingredients:
- 3/4 cup raw cashews, soaked overnight and drained
- 2 tablespoons fresh lime juice
- 1/4 cup water
- 1/2 teaspoon deli mustard
- 1 teaspoon maple syrup
- 1/4 teaspoon garlic powder
- 1/4 teaspoon dried dill weed
- 1/2 teaspoon sea salt

Directions:
1. Blitz all the ingredients using a high-speed blender or food processor until smooth, creamy and uniform.
2. Add more spices, if needed.
3. Place in your refrigerator until ready to serve. Bon appétit!

Favorite Cranberry Sauce

Servings: 8
Cooking Time: 15 Minutes
Ingredients:
- 1/2 cup brown sugar
- 1/2 cup water
- 8 ounces cranberries, fresh or frozen
- A pinch of allspice
- A pinch of sea salt
- 1 tablespoon crystallized ginger

Directions:
1. In a heavy-bottomed saucepan, bring the sugar and water to a rolling boil.
2. Stir until the sugar has dissolved.
3. Add in the cranberries, followed by the remaining ingredients. Turn the heat to a simmer and continue to cook for 10 to 12 minutes or until the cranberries burst.
4. Let it cool at room temperature. Store in a glass jar in your refrigerator. Bon appétit!

Classic Ranch Dressing

Servings: 8
Cooking Time: 10 Minutes
Ingredients:
- 1 cup vegan mayonnaise
- 1/4 almond milk, unsweetened
- 1 teaspoon sherry vinegar
- 1/2 teaspoon kosher salt
- 1/4 teaspoon black pepper
- 2 cloves garlic, minced
- 1/2 teaspoon dried chives
- 1/2 teaspoon dried dill weed
- 1 teaspoon dried parsley flakes
- 1/2 teaspoon onion powder
- 1/3 teaspoon paprika

Directions:
1. Using a wire whisk, thoroughly combine all the ingredients in a bowl.
2. Cover and place in your refrigerator until ready to serve.
3. Bon appétit!

Creamy Mustard Sauce

Servings: 4
Cooking Time: 35 Minutes
Ingredients:
- 1/2 plain hummus
- 1 teaspoon fresh garlic, minced
- 1 tablespoon deli mustard
- 1 tablespoon extra-virgin olive oil
- 1 tablespoon fresh lime juice
- 1 teaspoon red pepper flakes
- 1/2 teaspoon sea salt
- 1/4 teaspoon ground black pepper

Directions:
1. Thoroughly combine all ingredients in a mixing bowl.
2. Let it sit in your refrigerator for about 30 minutes before serving.
3. Bon appétit!

Cinnamon Vanilla Sunflower Butter

Servings: 16
Cooking Time: 10 Minutes
Ingredients:
- 2 cups roasted sunflower seeds, hulled
- 1/2 cup maple syrup
- 1 teaspoon vanilla extract
- 1 teaspoon cinnamon powder
- A pinch of grated nutmeg
- A pinch of sea salt

Directions:
1. Blitz the sunflower seeds in your food processor until a butter forms.
2. Add in the remaining ingredients and continue to blend until creamy, smooth and uniform.
3. Taste and adjust the flavor as needed. Bon appétit!

Traditional Balkan-style Ajvar

Servings: 6
Cooking Time: 30 Minutes
Ingredients:
- 4 red bell peppers
- 1 small eggplant
- 1 garlic clove, smashed
- 2 tablespoons olive oil
- 1 teaspoon white vinegar
- Kosher salt and ground black pepper, to taste

Directions:
1. Grill the peppers and eggplant until they are soft and charred.
2. Place the peppers in a plastic bag and let them steam for about 15 minutes. Remove the skin, seeds and core of the peppers and eggplant.

3. Then, transfer them to the bowl of your food processor. Add in the garlic, olive oil, vinegar, salt and black pepper and continue to blend until well combined.
4. Store in the refrigerator for up to 1 week. Bon appétit!

Herb Avocado Salad Dressing

Servings: 6
Cooking Time: 10 Minutes
Ingredients:
- 1 medium-sized avocado, pitted, peeled and mashed
- 4 tablespoons extra-virgin olive oil
- 4 tablespoons almond milk
- 2 tablespoons cilantro, minced
- 2 tablespoons parsley, minced
- 1 lemon, juiced
- 2 garlic cloves, minced
- 1/2 teaspoon mustard seeds
- 1/2 teaspoon red pepper flakes
- Kosher salt and cayenne pepper, to taste

Directions:
1. Mix all the above ingredients in your food processor or blender.
2. Blend until uniform, smooth and creamy.
3. Bon appétit!

Homemade Chocolate Sauce

Servings: 9
Cooking Time: 10 Minutes
Ingredients:
- 5 tablespoons coconut oil, melted
- 3 tablespoons agave syrup
- 3 tablespoons cacao powder
- A pinch of grated nutmeg
- A pinch of kosher salt
- 1/2 teaspoon cinnamon powder
- 1/2 teaspoon vanilla paste

Directions:
1. Thoroughly combine all the ingredients using a wire whisk.
2. Store the chocolate sauce in your refrigerator. To soften the sauce, heat it up over low heat just before serving.
3. Bon appétit!

Easy Tofu Hollandaise

Servings: 12
Cooking Time: 15 Minutes
Ingredients:
- 1/4 cup vegan butter, at room temperature
- 1 cup silken tofu
- 1 cup unsweetened rice milk
- Sea salt and ground black pepper, to taste
- 1/4 cup nutritional yeast
- 1/2 teaspoon turmeric powder
- 2 tablespoons fresh lime juice

Directions:
1. Puree all the ingredients in a high-speed blender or food processor.

2. Then, heat the mixture in a small saucepan over low-medium heat; cook, stirring occasionally, until the sauce has reduced and thickened.
3. Bon appétit!

Classic Espagnole Sauce

Servings: 6
Cooking Time: 55 Minutes
Ingredients:
- 3 tablespoons vegan butter
- 4 tablespoons rice flour
- 1/2 cup mirepoix
- 1 teaspoon garlic cloves, chopped
- 3 cups vegetable broth
- 1/4 cup canned tomatoes, puréed
- 1 bay laurel
- 1 teaspoon thyme
- Sea salt and black pepper, to taste

Directions:
1. Melt the vegan butter in a saucepan over a moderately high heat. Then, add in the flour and cook, stirring continuously, for about 8 minutes or until brown.
2. Then, sauté the mirepoix for about 5 minutes or until tender and fragrant.
3. Now, add in the mirepoix, garlic, vegetable broth, canned tomatoes and spices. Turn the heat to a bare simmer. Let it simmer for about 40 minutes.
4. Pour the sauce through a fine-mesh sieve into a bowl. Enjoy!

Traditional French Sauce

Servings: 9
Cooking Time: 10 Minutes
Ingredients:
- 1 cup vegan mayonnaise
- 1 tablespoon fresh basil leaves, chopped
- 1 tablespoon fresh parsley leaves, chopped
- 1 tablespoon fresh scallions, chopped
- 3 small cornichon pickles, coarsely chopped
- 2 tablespoons capers, coarsely chopped
- 2 teaspoons fresh lemon juice
- 1 teaspoon Dijon mustard
- Sea salt and ground black pepper, to taste

Directions:
1. Thoroughly combine all ingredients in your food processor or blender.
2. Blend until uniform and creamy.
3. Bon appétit!

Authentic French Remoulade

Servings: 9
Cooking Time: 10 Minutes
Ingredients:
- 1 cup vegan mayonnaise
- 1 tablespoon Dijon mustard
- 1 scallion, finely chopped
- 1 teaspoon garlic, minced
- 2 tablespoons capers, coarsely chopped

- 1 tablespoon hot sauce
- 1 tablespoon fresh lemon juice
- 1 tablespoon flat-leaf parsley, chopped

Directions:
1. Thoroughly combine all the ingredients in your food processor or blender.
2. Blend until uniform and creamy.
3. Bon appétit!

Lime Coconut Sauce

Servings: 7
Cooking Time: 10 Minutes
Ingredients:
- 1 teaspoon coconut oil
- 1 large garlic clove, minced
- 1 teaspoon fresh ginger, minced
- 1 cup coconut milk
- 1 lime, freshly squeezed and zested
- A pinch of Himalayan rock salt

Directions:
1. In a small saucepan, melt the coconut oil over medium heat. Once hot, cook the garlic and ginger for about 1 minute or until aromatic.
2. Turn the heat to a simmer and add in the coconut milk, lime juice, lime zest and salt; continue to simmer for 1 minute or until heated through.
3. Bon appétit!

Classic Velouté Sauce

Servings: 5
Cooking Time: 10 Minutes
Ingredients:
- 2 tablespoons vegan butter
- 2 tablespoons all-purpose flour
- 1 ½ cups vegetable stock
- 1/4 teaspoon white pepper

Directions:
1. Melt the vegan butter in a saucepan over a moderate flame. Add in the flour and continue to cook, whisking continuously to avoid lumps.
2. Gradually and slowly pour in the vegetable stock and continue whisking for about 5 minutes until the sauce has thickened.
3. Add in white pepper and stir to combine well. Bon appétit!

Thai-style Coconut Sauce

Servings: 4
Cooking Time: 10 Minutes
Ingredients:
- 1 tablespoon coconut oil
- 1 teaspoon garlic, minced
- 1 teaspoon fresh ginger, minced
- 1 lemon, juiced and zested
- 1 teaspoon turmeric powder
- 1/2 cup coconut milk
- 1 tablespoon soy sauce
- 1 teaspoon coconut sugar, or more to taste

- A pinch of salt
- A pinch of grated nutmeg

Directions:
1. In a small saucepan, melt the coconut oil over medium heat. Once hot, cook the garlic and ginger for about 1 minute or until aromatic.
2. Turn the heat to a simmer and add in the lemon, turmeric, coconut milk, soy sauce, coconut sugar, salt and nutmeg; continue to simmer for 1 minute or until heated through.
3. Bon appétit!

Classic Homemade Ketchup

Servings: 10
Cooking Time: 25 Minutes
Ingredients:
- 4 ounces canned tomato paste
- 2 tablespoons agave syrup
- 1/4 cup red wine vinegar
- 1/4 cup water
- 1/2 teaspoon kosher salt
- 1/4 teaspoon garlic powder

Directions:
1. Preheat a saucepan over medium flame. Then, add all the ingredients to a saucepan and bring it to a boil.
2. Turn the heat to a simmer; let it simmer, stirring continuously, for about 20 minutes or until the sauce has thickened.
3. Store in a glass jar in your refrigerator. Bon appétit!

Vegan Barbecue Sauce

Servings: 10
Cooking Time: 25 Minutes
Ingredients:
- 1 cup tomato paste
- 2 tablespoons apple cider vinegar
- 2 tablespoons lime juice
- 1 tablespoon brown sugar
- 1 tablespoon mustard powder
- 1 teaspoon red pepper flakes, crushed
- 1 teaspoon onion powder
- 1 teaspoon garlic powder
- 1 teaspoon chili powder
- 2 tablespoons vegan Worcestershire
- 1/2 cup water

Directions:
1. Thoroughly combine all the ingredients in a saucepan over medium-high heat. Bring to a rolling boil.
2. Turn the heat to a bare simmer.
3. Let it simmer for about 20 minutes or until the sauce has reduced and thickened.
4. Place in your refrigerator for up to 3 weeks. Bon appétit!

Classic Béarnaise Sauce

Servings: 8
Cooking Time: 30 Minutes
Ingredients:
- 4 tablespoons soy butter non-dairy
- 2 tablespoons all-purpose flour
- 1 teaspoon garlic, minced
- 1 cup soy milk
- 1 tablespoon fresh lime juice
- 1/4 teaspoon turmeric powder
- Kosher salt and ground black pepper, to taste
- 1 tablespoon fresh parsley, chopped

Directions:
1. Melt the butter in a saucepan over a moderately high heat. Then, add in the flour and cook, stirring continuously, for about 8 minutes or until brown.
2. Then, sauté the garlic for about 30 seconds or until fragrant.
3. Now, add in the milk, fresh lime juice, turmeric, salt and black pepper. Turn the heat to a bare simmer. Let it simmer for about 20 minutes.
4. Top with fresh parsley just before serving. Bon appétit!

Sunflower And Hemp Seed Butter

Servings: 16
Cooking Time: 15 Minutes
Ingredients:
- 2 cups sunflower seeds, hulled and roasted
- 4 tablespoons hemp seeds
- 2 tablespoons flaxseed meal
- A pinch of salt
- A pinch of grated nutmeg
- 2 dates, pitted

Directions:
1. Blitz the sunflower seeds in your food processor until a butter forms.
2. Add in the remaining ingredients and continue to blend until creamy and uniform.
3. Taste and adjust the flavor as needed. Bon appétit!

Authentic Béchamel Sauce

Servings: 5
Cooking Time: 10 Minutes
Ingredients:
- 2 tablespoons soy butter
- 2 tablespoons all-purpose flour
- 1 ½ cups oat milk
- Coarse sea salt, to taste
- 1/4 teaspoon turmeric powder
- 1/4 teaspoon ground black pepper, to taste
- A pinch of grated nutmeg

Directions:
1. Melt the soy butter in a sauté pan over a moderate flame. Add in the flour and continue to cook, whisking continuously to avoid lumps.
2. Pour the milk and continue whisking for about 4 minutes until the sauce has thickened.
3. Add in the spices and stir to combine well. Bon appétit!

Basic Tomato Sauce

Servings: 8
Cooking Time: 25 Minutes
Ingredients:
- 2 tablespoons olive oil
- 1 shallot, chopped
- 2 cloves garlic, minced
- 1 red chili pepper, seeded and minced
- 20 ounces canned tomatoes, puréed
- 2 tablespoons tomato paste
- 1 teaspoon cayenne pepper
- 1/2 teaspoon coarse sea salt

Directions:
1. In a medium saucepan, heat the olive oil over a moderately high heat. Sauté the shallot until tender and aromatic.
2. Add in the garlic and chili pepper; continue to sauté for 1 minute or until fragrant.
3. Add in the tomatoes, tomato paste, cayenne pepper and salt; turn the heat to a simmer. Continue to cook for about 22 minutes.
4. Bon appétit!

Homemade Guacamole

Servings: 7
Cooking Time: 10 Minutes
Ingredients:
- 2 avocados, peeled, pitted
- 1 lemon, juiced
- Sea salt and ground black pepper, to taste
- 1 small onion, diced
- 2 tablespoons chopped fresh cilantro
- 1 large tomato, diced

Directions:
1. Mash the avocados, together with the remaining ingredients in a mixing bowl.
2. Place the guacamole in your refrigerator until ready to serve. Bon appétit!

Red Pepper And Tomato Sauce

Servings: 6
Cooking Time: 1 Hour 20 Minutes
Ingredients:
- 1 pound red peppers
- 2 tablespoons olive oil
- 1 shallot, chopped
- 2 garlic cloves, minced
- 1 pound tomatoes, chopped
- 1/2 cup vegetable broth
- 1 teaspoon cayenne pepper
- 1 teaspoon dried basil
- 1/2 teaspoon dried oregano
- 2 tablespoons red wine
- Sea salt and freshly ground pepper, to taste

Directions:
1. Place the peppers directly over a low gas flame; roast the peppers for about 8 minutes until they are charred on all sides.

2. Let the peppers steam in a plastic bag or covered bowl for about 30 minutes. Remove the blackened skin and core and transfer the flesh to your food processor
3. Blitz until a smooth paste forms.
4. Heat the prepared paste in a saucepan; add in the remaining ingredients and stir to combine well. Turn the heat to a simmer and let it cook, partially covered, for about 40 minutes or until the sauce has reduced to your desired consistency.
5. Bon appétit!

Classic Barbecue Sauce

Servings: 20
Cooking Time: 5 Minutes
Ingredients:
- 1 cup brown sugar
- 1 cup ketchup
- 1/4 cup wine vinegar
- 1/3 cup water
- 1 tablespoon soy sauce
- 2 tablespoon mustard powder
- 1 teaspoon black pepper
- 2 teaspoons sea salt

Directions:
1. Mix all the ingredients in your blender or food processor.
2. Blend until uniform and smooth.
3. Bon appétit!

Perfect Cheese Sauce

Servings: 8
Cooking Time: 30 Minutes
Ingredients:
- 1 ½ cups cashews
- 1/2 cup water
- 1 teaspoon apple cider vinegar
- 1 teaspoon lime juice
- 1/2 teaspoon granulated garlic
- Sea salt and cayenne pepper, to taste
- 1 tablespoon coconut oil
- 1/4 cup nutritional yeast

Directions:
1. Process the cashews and water in your blender until creamy and uniform.
2. Add in the remaining ingredients and continue to blend until everything is well incorporated.
3. Keep in your refrigerator for up to a week. Bon appétit!

Basic Basil Pesto

Servings: 8
Cooking Time: 10 Minutes
Ingredients:
- 1 cup fresh basil, packed
- 4 tablespoons pine nuts
- 2 cloves garlic, peeled
- 1 tablespoon fresh lime juice
- 2 tablespoons nutritional yeast
- 2 tablespoons extra-virgin olive oil
- Sea salt, to taste

- 4 tablespoons water

Directions:
1. In your food processor, place all ingredients, except for the oil. Process until well combined.
2. Continue to blend, gradually adding the oil, until the mixture comes together.
3. Bon appétit!

Spicy Homemade Ketchup

Servings: 12
Cooking Time: 25 Minutes
Ingredients:
- 2 tablespoons sunflower oil
- 4 tablespoons shallots, chopped
- 2 cloves garlic, crushed
- 30 ounces canned tomatoes, crushed
- 1/4 cup brown sugar
- 1/4 cup white vinegar
- 1 teaspoon hot sauce
- 1/4 teaspoon allspice

Directions:
1. In a medium saucepan, heat the oil over a moderately high heat. Sauté the shallots until tender and aromatic.
2. Add in the garlic and continue to sauté for 1 minute or until fragrant.
3. Add in the remaining ingredients and bring to a simmer. Continue to simmer for 22 to 25 minutes.
4. Process the mixture in your blender until smooth and uniform. Bon appétit!

Smoked Cheese Sauce

Servings: 6
Cooking Time: 10 Minutes
Ingredients:
- 1/2 cup raw cashews, soaked and drained
- 4 tablespoons water
- 2 tablespoons raw tahini
- Fresh juice of 1/2 lemon
- 1 tablespoon apple cider vinegar
- 2 carrots, cooked
- 1 teaspoon smoked paprika
- Sea salt, to taste
- 1 clove garlic
- 1 teaspoon fresh dill weed
- 1/2 cup frozen corn kernels, thawed and squeezed

Directions:
1. Process the cashews and water in your blender until creamy and uniform.
2. Add in the remaining ingredients and continue to blend until everything is well incorporated.
3. Keep in your refrigerator for up to a week. Bon appétit!

Garden Herb Mustard

Servings: 10
Cooking Time: 35 Minutes
Ingredients:
- 1/2 cup mustard powder
- 5 tablespoons mustard seeds, ground
- 1/4 cup water
- 1/4 cup beer
- 2 tablespoons sherry vinegar
- 1 ½ teaspoons coarse sea salt
- 1 tablespoon agave syrup
- 1 tablespoon dried cilantro
- 1 tablespoon dried basil

Directions:
1. Thoroughly combine the mustard powder, ground mustard seeds, water and beer in a mixing bowl; let it stand for about 30 minutes.
2. Add in the remaining ingredients and stir to combine well.
3. Let it sit at least 12 hours before serving. Bon appétit!

Easy Caramel Sauce

Servings: 12
Cooking Time: 20 Minutes
Ingredients:
- 1 ½ cups granulated sugar
- 1/2 cup water
- 1 cup coconut cream
- 3 tablespoons coconut oil
- A pinch of salt
- A pinch of ground allspice
- 1 teaspoon vanilla essence

Directions:
1. In a saucepan, place the sugar and water over medium-low heat; let it cook until the sugar has dissolved.
2. Turn the heat to medium and continue to cook for 9 to 11 minutes or until the sugar turns into a thick, brown liquid.
3. Remove from the heat and stir in the coconut cream, coconut oil, salt, allspices and vanilla essence.
4. Cook for a few more minutes over a moderate heat until the sauce is smooth. The caramel sauce thickens as it cools.
5. Store in your refrigerator for up to one month. Bon appétit!

Chapter 7. Desserts & Sweet Treats

Coconut Cream Pie

Servings: 12
Cooking Time: 15 Minutes
Ingredients:
- Crust:
- 2 cups walnuts
- 10 fresh dates, pitted
- 2 tablespoons coconut oil at room temperature
- 1/4 teaspoon groin cardamom
- 1/2 teaspoon ground cinnamon
- 1 teaspoon vanilla extract
- Filling:
- 2 medium over-ripe bananas
- 2 frozen bananas
- 1 cup full-fat coconut cream, well-chilled
- 1/3 cup agave syrup
- Garnish:
- 3 ounces vegan dark chocolate, shaved

Directions:
1. In your food processor, blend the crust ingredients until the mixture comes together; press the crust into a lightly oiled baking pan.
2. Then, blend the filling layer. Spoon the filling onto the crust, creating a flat surface with a spatula.

3. Transfer the cake to your freezer for about 3 hours. Store in your freezer.
4. Garnish with chocolate curls just before serving. Bon appétit!

Easy Blueberry Cheesecakes

Servings: 12
Cooking Time: 10 Minutes
Ingredients:
- 1 cup almonds, ground
- 1 ½ cups dates, pitted
- 1 ½ cups vegan cream cheese
- 1/4 cup coconut oil, softened
- 1/2 cup fresh or frozen blueberries

Directions:
1. In your food processor, blend the almonds and 1 cup of dates until the mixture comes together; press the crust into a lightly greased muffin tin.
2. Then, blend the remaining 1/2 cup of dates along with the vegan cheese, coconut oil and blueberries until creamy and smooth. Spoon the topping mixture onto the crust.
3. Place these mini cheesecakes in your freezer for about 3 hours. Bon appétit!

Almond And Chocolate Chip Bars

Servings: 10
Cooking Time: 40 Minutes
Ingredients:
- 1/2 cup almond butter
- 1/4 cup coconut oil, melted
- 1/4 cup agave syrup
- 1 teaspoon vanilla extract
- 1/4 teaspoon sea salt
- 1/4 teaspoon grated nutmeg
- 1/2 teaspoon ground cinnamon
- 2 cups almond flour
- 1/4 cup flaxseed meal
- 1 cup vegan chocolate, cut into chunks
- 1 1/3 cups almonds, ground
- 2 tablespoons cacao powder
- 1/4 cup agave syrup

Directions:
1. In a mixing bowl, thoroughly combine the almond butter, coconut oil, 1/4 cup of agave syrup, vanilla, salt, nutmeg and cinnamon.
2. Gradually stir in the almond flour and flaxseed meal and stir to combine. Add in the chocolate chunks and stir again.
3. In a small mixing bowl, combine the almonds, cacao powder and agave syrup. Now, spread the ganache onto the cake. Freeze for about 30 minutes, cut into bars and serve well chilled. Enjoy!

Everyday Energy Bars

Servings: 16
Cooking Time: 35 Minutes
Ingredients:
- 1 cup vegan butter
- 1 cup brown sugar
- 2 tablespoons agave syrup
- 2 cups old-fashioned oats
- 1/2 cup almonds, slivered
- 1/2 cup walnuts, chopped
- 1/2 cup dried currants
- 1/2 cup pepitas

Directions:
1. Begin by preheating your oven to 320 degrees F. Line a baking pan with parchment paper or Silpat mat.
2. Thoroughly combine all the ingredients until everything is well incorporated.
3. Spread the mixture onto the prepared baking pan using a wide spatula.
4. Bake for about 33 minutes or until golden brown. Cut into bars using a sharp knife and enjoy!

Turkish Irmik Helvasi

Servings: 8
Cooking Time: 35 Minutes
Ingredients:
- 1 cup semolina flour
- 1/2 cup coconut, shredded
- 1/2 teaspoon baking powder
- A pinch of salt

- 1 teaspoon pure vanilla extract
- 1 cup vegan butter
- 1 cup coconut milk
- 1/2 cup walnuts, ground

Directions:
1. Thoroughly combine the flour, coconut, baking powder, salt and vanilla. Add in the butter and milk; mix to combine.
2. Fold in the walnuts and let it rest for about 1 hour.
3. Bake in the preheated oven at 350 degrees F for approximately 30 minutes or until a tester inserted in the center of the cake comes out dry and clean.
4. Transfer to a wire rack to cool completely before slicing and serving. Bon appétit!

Old-fashioned Cookies

Servings: 12
Cooking Time: 45 Minutes
Ingredients:
- 1 cup all-purpose flour
- 1 teaspoon baking powder
- A pinch of salt
- A pinch of grated nutmeg
- 1/2 teaspoon ground cinnamon
- 1/4 teaspoon ground cardamom
- 1/2 cup peanut butter
- 2 tablespoons coconut oil, room temperature
- 2 tablespoons almond milk
- 1/2 cup brown sugar
- 1 teaspoon vanilla extract
- 1 cup vegan chocolate chips

Directions:
1. In a mixing bowl, combine the flour, baking powder and spices.
2. In another bowl, combine the peanut butter, coconut oil, almond milk, sugar and vanilla. Stir the wet mixture into the dry ingredients and stir until well combined.
3. Fold in the chocolate chips. Place the batter in your refrigerator for about 30 minutes. Shape the batter into small cookies and arrange them on a parchment-lined cookie pan.
4. Bake in the preheated oven at 350 degrees F for approximately 11 minutes. Transfer them to a wire rack to cool slightly before serving. Bon appétit!

Famous Haystack Cookies

Servings: 9
Cooking Time: 20 Minutes
Ingredients:
- 1 cup instant oats
- 1/2 cup almond butter
- 2 ounces almonds, ground
- 1/4 cup cocoa powder, unsweetened
- 1/2 teaspoon vanilla
- 1/2 teaspoon ground cinnamon
- 1/2 teaspoon ground anise
- 1/4 cup almond milk
- 3 tablespoons vegan butter
- 1 cup brown sugar

Directions:

1. In mixing bowl, thoroughly combine the oats, almond butter, ground almonds, cocoa, vanilla, cinnamon and anise; reserve.
2. In a medium saucepan, bring the milk, butter and sugar to a boil. Let it boil for approximately 1 minute, stirring frequently.
3. Pour the milk/butter mixture over the oat mixture; stir to combine well.
4. Drop by teaspoonfuls onto a parchment-lined cookie sheet and let them cool completely. Enjoy!

Mom's Raspberry Cobbler

Servings: 7
Cooking Time: 50 Minutes
Ingredients:
- 1 pound fresh raspberries
- 1/2 teaspoon fresh ginger, peeled and minced
- 1/2 teaspoon lime zest
- 2 tablespoons brown sugar
- 1 cup all-purpose flour
- 1 teaspoon baking powder
- 1/4 teaspoon sea salt
- 2 ounces agave syrup
- 1/4 teaspoon ground cloves
- 1/2 teaspoon ground cinnamon
- 1/8 teaspoon freshly grated nutmeg
- 1/2 cup coconut cream
- 1/2 cup coconut milk

Directions:
1. Arrange the raspberries on the bottom of a lightly oiled baking pan. Sprinkle ginger, lime zest and brown sugar over them.
2. In a mixing bowl, thoroughly combine the flour, baking powder, salt, agave syrup, ground cloves, cinnamon and nutmeg.
3. Add in the coconut cream and milk and mix until everything is well incorporated. Spread the topping mixture over the raspberry layer.
4. Bake your cobbler at 350 degrees F for about 45 minutes or until golden brown. Bon appétit!

Lime Avocado Ice Cream

Servings:4
Cooking Time:10 Minutes
Ingredients:
- 2 large avocados, pitted
- Juice and zest of 3 limes
- 1/3 cup erythritol
- 1 ¾ cups coconut cream
- ¼ tsp vanilla extract

Directions:
1. In a blender, combine the avocado pulp, lime juice and zest, erythritol, coconut cream, and vanilla extract. Process until the mixture is smooth. Pour the mixture into your ice cream maker and freeze based on the manufacturer's instructions. When ready, remove and scoop the ice cream into bowls. Serve immediately.

Mom's Raspberry Cheesecake

Servings: 9
Cooking Time: 15 Minutes
Ingredients:
- Crust:
- 1 cup almond flour
- 1/2 cup macadamia nuts
- 1 cup dried desiccated coconut
- 1/2 teaspoon cinnamon
- 1/4 teaspoon grated nutmeg
- Topping:
- 1 cup raw cashew nuts, soaked overnight and drained
- 1 cup raw sunflower seeds, soaked overnight and drained
- 1/4 cup coconut oil, at room temperature
- 1/2 cup pure agave syrup
- 1/2 cup freeze-dried raspberries

Directions:
1. In your food processor, blend the crust ingredients until the mixture comes together; press the crust into a lightly greased springform pan.
2. Then, blend the topping ingredients until creamy and smooth. Spoon the topping mixture onto the crust.
3. Place the cheesecake in your freezer for about 3 hours. Garnish with some extra raspberries and coconut flakes. Bon appétit!

White Chocolate Fudge

Servings:6
Cooking Time:20 Minutes + Chilling Time
Ingredients:
- 2 cups coconut cream
- 1 tsp vanilla extract
- 3 oz plant butter
- 3 oz vegan white chocolate
- Swerve sugar for sprinkling

Directions:
1. Pour coconut cream and vanilla into a saucepan and bring to a boil over medium heat, then simmer until reduced by half, 15 minutes. Stir in plant butter until the batter is smooth. Chop white chocolate into bits and stir in the cream until melted. Pour the mixture into a baking sheet; chill in the fridge for 3 hours. Cut into squares, sprinkle with swerve sugar, and serve.

French-style Chocolate Custard

Servings: 2
Cooking Time: 10 Minutes
Ingredients:
- 1/2 cup raw cashews, soaked and drained
- 1/4 cup vegan half-and-half
- 2 tablespoons agave syrup
- 4 tablespoons vegan chocolate chips
- 1/8 teaspoon coarse salt
- 1/8 teaspoon grated nutmeg
- 2 dollops coconut whipped cream

Directions:

1. Place the cashews in the bowl of your high-speed blender. Add in the remaining ingredients and blend until uniform and smooth.
2. Pour the mixture into 2 ramekins and refrigerate for at least 2 hours or until well-chilled.
3. Garnish with coconut whipped cream and serve. Bon appétit!

Macedonia Salad With Coconut & Pecans

Servings:4
Cooking Time:15 Minutes + Cooling Time
Ingredients:
- 1 cup pure coconut cream
- ½ tsp vanilla extract
- 2 bananas, cut into chunks
- 1 ½ cups coconut flakes
- 4 tbsp toasted pecans, chopped
- 1 cup pineapple tidbits, drained
- 1 can mandarin oranges
- ¾ cup maraschino cherries, stems removed

Directions:
1. In a medium bowl, mix the coconut cream and vanilla extract until well combined.
2. In a larger bowl, combine the bananas, coconut flakes, pecans, pineapple, oranges, and cherries until evenly distributed. Pour on the coconut cream mixture and fold well into the salad. Chill in the refrigerator for 1 hour and serve afterward.

Fluffy Coconut Blondies With Raisins

Servings: 9
Cooking Time: 30 Minutes
Ingredients:
- 1 cup coconut flour
- 1 cup all-purpose flour
- 1/2 teaspoon baking powder
- 1/4 teaspoon salt
- 1 cup desiccated coconut, unsweetened
- 3/4 cup vegan butter, softened
- 1 ½ cups brown sugar
- 3 tablespoons applesauce
- 1/2 teaspoon vanilla extract
- 1/2 teaspoon ground anise
- 1 cup raisins, soaked for 15 minutes

Directions:
1. Start by preheating your oven to 350 degrees F. Brush a baking pan with a nonstick cooking oil.
2. Thoroughly combine the flour, baking powder, salt and coconut. In another bowl, mix the butter, sugar, applesauce, vanilla and anise. Stir the butter mixture into the dry ingredients; stir to combine well.
3. Fold in the raisins. Press the batter into the prepared baking pan.
4. Bake for approximately 25 minutes or until it is set in the middle. Place the cake on a wire rack to cool slightly.
5. Bon appétit!

Almond Granola Bars

Servings: 12
Cooking Time: 25 Minutes
Ingredients:
- 1/2 cup spelt flour
- 1/2 cup oat flour
- 1 cup rolled oats
- 1 teaspoon baking powder
- 1/2 teaspoon cinnamon
- 1/2 teaspoon ground cardamom
- 1/4 teaspoon freshly grated nutmeg
- 1/8 teaspoon kosher salt
- 1 cup almond milk
- 3 tablespoons agave syrup
- 1/2 cup peanut butter
- 1/2 cup applesauce
- 1/2 teaspoon pure almond extract
- 1/2 teaspoon pure vanilla extract
- 1/2 cup almonds, slivered

Directions:
1. Begin by preheating your oven to 350 degrees F.
2. In a mixing bowl, thoroughly combine the flour, oats, baking powder and spices. In another bowl, combine the wet ingredients.
3. Then, stir the wet mixture into the dry ingredients; mix to combine well. Fold in the slivered almonds.
4. Scrape the batter mixture into a parchment-lined baking pan. Bake in the preheated oven for about 20 minutes. Let it cool on a wire rack. Cut into bars and enjoy!

Layered Raspberry & Tofu Cups

Servings:4
Cooking Time:60 Minutes
Ingredients:
- ½ cup unsalted raw cashews
- 3 tbsp pure date sugar
- ½ cup soy milk
- ¾ cup firm silken tofu, drained
- 1 tsp vanilla extract
- 2 cups sliced raspberries
- 1 tsp fresh lemon juice
- Fresh mint leaves

Directions:
1. Grind the cashews and 3 tbsp of date sugar in a blender until a fine powder is obtained. Pour in soy milk and blitz until smooth. Add in tofu and vanilla and pulse until creamy. Remove to a bowl and refrigerate covered for 30 minutes.
2. In a bowl, mix the raspberries, lemon juice, and remaining date sugar. Let sit for 20 minutes. Assemble by alternating into small cups, one layer of raspberries, and one cashew cream layer, ending with the cashew cream. Serve garnished with mint leaves.

Tangy Fruit Salad With Lemon Dressing

Servings: 4
Cooking Time: 15 Minutes
Ingredients:
- Salad:
- 1/2 pound mixed berries
- 1/2 pound apples, cored and diced
- 8 ounces red grapes
- 2 kiwis, peeled and diced
- 2 large oranges, peeled and sliced
- 2 bananas, sliced
- Lemon Dressing:
- 2 tablespoons fresh lemon juice
- 1 teaspoon fresh ginger, peeled and minced
- 4 tablespoons agave syrup

Directions:
1. Mix all the ingredients for the salad until well combined.
2. Then, in a small mixing bowl, whisk all the lemon dressing ingredients.
3. Dress your salad and serve well chilled. Bon appétit!

Summer Banana Pudding

Servings:4
Cooking Time:25 Minutes + Cooling Time
Ingredients:
- 1 cup unsweetened almond milk
- 2 cups cashew cream
- ¾ cup + 1 tbsp pure date sugar
- ¼ tsp salt
- 3 tbsp cornstarch
- 2 tbsp plant butter, cut into 4 pieces
- 1 tsp vanilla extract
- 2 banana, sliced

Directions:
1. In a medium pot, mix almond milk, cashew cream, date sugar, and salt. Cook over medium heat until slightly thickened, 10-15 minutes. Stir in the cornstarch, plant butter, vanilla extract, and banana extract. Cook further for 1 to 2 minutes or until the pudding thickens. Dish the pudding into 4 serving bowls and chill in the refrigerator for at least 1 hour. To serve, top with the bananas and enjoy!

German-style Apple Crumble

Servings: 8
Cooking Time: 50 Minutes
Ingredients:
- 4 apples, cored, peeled and sliced
- 1/2 cup brown sugar
- 1 cup all-purpose flour
- 1/2 cup coconut flour
- 2 tablespoons flaxseed meal
- 1 teaspoon baking powder
- 1/2 teaspoon baking soda
- A pinch of sea salt
- A pinch of freshly grated nutmeg
- 1/2 teaspoon ground cinnamon

- 1/2 teaspoon ground anise
- 1/2 teaspoon pure vanilla extract
- 1/2 teaspoon pure coconut extract
- 1 cup coconut milk
- 1/2 cup coconut oil, softened

Directions:
1. Arrange the apples on the bottom of a lightly oiled baking pan. Sprinkle brown sugar over them.
2. In a mixing bowl, thoroughly combine the flour, flaxseed meal, baking powder, baking soda, salt, nutmeg, cinnamon, anise, vanilla and coconut extract.
3. Add in the coconut milk and softened oil and mix until everything is well incorporated. Spread the topping mixture over the fruit layer.
4. Bake the apple crumble at 350 degrees F for about 45 minutes or until golden brown. Bon appétit!

Coconut & Chocolate Brownies

Servings:4
Cooking Time:40 Minutes
Ingredients:
- 1 cup whole-grain flour
- ½ cup unsweetened cocoa powder
- 1 tsp baking powder
- ½ tsp salt
- 1 cup pure date sugar
- ½ cup canola oil
- ¾ cup almond milk
- 1 tsp pure vanilla extract
- 1 tsp coconut extract
- ½ cup vegan chocolate chips
- ½ cup sweetened shredded coconut

Directions:
1. Preheat oven to 360 F. In a bowl, combine the flour, cocoa, baking powder, and salt.
2. In another bowl, whisk the date sugar and oil until creamy. Add in almond milk, vanilla, and coconut extracts. Mix until smooth. Pour into the flour mixture and stir to combine. Fold in the coconut and chocolate chips. Pour the batter into a greased baking pan and bake for 35-40 minutes. Let cool before serving.

Raw Walnut And Berry Cake

Servings: 8
Cooking Time: 10 Minutes
Ingredients:
- Crust:
- 1 ½ cups walnuts, ground
- 2 tablespoons maple syrup
- 1/4 cup raw cacao powder
- 1/4 teaspoon ground cinnamon
- A pinch of coarse salt
- A pinch of freshly grated nutmeg
- Berry layer:
- 6 cups mixed berries
- 2 frozen bananas
- 1/2 cup agave syrup

Directions:

1. In your food processor, blend the crust ingredients until the mixture comes together; press the crust into a lightly oiled baking pan.
2. Then, blend the berry layer. Spoon the berry layer onto the crust, creating a flat surface with a spatula.
3. Transfer the cake to your freezer for about 3 hours. Store in your freezer. Bon appétit!

Blueberry Lime Granizado

Servings:1
Cooking Time:15 Minutes
Ingredients:
- ½ cup pure date sugar
- 2 cups blueberries
- 2 tsp fresh lemon juice

Directions:
1. Place the sugar and ½ cup water in a pot. Cook for 3 minutes on low heat until the sugar is dissolved. Remove to a heatproof bowl and chill for 2 hours in the fridge. Blitz the blueberries and lemon juice in a blender until smooth. Add in cooled sugar and pulse until smooth. Place in an ice cream maker and follow the directions. Once ready, serve immediately or freeze another 1-2 hours for a firm texture.

Almond & Chia Bites With Cherries

Servings:2
Cooking Time:20 Minutes
Ingredients:
- 1 cup cherries, pitted
- 1 cup shredded coconut
- ¼ cup chia seeds
- ¾ cup ground almonds
- ¼ cup cocoa nibs

Directions:
1. Blend cherries, coconut, chia seeds, almonds, and cocoa nibs in a food processor until crumbly. Shape the mixture into 24 balls and arrange on a lined baking sheet. Let sit in the fridge for 15 minutes.

Pistachios & Chocolate Popsicles

Servings:4
Cooking Time:5 Minutes + Cooling Time
Ingredients:
- ½ cup chocolate chips, melted
- 1 ½ cups oat milk
- 1 tbsp unsweetened cocoa powder
- 3 tbsp pure date syrup
- 1 tsp vanilla extract
- A handful of pistachios, chopped

Directions:
1. In a blender, add chocolate, oat milk, cocoa powder, date syrup, vanilla, pistachios, and process until smooth. Divide the mixture into popsicle molds and freeze for 3 hours. Dip the popsicle molds in warm water to loosen the popsicles and pull out the popsicles.

Lemon Blackberry Cake

Servings:4
Cooking Time:45 Minutes

Ingredients:
- 4 peaches, peeled and sliced
- 2 cups fresh blackberries
- 1 tbsp cornstarch
- ¾ cup pure date sugar
- 2 tsp fresh lemon juice
- 1 tsp ground cinnamon
- ½ cup whole-grain flour
- ½ cup old-fashioned oats
- 3 tbsp plant butter

Directions:
1. Preheat oven to 370 F. In a bowl, mix the peaches, blackberries, cornstarch, ¼ cup of sugar, lemon juice, and ½ tsp of cinnamon. Pour the batter into the pan. Set aside. In a bowl, stir the flour, oats, butter, remaining cup of sugar, and remaining cinnamon. Blend until crumbly. Drizzle the topping over the fruit. Bake for 30-40 minutes until browned. Serve.

Easy Maple Rice Pudding

Servings:4
Cooking Time:30 Minutes
Ingredients:
- 1 cup short-grain brown rice
- 1 ¾ cups non-dairy milk
- 4 tbsp pure maple syrup
- 1 tsp vanilla extract
- A pinch of salt
- ¼ cup dates, pitted and chopped

Directions:
1. In a pot over medium heat, place the rice, milk, 1 ½ cups water, maple, vanilla, and salt. Bring to a boil, then reduce the heat. Cook for 20 minutes, stirring occasionally. Mix in dates and cook for another 5 minutes. Serve chilled in cups.

Avocado Truffles With Chocolate Coating

Servings:6
Cooking Time:5 Minutes
Ingredients:
- 1 ripe avocado, pitted
- ½ tsp vanilla extract
- ½ tsp lemon zest
- 5 oz dairy-free dark chocolate
- 1 tbsp coconut oil
- 1 tbsp unsweetened cocoa powder

Directions:
1. Scoop the pulp of the avocado into a bowl and mix with the vanilla using an immersion blender. Stir in the lemon zest and a pinch of salt. Pour the chocolate and coconut oil into a safe microwave bowl and melt in the microwave for 1 minute. Add to the avocado mixture and stir. Allow cooling to firm up a bit. Form balls out of the mix. Roll each ball in the cocoa powder and serve immediately.

Homemade Chocolates With Coconut And Raisins

Servings: 20
Cooking Time: 10 Minutes
Ingredients:
- 1/2 cup cacao butter, melted
- 1/3 cup peanut butter
- 1/4 cup agave syrup
- A pinch of grated nutmeg
- A pinch of coarse salt
- 1/2 teaspoon vanilla extract
- 1 cup dried coconut, shredded
- 6 ounces dark chocolate, chopped
- 3 ounces raisins

Directions:
1. Thoroughly combine all the ingredients, except for the chocolate, in a mixing bowl.
2. Spoon the mixture into molds. Leave to set hard in a cool place.
3. Melt the dark chocolate in your microwave. Pour in the melted chocolate until the fillings are covered. Leave to set hard in a cool place.
4. Enjoy!

Vanilla Cranberry & Almond Balls

Servings: 12
Cooking Time: 25 Minutes
Ingredients:
- 2 tbsp almond butter
- 2 tbsp maple syrup
- ¾ cup cooked millet
- ¼ cup sesame seeds, toasted
- 1 tbsp chia seeds
- ½ tsp almond extract
- Zest of 1 orange
- 1 tbsp dried cranberries
- ¼ cup ground almonds

Directions:
1. Whisk the almond butter and syrup in a bowl until creamy. Mix in millet, sesame seeds, chia seeds, almond extract, orange zest, cranberries, and almonds. Shape the mixture into balls and arrange on a parchment paper-lined baking sheet. Let chill in the fridge for 15 minutes.

Decadent Hazelnut Halvah

Servings: 16
Cooking Time: 10 Minutes
Ingredients:
- 1/2 cup tahini
- 1/2 cup almond butter
- 1/4 cup coconut oil, melted
- 4 tablespoons agave nectar
- 1/2 teaspoon pure almond extract
- 1/2 teaspoon pure vanilla extract
- 1/8 teaspoon salt
- 1/8 teaspoon freshly grated nutmeg
- 1/2 cup hazelnuts, chopped

Directions:
1. Line a square baking pan with parchment paper.
2. Mix the ingredients, except for the hazelnuts, until everything is well incorporated.
3. Scrape the batter into the parchment-lined pan. Press the hazelnuts into the batter.
4. Place in your freezer until ready to serve. Bon appétit!

Chocolate Dream Balls

Servings: 8
Cooking Time: 10 Minutes
Ingredients:
- 3 tablespoons cocoa powder
- 8 fresh dates, pitted and soaked for 15 minutes
- 2 tablespoons tahini, at room temperature
- 1/2 teaspoon ground cinnamon
- 1/2 cup vegan chocolate, broken into chunks
- 1 tablespoon coconut oil, at room temperature

Directions:
1. Add the cocoa powder, dates, tahini and cinnamon to the bowl of your food processor. Process until the mixture forms a ball.
2. Use a cookie scoop to portion the mixture into 1-ounce portions. Roll the balls and refrigerate them for at least 30 minutes.
3. Meanwhile, microwave the chocolate until melted; add in the coconut oil and whisk to combine well.
4. Dip the chocolate balls in the coating and store them in your refrigerator until ready to serve. Bon appétit!

Oatmeal Squares With Cranberries

Servings: 20
Cooking Time: 25 Minutes
Ingredients:
- 1 ½ cups rolled oats
- 1/2 cup brown sugar
- 1 teaspoon baking soda
- A pinch of coarse salt
- A pinch of grated nutmeg
- 1/2 teaspoon cinnamon
- 2/3 cup peanut butter
- 1 medium banana, mashed
- 1/3 cup oat milk
- 1 teaspoon vanilla extract
- 1/2 cup dried cranberries

Directions:
1. Begin by preheating your oven to 350 degrees F.
2. In a mixing bowl, thoroughly combine the dry ingredients. In another bowl, combine the wet ingredients.
3. Then, stir the wet mixture into the dry ingredients; mix to combine well.
4. Spread the batter mixture in a parchment-lined baking pan. Bake in the preheated oven for about 20 minutes.
5. Let it cool on a wire rack. Cut into squares and enjoy!

Tropical Bread Pudding

Servings: 5
Cooking Time: 2 Hours
Ingredients:

- 6 cups stale bread, cut into cubes
- 2 cups rice milk, sweetened
- 1/2 cup agave syrup
- 1 teaspoon vanilla extract
- 1/2 teaspoon ground cloves
- 1 teaspoon ground cinnamon
- 1/4 teaspoon coarse sea salt
- 5 tablespoons pineapple, crushed and drained
- 1 firm banana, sliced

Directions:

1. Place the bread cubes in a lightly oiled baking dish.
2. Now, blend the milk, agave syrup, vanilla, ground cloves, cinnamon and coarse sea salt until creamy and uniform.
3. Fold in the pineapple and banana and mix to combine well.
4. Spoon the mixture all over the bread cubes; press down slightly and set aside for about 1 hour.
5. Bake in the preheated oven at 350 degrees F for about 1 hour or until the top of your pudding is golden brown.
6. Bon appétit!

Southern Apple Cobbler With Raspberries

Servings:4
Cooking Time:50 Minutes
Ingredients:

- 3 apples, chopped
- 2 tbsp pure date sugar
- 1 cup fresh raspberries
- 2 tbsp unsalted plant butter
- ½ cup whole-wheat flour
- 1 cup toasted rolled oats
- 2 tbsp pure date sugar
- 1 tsp cinnamon powder

Directions:

1. Preheat the oven to 350 F and grease a baking dish with some plant butter.
2. Add apples, date sugar, and 3 tbsp of water to a pot. Cook over low heat until the date sugar melts and then mix in the raspberries. Cook until the fruits soften, 10 minutes. Pour and spread the fruit mixture into the baking dish and set aside.
3. In a blender, add the plant butter, flour, oats, date sugar, and cinnamon powder. Pulse a few times until crumbly. Spoon and spread the mixture on the fruit mix until evenly layered. Bake in the oven for 25 to 30 minutes or until golden brown on top. Remove the dessert, allow cooling for 2 minutes, and serve.

Raw Coconut Ice Cream

Servings: 2
Cooking Time: 10 Minutes
Ingredients:

- 4 over-ripe bananas, frozen
- 4 tablespoons coconut milk
- 6 fresh dates, pitted
- 1/4 teaspoon pure coconut extract
- 1/2 teaspoon pure vanilla extract
- 1/2 cup coconut flakes

Directions:

1. Place all the ingredients in the bowl of your food processor or high-speed blender.
2. Blitz the ingredients until creamy or until your desired consistency is achieved.
3. Serve immediately or store in your freezer.
4. Bon appétit!

Poppy-granola Balls With Chocolate

Servings:8
Cooking Time:25 Minutes
Ingredients:

- ½ cup granola
- ¼ cup pure date sugar
- ½ cup golden raisins
- ½ cup shelled sunflower seeds
- ¼ cup poppy seeds
- 1 ½ cups creamy almond butter
- 2 cups vegan chocolate chips

Directions:

1. Blend the granola, sugar, raisins, sunflower seeds, and poppy seeds in a food processor. Stir in the almond butter and pulse until a smooth dough is formed. Leave in the fridge overnight. Shape small balls out of the mixture. Set aside.
2. Melt the chocolate in the microwave oven. Dip the balls into the melted chocolate and place on a baking sheet. Chill in the fridge for 30 minutes, until firm. Serve.

Raw Raspberry Cheesecake

Servings: 9
Cooking Time: 15 Minutes
Ingredients:

- Crust:
- 2 cups almonds
- 1 cup fresh dates, pitted
- 1/4 teaspoon ground cinnamon
- Filling:
- 2 cups raw cashews, soaked overnight and drained
- 14 ounces blackberries, frozen
- 1 tablespoon fresh lime juice
- 1/4 teaspoon crystallized ginger
- 1 can coconut cream
- 8 fresh dates, pitted

Directions:

1. In your food processor, blend the crust ingredients until the mixture comes together; press the crust into a lightly oiled springform pan.
2. Then, blend the filling layer until completely smooth. Spoon the filling onto the crust, creating a flat surface with a spatula.

3. Transfer the cake to your freezer for about 3 hours. Store in your freezer.

4. Garnish with organic citrus peel. Bon appétit!

Tofu & Almond Pancakes

Servings:10
Cooking Time:15 Minutes
Ingredients:
- 1 ⅓ cups almond milk
- 1 cup almond flour
- ⅓ cup firm tofu, crumbled
- 3 tbsp plant butter, melted
- 2 tbsp pure date sugar
- 1 ½ tsp pure vanilla extract
- ½ tsp baking powder
- ⅛ tsp salt

Directions:
1. Blitz almond milk, tofu, butter, sugar, vanilla, baking powder, and salt in a blender until smooth. Heat a pan and coat with oil. Scoop a ladle of batter at the center and spread all over. Cook for 3-4 minutes until golden, turning once. Transfer to a plate and repeat the process until no batter is left. Serve.

Orange Mini Cheesecakes

Servings: 12
Cooking Time: 10 Minutes
Ingredients:
- Crust:
- 1 cup raw almonds
- 1 cup fresh dates, pitted
- Topping:
- 1/2 cup raw sunflower seeds, soaked overnight and drained
- 1 cup raw cashew nuts, soaked overnight and drained
- 1 orange, freshly squeezed
- 1/4 cup coconut oil, softened
- 1/2 cup dates, pitted
- Garnish:
- 2 tablespoons caramel topping

Directions:
1. In your food processor, blend the crust ingredients until the mixture comes together; press the crust into a lightly greased muffin tin.

2. Then, blend the topping ingredients until creamy and smooth. Spoon the topping mixture onto the crust, creating a flat surface with a spatula.

3. Place these mini cheesecakes in your freezer for about 3 hours. Garnish with caramel topping. Bon appétit!

Mango Chocolate Fudge

Servings:3
Cooking Time:10 Minutes + Chilling Time
Ingredients:
- 1 mango
- ¾ cup vegan chocolate chips
- 4 cups pure date sugar

Directions:

1. In a food processor, blend the mango until smooth.

2. Microwave the chocolate until melted. Add in the pureed mango and date sugar and stir to combine. Spread on a lined with waxed paper baking pan and chill in the fridge for 2 hours. Once chilled, take out the fudge and lay on a cutting board. Discard the waxed paper. Slice into small pieces and serve.

Kiwi & Peanut Bars

Servings:9
Cooking Time:5 Minutes
Ingredients:
- 2 kiwis, mashed
- 1 tbsp maple syrup
- ½ tsp vanilla extract
- 2 cups old-fashioned rolled oats
- ½ tsp salt
- ¼ cup chopped peanuts

Directions:
1. Preheat oven to 360 F.

2. In a bowl, add kiwi, maple syrup, and vanilla and stir. Mix in oats, salt, and peanuts. Pour into a greased baking dish and bake for 25-30 minutes until crisp. Let completely cool and slice into bars to serve.

Coconut Bars With Chocolate Chips

Servings:16
Cooking Time:45 Minutes
Ingredients:
- ¼ cup coconut oil
- 1 cups shredded coconut
- ¼ cup pure date sugar
- 2 tbsp agave syrup
- 1 cup vegan chocolate chips

Directions:
1. Grease a dish with coconut oil. Set aside. In a bowl, mix the coconut, sugar, agave syrup, and coconut oil. Spread the mixture onto the dish, pressing down. Place the chocolate chips in a heatproof bowl and microwave for 1 minute. Stir and heat 30 seconds more until the chocolate is melted. Pour over the coconut and let harden for 20 minutes. Chop into 16 bars. Store in a container for up to 1 week.

Berry Macedonia With Mint

Servings:4
Cooking Time:20 Minutes
Ingredients:
- ¼ cup lemon juice
- 4 tsp agave syrup
- 2 cups chopped pears
- 2 cups chopped strawberries
- 3 cups mixed berries
- 8 fresh mint leaves

Directions:
1. Chop half of the mint leaves; reserve.

2. In a large bowl, combine together pears, strawberries, raspberries, blackberries, and half of the mint leaves. Divide the Macedonia salad between 4 small cups. Top with lemon juice, agave syrup, and mint leaves and serve chilled.

Oatmeal Cookies With Hazelnuts

Servings:2
Cooking Time:15 Minutes
Ingredients:

- 1 ½ cups whole-grain flour
- 1 tsp baking powder
- ⅛ tsp salt
- 1 tsp ground cinnamon
- ¼ tsp ground nutmeg
- 1 ½ cups old-fashioned oats
- 1 cup chopped hazelnuts
- ½ cup plant butter, melted
- ½ cup pure maple syrup
- ¼ cup pure date sugar
- 2 tsp pure vanilla extract

Directions:
1. Preheat oven to 360 F.
2. Combine the flour, baking powder, salt, cinnamon, and nutmeg in a bowl. Add in oats and hazelnuts. In another bowl, whisk the butter, maple syrup, sugar, and vanilla. Pour over the flour mixture. Mix well. Spoon a small ball of cookie dough on a baking sheet and press down with a fork. Bake for 10-12 minutes until browned. Let completely cool on a rack.

Last-minute Macaroons

Servings: 10
Cooking Time: 15 Minutes
Ingredients:

- 3 cups coconut flakes, sweetened
- 9 ounces canned   coconut milk, sweetened
- 1 teaspoon ground anise
- 1 teaspoon vanilla extract

Directions:
1. Begin by preheating your oven to 325 degrees F. Line the cookie sheets with parchment paper.
2. Thoroughly combine all the ingredients until everything is well incorporated.
3. Use a cookie scoop to drop mounds of the batter onto the prepared cookie sheets.
4. Bake for about 11 minutes until they are lightly browned. Bon appétit!

Traditional Greek Koufeto

Servings: 8
Cooking Time: 15 Minutes
Ingredients:

- 1 pound pumpkin
- 8 ounces brown sugar
- 1 vanilla bean
- 3-4 cloves
- 1 cinnamon stick
- 1 cup almonds, slivered and lightly toasted

Directions:
1. Bring the pumpkin and brown sugar to a boil; add in the vanilla, cloves and cinnamon.
2. Stir continuously to prevent from sticking.

3. Cook until your Koufeto has thickened; fold in the almonds; let it cool completely. Enjoy!

Berry Cupcakes With Cashew Cheese Icing

Servings:4
Cooking Time:35 Minutes + Cooling Time
Ingredients:

- 2 cups whole-wheat flour
- ¼ cup cornstarch
- 2 ½ tsp baking powder
- 1 ½ cups pure date sugar
- ½ tsp salt
- ¾ cup plant butter, softened
- 3 tsp vanilla extract
- 1 cup strawberries, pureed
- 1 cup oat milk, room temperature
- ¾ cup cashew cream
- 2 tbsp coconut oil, melted
- 3 tbsp pure maple syrup
- 1 tsp vanilla extract
- 1 tsp freshly squeezed lemon juice

Directions:
1. Preheat the oven to 350 F and line a 12-holed muffin tray with cupcake liners. Set aside.
2. In a bowl, mix flour, cornstarch, baking powder, date sugar, and salt. Whisk in plant butter, vanilla extract, strawberries, and oat milk until well combined. Divide the mixture into the muffin cups two-thirds way up and bake for 20-25 minutes. Allow cooling while you make the frosting.
3. In a blender, add cashew cream, coconut oil, maple syrup, vanilla, and lemon juice. Process until smooth. Pour the frosting into a medium bowl and chill for 30 minutes. Transfer the mixture into a piping bag and swirl mounds of the frosting onto the cupcakes. Serve immediately.

Mini Lemon Tarts

Servings: 9
Cooking Time: 15 Minutes
Ingredients:

- 1 cup cashews
- 1 cup dates, pitted
- 1/2 cup coconut flakes
- 1/2 teaspoon anise, ground
- 3 lemons, freshly squeezed
- 1 cup coconut cream
- 2 tablespoons agave syrup

Directions:
1. Brush a muffin tin with a nonstick cooking oil.
2. Blend the cashews, dates, coconut and anise in your food processor or a high-speed blender. Press the crust into the peppered muffin tin.
3. Then, blend the lemon, coconut cream and agave syrup. Spoon the cream into the muffin tin.
4. Store in your freezer. Bon appétit!

Raspberries Turmeric Panna Cotta

Servings:6
Cooking Time:10 Minutes + Chilling Time
Ingredients:

- ½ tbsp powdered vegetarian gelatin
- 2 cups coconut cream
- ¼ tsp vanilla extract
- 1 pinch turmeric powder
- 1 tbsp erythritol
- 1 tbsp chopped toasted pecans
- 12 fresh raspberries

Directions:

1. Mix gelatin and ½ tsp water and allow sitting to dissolve. Pour coconut cream, vanilla extract, turmeric, and erythritol into a saucepan and bring to a boil over medium heat, then simmer for 2 minutes. Turn the heat off. Stir in the gelatin until dissolved. Pour the mixture into 6 glasses, cover with plastic wrap, and refrigerate for 2 hours or more. Top with the pecans and raspberries and serve.

Melon Chocolate Pudding

Servings:4
Cooking Time:25 Minutes
Ingredients:

- 1 cup cubed melon
- 4 tbsp non-dairy milk
- 2 tbsp unsweetened cocoa powder
- 2 tbsp pure date sugar
- ½ ripe avocado

Directions:

1. Blitz the milk, cocoa powder, sugar, and avocado in a blender until smooth. Mash the melon with a fork in a bowl. Mix in the cocoa mixture and serve.

Chocolate Fudge With Nuts

Servings:4
Cooking Time:10 Minutes + Cooling Time
Ingredients:

- 3 cups chocolate chips
- ¼ cup thick coconut milk
- 1 ½ tsp vanilla extract
- A pinch salt
- 1 cup chopped mixed nuts

Directions:

1. Line a square pan with baking paper. Melt the chocolate chips, coconut milk, and vanilla in a medium pot over low heat. Mix in the salt and nuts until well distributed and pour the mixture into the square pan. Refrigerate for at least 2 hours. Remove from the fridge, cut into squares, and serve.

Berry Compote With Red Wine

Servings: 4
Cooking Time: 15 Minutes
Ingredients:

- 4 cups mixed berries, fresh or frozen
- 1 cup sweet red wine
- 1 cup agave syrup
- 1/2 teaspoon star anise

- 1 cinnamon stick
- 3-4 cloves
- A pinch of grated nutmeg
- A pinch of sea salt

Directions:

1. Add all ingredients to a saucepan. Cover with water by 1 inch. Bring to a boil and immediately reduce the heat to a simmer.
2. Let it simmer for 9 to 11 minutes. Allow it to cool completely.
3. Bon appétit!

Holiday Pecan Tart

Servings:4
Cooking Time:50 Minutes + Cooling Time
Ingredients:

- 4 tbsp flaxseed powder
- 1/3 cup whole-wheat flour
- ½ tsp salt
- ¼ cup cold plant butter, crumbled
- 3 tbsp pure malt syrup
- For the filling:
- 3 tbsp flaxseed powder + 9 tbsp water
- 2 cups toasted pecans, chopped
- 1 cup light corn syrup
- ½ cup pure date sugar
- 1 tbsp pure pomegranate molasses
- 4 tbsp plant butter, melted
- ½ tsp salt
- 2 tsp vanilla extract

Directions:

1. Preheat oven to 350 F. In a bowl, mix the flaxseed powder with 12 tbsp water and allow thickening for 5 minutes. Do this for the filling's vegan "flax egg" too in a separate bowl. In a bowl, combine flour and salt. Add in plant butter and whisk until crumbly. Pour in the crust's vegan "flax egg" and maple syrup and mix until smooth dough forms. Flatten the dough on a flat surface, cover with plastic wrap, and refrigerate for 1 hour. Dust a working surface with flour, remove the dough onto the surface, and using a rolling pin, flatten the dough into a 1-inch diameter circle. Lay the dough on a greased pie pan and press to fit the shape of the pan. Trim the edges of the pan. Lay a parchment paper on the dough, pour on some baking beans and bake for 20 minutes. Remove, pour out baking beans, and allow cooling.

2. In a bowl, mix the filling's vegan "flax egg," pecans, corn syrup, date sugar, pomegranate molasses, plant butter, salt, and vanilla. Pour and spread the mixture on the piecrust. Bake for 20 minutes or until the filling sets. Remove from the oven, decorate with more pecans, slice, and cool. Slice and serve.

Almond Butter Cookies

Servings: 10
Cooking Time: 45 Minutes
Ingredients:

- 3/4 cup all-purpose flour
- 1/2 teaspoon baking soda
- 1/4 teaspoon kosher salt
- 1 flax egg
- 1/4 cup coconut oil, at room temperature
- 2 tablespoons almond milk
- 1/2 cup brown sugar
- 1/2 cup almond butter
- 1/2 teaspoon ground cinnamon
- 1/2 teaspoon vanilla

Directions:

1. In a mixing bowl, combine the flour, baking soda and salt.
2. In another bowl, combine the flax egg, coconut oil, almond milk, sugar, almond butter, cinnamon and vanilla. Stir the wet mixture into the dry ingredients and stir until well combined.
3. Place the batter in your refrigerator for about 30 minutes. Shape the batter into small cookies and arrange them on a parchment-lined cookie pan.
4. Bake in the preheated oven at 350 degrees F for approximately 12 minutes. Transfer the pan to a wire rack to cool at room temperature. Bon appétit!

Jasmine Rice Pudding With Dried Apricots

Servings: 4
Cooking Time: 20 Minutes
Ingredients:

- 1 cup jasmine rice, rinsed
- 1 cup water
- 1 cup almond milk
- 1/2 cup brown sugar
- A pinch of salt
- A pinch of grated nutmeg
- 1/2 cup dried apricots, chopped
- 1/4 teaspoon cinnamon powder
- 1 teaspoon vanilla extract

Directions:

1. Add the rice and water to a saucepan. Cover the saucepan and bring the water to a boil.
2. Turn the heat to low; let it simmer for another 10 minutes until all the water is absorbed.
3. Then, add in the remaining ingredients and stir to combine. Let it simmer for 10 minutes more or until the pudding has thickened. Bon appétit!

Balsamic-glazed Caramelized Quinces

Servings:4
Cooking Time:20 Minutes
Ingredients:

- 1 cup balsamic vinegar
- ¼ cup + 3 tbsp pure date sugar
- ¼ tsp grated nutmeg
- A pinch of salt
- ¼ cup coconut oil
- 2 quinces, cored and cut into slices

Directions:

1. Heat a saucepan over medium heat and add in the balsamic vinegar, ¼ cup of date sugar, nutmeg, and salt. Cook for 10-15 minutes, stirring occasionally until the liquid has reduced by half.
2. Melt the coconut oil in a skillet over medium heat and in place in the quinces; cook for 5 minutes until golden. Stir in 3 tbsp of date sugar and cook for another 5 minutes until caramelized. Serve in a plate drizzled with the balsamic glaze.

Crispy Oat And Pecan Treats

Servings: 10
Cooking Time: 25 Minutes
Ingredients:

- 1 cup all-purpose flour
- 2 ½ cups instant oats
- 1 teaspoon baking soda
- A pinch of coarse salt
- 1 cup brown sugar
- 1/2 cup coconut oil, room temperature
- 4 tablespoons agave syrup
- 1 teaspoon vanilla extract
- 1/4 teaspoon ground cinnamon
- 1/4 teaspoon ground anise
- 1/4 teaspoon ground cloves
- 2 tablespoons applesauce
- 1/2 cup pecans, roughly chopped

Directions:

1. In a mixing bowl, thoroughly combine the flour, oats, baking soda and salt.
2. Then, whip the sugar with coconut oil and agave syrup. Add in the spices and applesauce. Add the wet mixture to the dry ingredients.
3. Fold in the pecans and stir to combine. Spread the batter onto a parchment-lined baking sheet.
4. Bake your cake at 350 degrees F for about 25 minutes or until the center is set. Let it cool and cut into bars. Bon appétit!

Mint Ice Cream

Servings:4
Cooking Time:10 Minutes + Chilling Time
Ingredients:

- 2 avocados, pitted
- 1 ¼ cups coconut cream
- ½ tsp vanilla extract
- 2 tbsp erythritol
- 2 tsp chopped mint leaves

Directions:

1. Into a blender, spoon the avocado pulps, pour in the coconut cream, vanilla extract, erythritol, and mint leaves. Process until smooth. Pour the mixture into your ice cream maker and freeze according to the manufacturer's

instructions. When ready, remove and scoop the ice cream into bowls. Serve.

Mango Muffins With Chocolate Chips

Servings:12
Cooking Time:40 Minutes
Ingredients:

- 2 medium mangoes, chopped
- 1 cup non-dairy milk
- 2 tbsp almond butter
- 1 tsp apple cider vinegar
- 1 tsp pure vanilla extract
- 1 ¼ cups whole-wheat flour
- ½ cup rolled oats
- ¼ cup coconut sugar
- 1 tsp baking powder
- ½ tsp baking soda
- ½ cup unsweetened cocoa powder
- ¼ cup sesame seeds
- A pinch of salt
- ¼ cup dark chocolate chips

Directions:
1. Preheat oven to 360 F.
2. In a food processor, put the mangoes, milk, almond butter, vinegar, and vanilla. Blend until smooth.
3. In a bowl, combine the flour, oats, sugar, baking powder, baking soda, cocoa powder, sesame seeds, salt, and chocolate chips. Pour into the mango mixture and mix. Scoop into greased muffin cups and bake for 20-25 minutes. Let cool completely before removing it from the cups.

Aunt´s Apricot Tarte Tatin

Servings:4
Cooking Time:30 Minutes+ Cooling Time
Ingredients:

- 4 tbsp flaxseed powder
- ¼ cup almond flour
- 3 tbsp whole-wheat flour
- ½ tsp salt
- ¼ cup cold plant butter, crumbled
- 3 tbsp pure maple syrup
- 4 tbsp melted plant butter
- 3 tsp pure maple syrup
- 1 tsp vanilla extract
- 1 lemon, juiced
- 12 apricots, halved and pitted
- ½ cup coconut cream
- 4 fresh basil leaves

Directions:
1. Preheat the oven to 350 F and grease a large pie pan with cooking spray.
2. In a medium bowl, mix the flaxseed powder with 12 tbsp water and allow thickening for 5 minutes.
3. In a large bowl, combine the flours and salt. Add the plant butter, and using an electric hand mixer, whisk until crumbly. Pour in the vegan "flax egg" and maple syrup and mix until smooth dough forms. Flatten the dough on a flat surface, cover with plastic wrap, and refrigerate for 1 hour.

4. Dust a working surface with almond flour, remove the dough onto the surface, and using a rolling pin, flatten the dough into a 1-inch diameter circle. Set aside. In a large bowl, mix the plant butter, maple syrup, vanilla, and lemon juice. Add the apricots to the mixture and coat well.
5. Arrange the apricots (open side down) in the pie pan and lay the dough on top. Press to fit and cut off the dough hanging on the edges. Brush the top with more plant butter and bake in the oven for 35 to 40 minutes or until golden brown and puffed up.
6. Remove the pie pan from the oven, allow cooling for 5 minutes, and run a butter knife around the edges of the pastry. Invert the dessert onto a large plate, spread the coconut cream on top, and garnish with the basil leaves. Slice and serve.

Old-fashioned Fudge Penuche

Servings: 12
Cooking Time: 15 Minutes
Ingredients:

- 4 ounces dark vegan chocolate
- 1/2 cup almond milk
- 1 cup brown sugar
- 1/4 cup coconut oil, softened
- 1/2 cup walnuts, chopped
- 1/4 teaspoon ground cloves
- 1/2 teaspoon ground cinnamon

Directions:
1. Microwave the chocolate until melted.
2. In a saucepan, heat the milk and add the warm milk to the melted chocolate.
3. Add in the remaining ingredients and mix to combine well.
4. Pour the mixture into a well-greased pan and place it in your refrigerator until set. Bon appétit

Roasted Apples Stuffed With Pecans & Dates

Servings:4
Cooking Time:40 Minutes
Ingredients:

- 4 apples, cored, halved lengthwise
- ½ cup finely chopped pecans
- 4 dates, pitted and chopped
- 1 tbsp plant butter
- 1 tbsp pure maple syrup
- ¼ tsp ground cinnamon

Directions:
1. Preheat oven to 360 F.
2. Mix the pecans, dates, butter, maple syrup, and cinnamon in a bowl. Arrange the apple on a greased baking pan and fill them with the pecan mixture. Pour 1 tbsp of water into the baking pan. Bake for 30-40 minutes, until soft and lightly browned. Serve immediately.

Baked Apples Filled With Nuts

Servings:4
Cooking Time:35 Minutes + Cooling Time
Ingredients:
- 4 gala apples
- 3 tbsp pure maple syrup
- 4 tbsp almond flour
- 6 tbsp pure date sugar
- 6 tbsp plant butter, cold and cubed
- 1 cup chopped mixed nuts

Directions:
1. Preheat the oven the 400 F.
2. Slice off the top of the apples and use a melon baller or spoon to scoop out the cores of the apples. In a bowl, mix the maple syrup, almond flour, date sugar, butter, and nuts. Spoon the mixture into the apples and then bake in the oven for 25 minutes or until the nuts are golden brown on top and the apples soft. Remove the apples from the oven, allow cooling, and serve.

Cinnamon Pumpkin Pie

Servings:4
Cooking Time:1 Hr 10 Min + Cooling Time
Ingredients:
- For the piecrust:
- 4 tbsp flaxseed powder
- 1/3 cup whole-wheat flour
- ½ tsp salt
- ¼ cup cold plant butter, crumbled
- 3 tbsp pure malt syrup
- For the filling:
- 2 tbsp flaxseed powder + 6 tbsp water
- 4 tbsp plant butter
- ¼ cup pure maple syrup
- ¼ cup pure date sugar
- 1 tsp cinnamon powder
- ½ tsp ginger powder
- 1/8 tsp cloves powder
- 1 can pumpkin purée
- 1 cup almond milk

Directions:
1. Preheat oven to 350 F. In a bowl, mix flaxseed powder with 12 tbsp water and allow thickening for 5 minutes. Do this for the filling's vegan "flax egg" too in another bowl. In a bowl, combine flour and salt. Add in plant butter and whisk until crumbly. Pour in crust's vegan "flax egg," maple syrup, vanilla, and mix until smooth dough forms. Flatten, cover with plastic wrap, and refrigerate for 1 hour.
2. Dust a working surface with flour, remove the dough onto the surface and flatten it into a 1-inch diameter circle. Lay the dough on a greased pie pan and press to fit the shape of the pan. Use a knife to trim the edges of the pan. Lay a parchment paper on the dough, pour on some baking beans and bake for 15-20 minutes. Remove, pour out the baking beans, and allow cooling. In a bowl, whisk filling's flaxseed, butter, maple syrup, date sugar, cinnamon powder, ginger powder, cloves powder, pumpkin puree, and almond milk.

Pour the mixture onto the piecrust and bake for 35-40 minutes.

Coconut Chocolate Truffles

Servings:12
Cooking Time:1 Hour 15 Minutes
Ingredients:
- 1 cup raw cashews, soaked overnight
- ¾ cup pitted cherries
- 2 tbsp coconut oil
- 1 cup shredded coconut
- 2 tbsp cocoa powder

Directions:
1. Line a baking sheet with parchment paper and set aside.
2. Blend cashews, cherries, coconut oil, half of the shredded coconut, and cocoa powder in a food processor until ingredients are evenly mixed. Spread the remaining shredded coconut on a dish. Mold the mixture into 12 truffle shapes. Roll the truffles in the coconut dish, shaking off any excess, then arrange on the prepared baking sheet. Refrigerate for 1 hour.

Raisin Oatmeal Biscuits

Servings:8
Cooking Time:20 Minutes
Ingredients:
- ½ cup plant butter
- 1 cup date sugar
- ¼ cup pineapple juice
- 1 cup whole-grain flour
- 1 tsp baking powder
- ½ tsp salt
- 1 tsp pure vanilla extract
- 1 cup old-fashioned oats
- ½ cup vegan chocolate chips
- ½ cup raisins

Directions:
1. Preheat oven to 370 F. Beat the butter and sugar in a bowl until creamy and fluffy. Pour in the juice and blend. Mix in flour, baking powder, salt, and vanilla. Stir in oats, chocolate chips, and raisins. Spread the dough on a baking sheet and bake for 15 minutes. Let completely cool on a rack.

Peanut Chocolate Brownies

Servings:12
Cooking Time:40 Minutes
Ingredients:
- 1 ¾ cups whole-grain flour
- 1 tsp baking powder
- ½ tsp salt
- 1 tbsp ground nutmeg
- ½ tsp ground cinnamon
- 3 tbsp unsweetened cocoa powder
- ½ cup vegan chocolate chips
- ½ cup chopped peanuts
- ¼ cup canola oil
- ½ cup dark molasses ½ cup water
- 1/3 cup pure date sugar

- 2 tsp grated fresh ginger

Directions:

1. Preheat oven to 360 F.
2. Combine the flour, baking powder, salt, nutmeg, cinnamon, and cocoa in a bowl. Add in chocolate chips and peanuts and stir. Set aside. In another bowl, mix the oil, molasses, water, sugar, and ginger. Pour into the flour mixture and stir to combine. Transfer to a greased baking pan and bake for 30-35 minutes. Let cool before slicing.

Mint Chocolate Cake

Servings: 16
Cooking Time: 45 Minutes
Ingredients:

- 1/2 cup vegan butter
- 1/2 cup brown sugar
- 2 chia eggs
- 3/4 cup all-purpose flour
- 1 teaspoon baking powder
- A pinch of salt
- A pinch of ground cloves
- 1 teaspoon ground cinnamon
- 1 teaspoon pure vanilla extract
- 1/3 cup coconut flakes
- 1 cup vegan chocolate chunks
- A few drops peppermint essential oil

Directions:

1. In a mixing bowl, beat the vegan butter and sugar until fluffy.
2. Add in the chia eggs, flour, baking powder, salt, cloves, cinnamon and vanilla. Beat to combine well.
3. Add in the coconut and mix again.
4. Scrape the mixture into a lightly greased baking pan; bake at 350 degrees F for 35 to 40 minutes.
5. Melt the chocolate in your microwave and add in the peppermint essential oil; stir to combine well.
6. Afterwards, spread the chocolate ganache evenly over the surface of the cake. Bon appétit!

Raw Chocolate Mango Pie

Servings: 16
Cooking Time: 10 Minutes
Ingredients:

- Avocado layer:
- 3 ripe avocados, pitted and peeled
- A pinch of sea salt
- A pinch of ground anise
- 1/2 teaspoon vanilla paste
- 2 tablespoons coconut milk
- 5 tablespoons agave syrup
- 1/3 cup cocoa powder
- Crema layer:
- 1/3 cup almond butter
- 1/2 cup coconut cream
- 1 medium mango, peeled
- 1/2 coconut flakes
- 2 tablespoons agave syrup

Directions:

1. In your food processor, blend the avocado layer until smooth and uniform; reserve.
2. Then, blend the other layer in a separate bowl. Spoon the layers in a lightly oiled baking pan.
3. Transfer the cake to your freezer for about 3 hours. Store in your freezer. Bon appétit!

Raspberry Cream Pie

Servings: 10
Cooking Time: 10 Minutes
Ingredients:

- Crust:
- 2 cups almonds
- 2 cups dates
- A pinch of sea salt
- A pinch of ground cloves
- 1/4 teaspoon ground anise
- 2 tablespoons coconut oil, softened
- Filling:
- 2 ripe bananas
- 2 frozen bananas
- 2 cups raspberries
- 1 tablespoon agave syrup
- 2 tablespoons coconut oil, softened

Directions:

1. In your food processor, blend the crust ingredients until the mixture comes together; press the crust into a lightly oiled springform pan.
2. Then, blend the filling layer. Spoon the filling onto the crust, creating a flat surface with a spatula.
3. Transfer the cake to your freezer for about 3 hours. Store in your freezer.
4. Bon appétit!

Homemade Hazelnut Candy

Servings: 12
Cooking Time: 10 Minutes
Ingredients:

- 1 ½ cups vegan chocolate, broken into chunks
- 1 cup peanut butter
- 1/2 cup hazelnuts, roughly chopped

Directions:

1. Line a square baking pan with parchment paper. Microwave the chocolate until completely melted.
2. Mix the ingredients until everything is well incorporated.
3. Scrape the batter into the parchment-lined pan. Place in your freezer until ready to serve. Bon appétit!

Chocolate And Raisin Cookie Bars

Servings: 10
Cooking Time: 40 Minutes
Ingredients:

- 1/2 cup peanut butter, at room temperature
- 1 cup agave syrup
- 1 teaspoon pure vanilla extract
- 1/4 teaspoon kosher salt
- 2 cups almond flour
- 1 teaspoon baking soda

- 1 cup raisins
- 1 cup vegan chocolate, broken into chunks

Directions:

1. In a mixing bowl, thoroughly combine the peanut butter, agave syrup, vanilla and salt.
2. Gradually stir in the almond flour and baking soda and stir to combine. Add in the raisins and chocolate chunks and stir again.
3. Freeze for about 30 minutes and serve well chilled. Enjoy!

Coconut & Chocolate Cake

Servings:4
Cooking Time:40 Minutes + Cooling Time

Ingredients:

- 2/3 cup toasted almond flour
- ¼ cup unsalted plant butter, melted
- 2 cups chocolate bars, cubed
- 2 ½ cups coconut cream
- Fresh berries for topping

Directions:

1. Lightly grease a 9-inch springform pan with some plant butter and set aside.
2. Mix the almond flour and plant butter in a medium bowl and pour the mixture into the springform pan. Use the spoon to spread and press the mixture into the bottom of the pan. Place in the refrigerator to firm for 30 minutes.
3. Meanwhile, pour the chocolate in a safe microwave bowl and melt for 1 minute stirring every 30 seconds. Remove from the microwave and mix in the coconut cream and maple syrup.
4. Remove the cake pan from the oven, pour the chocolate mixture on top, and shake the pan and even the layer. Chill further for 4 to 6 hours. Take out the pan from the fridge, release the cake and garnish with the raspberries or strawberries. Slice and serve.

Nutty Date Cake

Servings:4
Cooking Time:1 Hour 30 Minutes

Ingredients:

- ½ cup cold plant butter, cut into pieces
- 1 tbsp flaxseed powder
- ½ cup whole-wheat flour
- ¼ cup chopped pecans and walnuts
- 1 tsp baking powder
- 1 tsp baking soda
- 1 tsp cinnamon powder
- 1 tsp salt
- 1/3 cup pitted dates, chopped
- ½ cup pure date sugar
- 1 tsp vanilla extract
- ¼ cup pure date syrup for drizzling.

Directions:

1. Preheat oven to 350 F and lightly grease a baking dish with some plant butter. In a small bowl, mix the flaxseed powder with 3 tbsp water and allow thickening for 5 minutes to make the vegan "flax egg."

2. In a food processor, add the flour, nuts, baking powder, baking soda, cinnamon powder, and salt. Blend until well combined. Add 1/3 cup of water, dates, date sugar, and vanilla. Process until smooth with tiny pieces of dates evident.
3. Pour the batter into the baking dish and bake in the oven for 1 hour and 10 minutes or until a toothpick inserted comes out clean. Remove the dish from the oven, invert the cake onto a serving platter to cool, drizzle with the date syrup, slice, and serve.

Almond And Banana Brownie

Servings: 8
Cooking Time: 30 Minutes

Ingredients:

- 1 ½ cups all-purpose flour
- 1 ½ cups brown sugar
- 1/2 teaspoon baking powder
- 1/4 teaspoon salt
- 1/4 teaspoon ground cinnamon
- 1/2 teaspoon pure vanilla extract
- 1/2 teaspoon pure almond extract
- 1/2 cup cocoa powder, unsweetened
- 1/2 cup almond milk
- 1 ripe banana, mashed
- 1/2 cup coconut oil, melted
- 1/4 cup almonds, slivered

Directions:

1. Start by preheating your oven to 350 degrees F.
2. In a mixing bowl, mix the flour, sugar, baking powder, spices and cocoa powder until well combined.
3. Then, gradually add in the almond milk, banana and coconut oil; fold in the almonds and mix to combine well.
4. Pour the batter into a lightly oiled baking pan. Bake in the preheated oven for about 25 minutes or until a tester inserted in the middle comes out clean.
5. Bon appétit!

Coconut & Chocolate Macaroons

Servings:4
Cooking Time:25 Minutes

Ingredients:

- 1 cup shredded coconut
- 2 tbsp cocoa powder
- 1 tbsp vanilla extract
- ⅔ cup coconut milk
- ¼ cup maple syrup
- A pinch of salt

Directions:

1. Preheat oven to 360 F.
2. Place the shredded coconut, cocoa powder, vanilla extract, coconut milk, maple syrup, and salt in a pot. Cook until a firm dough is formed. Shape balls out of the mixture. Arrange the balls on a lined with parchment paper baking sheet. Bake for 15 minutes. Allow cooling before serving.

Classic Bread Pudding With Sultanas

Servings: 4
Cooking Time: 2 Hours
Ingredients:

- 10 ounces day-old bread, cut into cubes
- 2 cups coconut milk
- 1/2 cup coconut sugar
- 1 teaspoon vanilla extract
- 1/2 teaspoon ground cloves
- 1/2 teaspoon ground cinnamon
- 1/2 cup Sultanas

Directions:

1. Place the bread cubes in a lightly oiled baking dish.
2. Now, blend the milk, sugar, vanilla, ground cloves and cinnamon until creamy and smooth.
3. Spoon the mixture all over the bread cubes, pressing them with a wide spatula to soak well; fold in Sultanas and set aside for about 1 hour.
4. Bake in the preheated oven at 350 degrees F for about 1 hour or until the top of your pudding is golden brown.
5. Bon appétit!

Vanilla Ice Cream

Servings: 4
Cooking Time: 10 Minutes
Ingredients:

- 1/2 cup raw cashews, soaked overnight and drained
- 1 cup coconut milk
- 1/4 cup agave syrup
- A pinch of ground anise
- A pinch of Himalayan salt
- 1 tablespoon pure vanilla extract

Directions:

1. Place all the ingredients in the bowl of your food processor or high-speed blender.
2. Blitz the ingredients until creamy, uniform and smooth.
3. Place your ice cream in the freezer for at least 3 hours. Bon appétit!

Homemade Goji Berry Chocolate Granita

Servings:4
Cooking Time:5 Minutes
Ingredients:

- 1 pear, chopped
- 1 tbsp almond butter
- 2 tbsp fresh mint, minced
- ¼ cup non-dairy milk
- 3 tbsp non-dairy chocolate chips
- 2 tbsp goji berries

Directions:

1. In a food processor, place the almond butter, pear, and mint. Pulse until smooth. Pour in milk while keep blending. Add in chocolate chips and berries. Transfer to a glass and serve.

Glazed Chili Chocolate Cake

Servings:4

Cooking Time:45 Minutes
Ingredients:

- 1 ¾ cups whole-grain flour
- 1 cup pure date sugar
- ¼ cup unsweetened cocoa powder
- 1 tsp baking soda
- ½ tsp baking powder
- 1 ½ tsp ground cinnamon
- ¼ tsp ground chili
- ⅓ cup olive oil
- 1 tbsp apple cider vinegar
- 1 ½ tsp pure vanilla extract
- 2 squares vegan chocolate
- ¼ cup soy milk
- ½ cup pure date sugar
- 3 tbsp plant butter
- ½ tsp pure vanilla extract

Directions:

1. Preheat oven to 360 F.
2. In a bowl, mix the flour, sugar, baking soda, baking powder, cinnamon, and chili.
3. In another bowl, whisk the oil, vinegar, vanilla, and 1 cup cold water. Pour into the flour mixture, stir to combine. Pour the batter into a greased baking pan. Bake for 30 minutes. Let cool for 10-15 minutes. Take out the cake inverted onto a wire rack and allow to cool completely.
4. Place the chocolate and soy milk in a pot. Cook until the chocolate is melted. Add in sugar, cook for 5 minutes. Turn the heat off and mix in butter and vanilla. Cover the cake with the glaze. Refrigerate until the glaze is set. Serve.

Chocolate Rice Pudding

Servings: 4
Cooking Time: 40 Minutes
Ingredients:

- 3/4 cup white rice, rinsed
- 2 cups coconut milk
- 1/2 cup brown sugar
- 1/2 teaspoon vanilla extract
- 1/2 teaspoon ground cinnamon
- 1/2 teaspoon ground cloves
- 2 ounces vegan chocolate, broken into chunks

Directions:

1. Bring 1 ½ cups of water to a boil in a saucepan; stir the rice into a boiling water. Reduce the heat to low and simmer, covered, for 20 minutes.
2. Then, add in the milk, sugar, vanilla, cinnamon and cloves and stir to combine. Let it simmer for 15 minutes more or until the pudding has thickened.
3. Fold the chocolate chunks into the warm pudding and gently stir to combine. Bon appétit!

Coconut & Date Truffles With Walnuts

Servings:8
Cooking Time:15 Minutes
Ingredients:
- 1 cup pitted dates
- 1 cup walnuts
- ½ cup sweetened cocoa powder, plus extra for coating
- ½ cup shredded coconut
- ¼ cup pure maple syrup
- 1 tsp vanilla extract
- ¼ tsp salt

Directions:
1. Blend the dates, walnuts, cocoa powder, maple syrup, vanilla extract, and salt in a food processor until smooth. Let chill in the fridge for 1 hour. Shape the mixture into balls and roll up the truffles in cocoa powder. Serve chilled.

Chocolate & Peanut Butter Cookies

Servings:4
Cooking Time:15 Minutes + Cooling Time
Ingredients:
- 1 tbsp flaxseed powder
- 1 cup pure date sugar + for dusting
- ½ cup vega butter, softened
- ½ cup creamy peanut butter
- 1 tsp vanilla extract
- 1 ¾ cup whole-wheat flour
- 1 tsp baking soda
- ¼ tsp salt
- ¼ cup unsweetened chocolate chips

Directions:
1. In a small bowl, mix the flaxseed powder with 3 tbsp water and allow thickening for 5 minutes to make the vegan "flax egg." In a medium bowl, whisk the date sugar, plant butter, and peanut butter until light and fluffy. Mix in the flax egg and vanilla until combined. Add in flour, baking soda, salt, and whisk well again. Fold in chocolate chips, cover the bowl with plastic wrap, and refrigerate for 1 hour.
2. Preheat oven to 375 F and line a baking sheet with parchment paper. Use a cookie sheet to scoop mounds of the batter onto the sheet with 1-inch intervals. Bake for 10 minutes. Remove the cookies from the oven, cool for 3 minutes, roll in some date sugar, and serve.

Berry Hazelnut Trifle

Servings:4
Cooking Time:10 Minutes
Ingredients:
- 1 ½ ripe avocados
- ¾ cup coconut cream
- Zest and juice of ½ a lemon
- 1 tbsp vanilla extract
- 3 oz fresh strawberries
- 2 oz toasted hazelnuts

Directions:
1. In a bowl, add avocado pulp, coconut cream, lemon zest and juice, and half of the vanilla extract. Mix with an immersion blender. Put the strawberries and remaining vanilla in another bowl and use a fork to mash the fruits. In a tall glass, alternate layering the cream and strawberry mixtures. Drop a few hazelnuts on each and serve the dessert immediately.

Cashew & Cranberry Truffles

Servings:4
Cooking Time:15 Minutes
Ingredients:
- 2 cups fresh cranberries
- 2 tbsp pure date syrup
- 1 tsp vanilla extract
- 16 oz cashew cream
- 4 tbsp plant butter
- 3 tbsp unsweetened cocoa powder
- 2 tbsp pure date sugar

Directions:
1. Set a silicone egg tray aside. Puree the cranberries, date syrup, and vanilla in a blender until smooth.
2. Add the cashew cream and plant butter to a medium pot. Heat over medium heat until the mixture is well combined. Turn the heat off. Mix in the cranberry mixture and divide the mixture into the muffin holes. Refrigerate for 40 minutes or until firm. Remove the tray and pop out the truffles.
3. Meanwhile, mix the cocoa powder and date sugar on a plate. Roll the truffles in the mixture until well dusted and serve.

Coconut Peach Tart

Servings:8
Cooking Time:10 Minutes
Ingredients:
- ½ cup rolled oats
- 1 cup cashews
- 1 cup soft pitted dates
- 1 cup canned coconut milk
- 2 large peaches, chopped
- ½ cup shredded coconut

Directions:
1. In a food processor, pulse the oats, cashews, and dates until a dough-like mixture forms. Press down into a greased baking pan.
2. Pulse the coconut milk, ½ cup water, peaches, and shredded coconut in the food processor until smooth. Pour this mixture over the crust and spread evenly. Freeze for 30 minutes. Soften 15 minutes before serving. Top with whipped coconut cream and shredded coconut.

Fruit And Almond Crisp

Servings: 8
Cooking Time: 45 Minutes
Ingredients:
- 4 cups peaches, pitted and sliced
- 3 cups plums, pitted and halved
- 1 tablespoon lemon juice, freshly squeezed
- 1 cup brown sugar
- For the topping:
- 2 cups rolled oats
- 1/2 cup oat flour

- 1 teaspoon baking powder
- 4 tablespoons water
- 1/2 cup almonds, slivered
- 1/2 teaspoon vanilla extract
- 1/2 teaspoon almond extract
- 1/4 teaspoon ground cloves
- 1/4 teaspoon ground cinnamon
- A pinch of kosher salt
- A pinch of grated nutmeg
- 5 ounces coconut oil, softened

Directions:
1. Start by preheating your oven to 350 degrees F.
2. Arrange the fruits on the bottom of a lightly oiled baking pan. Sprinkle lemon juice and 1/2 cup of brown sugar over them.
3. In a mixing bowl, thoroughly combine the oats, oat flour, baking powder, water, almonds, vanilla, almond extract, ground cloves, cinnamon, salt, nutmeg and coconut oil.
4. Spread the topping mixture over the fruit layer.
5. Bake in the preheated oven for about 45 minutes or until golden brown. Bon appétit!

Party Matcha & Hazelnut Cheesecake

Servings:4
Cooking Time:20 Minutes + Cooling Time
Ingredients:
- 2/3 cup toasted rolled oats
- ¼ cup plant butter, melted
- 3 tbsp pure date sugar
- 6 oz cashew cream cheese
- ¼ cup almond milk
- 1 tbsp matcha powder
- ¼ cup just-boiled water
- 3 tsp agar agar powder
- 2 tbsp toasted hazelnuts, chopped

Directions:
1. Process the oats, butter, and date sugar in a blender until smooth.
2. Pour the mixture into a greased 9-inch springform pan and press the mixture onto the bottom of the pan. Refrigerate for 30 minutes until firm while you make the filling.
3. In a large bowl, using an electric mixer, whisk the cashew cream cheese until smooth. Beat in the almond milk and mix in the matcha powder until smooth.
4. Mix the boiled water and agar agar until dissolved and whisk this mixture into the creamy mix. Fold in the hazelnuts until well distributed. Remove the cake pan from the fridge and pour in the cream mixture. Shake the pan to ensure smooth layering on top. Refrigerate further for at least 3 hours. Take out the cake pan, release the cake, slice, and serve.

Mixed Berry Yogurt Ice Pops

Servings:6
Cooking Time:5 Minutes + Chilling Time
Ingredients:
- 2/3 cup avocado, halved and pitted
- 2/3 cup frozen berries, thawed
- 1 cup dairy-free yogurt
- ½ cup coconut cream
- 1 tsp vanilla extract

Directions:
1. Pour the avocado pulp, berries, dairy-free yogurt, coconut cream, and vanilla extract. Process until smooth. Pour into ice pop sleeves and freeze for 8 or more hours. Enjoy the ice pops when ready.

Coconut Chocolate Barks

Servings:4
Cooking Time:35 Minutes
Ingredients:
- 1/3 cup coconut oil, melted
- ¼ cup almond butter, melted
- 2 tbsp unsweetened coconut flakes.
- 1 tsp pure maple syrup
- A pinch of ground rock salt
- ¼ cup unsweetened cocoa nibs

Directions:
1. Line a baking tray with baking paper and set aside. In a medium bowl, mix the coconut oil, almond butter, coconut flakes, maple syrup, and fold in the rock salt and cocoa nibs. Pour and spread the mixture on the baking sheet, chill in the refrigerator for 20 minutes or until firm. Remove the dessert, break into shards, and enjoy. Preserve extras in the refrigerator.

Cinnamon Faux Rice Pudding

Servings:6
Cooking Time:25 Minutes
Ingredients:
- 1 ¼ cups coconut cream
- 1 tsp vanilla extract
- 1 tsp cinnamon powder
- 1 cup mashed tofu
- 2 oz fresh strawberries

Directions:
1. Pour the coconut cream into a bowl and whisk until a soft peak forms. Mix in the vanilla and cinnamon. Lightly fold in the vegan cottage cheese and refrigerate for 10 to 15 minutes to set. Spoon into serving glasses, top with the strawberries and serve immediately.

The Best Granola Bars Ever

Servings: 16
Cooking Time: 25 Minutes
Ingredients:
- 1 cup vegan butter
- 1 cup rolled oats
- 1 cup all-purpose flour
- 1 cup oat flour
- 1 teaspoon baking powder
- A pinch of coarse sea salt
- A pinch of freshly grated nutmeg
- 1/4 teaspoon ground cloves
- 1/4 teaspoon ground cardamom
- 1/4 teaspoon ground cinnamon

- 1 heaping cup packed dates, pitted
- 4 ounces raspberry preserves

Directions:
1. Begin by preheating your oven to 350 degrees F.
2. In a mixing bowl, thoroughly combine the dry ingredients. In another bowl, combine the wet ingredients.
3. Then, stir the wet mixture into the dry ingredients; mix to combine well.
4. Spread the batter mixture in a parchment-lined baking pan. Bake in the preheated oven for about 20 minutes.
5. Let it cool on a wire rack and then, cut into bars. Bon appétit!

Vanilla Brownies

Servings:4
Cooking Time:30 Minutes + Chilling Time
Ingredients:
- 2 tbsp flaxseed powder
- ¼ cup cocoa powder
- ½ cup almond flour
- ½ tsp baking powder
- ½ cup erythritol
- 10 tablespoons plant butter
- 2 oz dairy-free dark chocolate
- ½ teaspoon vanilla extract

Directions:
1. Preheat oven to 375 F and line a baking sheet with parchment paper. Mix the flaxseed powder with 6 tbsp water in a bowl and allow thickening for 5 minutes. In a separate bowl, mix cocoa powder, almond flour, baking powder, and erythritol until no lumps. In another bowl, add the plant butter and dark chocolate and melt both in the microwave for 30 seconds to 1 minute.
2. Whisk the vegan "flax egg" and vanilla into the chocolate mixture, then pour the mixture into the dry ingredients. Combine evenly. Pour the batter onto the paper-lined baking sheet and bake for 20 minutes. Cool completely and refrigerate for 2 hours. When ready, slice into squares and serve.

Maple Fruit Crumble

Servings:4
Cooking Time:25 Minutes
Ingredients:
- 3 cups chopped apricots
- 3 cups chopped mangoes
- 4 tbsp pure maple syrup
- 1 cup gluten-free rolled oats
- ½ cup shredded coconut
- 2 tbsp coconut oil

Directions:
1. Preheat oven to 360 F.
2. Place the apricots, mangoes, and 2 tbsp of maple syrup in a round baking dish.
3. In a food processor, put the oats, coconut, coconut oil, and remaining maple syrup. Blend until combined. Pour over the fruit. Bake for 20-25 minutes. Allow cooling before slicing and serving.

Sicilian Papaya Sorbet

Servings:4
Cooking Time:5 Minutes Freezing Time
Ingredients:
- 8 cups papaya chunks
- 2 limes, juiced and zested
- ½ cup pure date sugar

Directions:
1. Blend the papaya, lime juice, and sugar in a food processor until smooth. Transfer the mixture to a glass dish. Freeze for 2 hours. Take out from the freezer and scrape the top ice layer with a fork. Back to the freezer for 1 hour. Repeat the process a few more times until all the ice is scraped up. Serve frozen garnished with lime zest strips.

Autumn Pear Crisp

Servings: 8
Cooking Time: 50 Minutes
Ingredients:
- 4 pears, peeled, cored and sliced
- 1 tablespoon fresh lemon juice
- 1/2 teaspoon ground cinnamon
- 1/2 teaspoon ground anise
- 1 cup brown sugar
- 1 ¼ cups quick-cooking oats
- 1/2 cup water
- 1/2 teaspoon baking powder
- 1/2 cup coconut oil, melted
- 1 teaspoon pure vanilla extract

Directions:
1. Start by preheating your oven to 350 degrees F.
2. Arrange the pears on the bottom of a lightly oiled baking pan. Sprinkle lemon juice, cinnamon, anise and 1/2 cup of brown sugar over them.
3. In a mixing bowl, thoroughly combine the quick-cooking oats, water, 1/2 of the brown sugar, baking powder, coconut oil and vanilla extract.
4. Spread the topping mixture over the fruit layer.
5. Bake in the preheated oven for about 45 minutes or until golden brown. Bon appétit!

Chocolate-glazed Cookies

Servings: 14
Cooking Time: 45 Minutes
Ingredients:
- 1/2 cup all-purpose flour
- 1/2 cup almond flour
- 1 teaspoon baking powder
- A pinch of sea salt
- A pinch of grated nutmeg
- 1/4 teaspoon ground cloves
- 1/2 cup cocoa powder
- 1/2 cup cashew butter
- 2 tablespoons almond milk
- 1 cup brown sugar
- 1 teaspoon vanilla paste
- 4 ounces vegan chocolate
- 1 ounce coconut oil

Directions:

1. In a mixing bowl, combine the flour, baking powder, salt, nutmeg, cloves and cocoa powder.

2. In another bowl, combine the cashew butter, almond milk, sugar and vanilla paste. Stir the wet mixture into the dry ingredients and stir until well combined.

3. Place the batter in your refrigerator for about 30 minutes. Shape the batter into small cookies and arrange them on a parchment-lined cookie pan.

4. Bake in the preheated oven at 330 degrees F for approximately 10 minutes. Transfer the pan to a wire rack to cool slightly.

5. Microwave the chocolate until melted; mix the melted chocolate with the coconut oil. Spread the glaze over your cookies and let it cool completely. Bon appétit!

Almond Berry Cream

Servings:4
Cooking Time:10 Minutes
Ingredients:

- 3 cans almond milk
- 3 tbsp maple syrup
- ½ tsp almond extract
- 1 cup blueberries
- 1 cup raspberries
- 1 cup strawberries, sliced

Directions:

1. Place almond milk in the fridge overnight. Open the can and reserve the liquid. In a bowl, mix almond solids, maple syrup, and almond extract. Share berries into 4 bowls. Serve topped with almond cream.

Pressure Cooker Apple Cupcakes

Servings:4
Cooking Time:25 Minutes
Ingredients:

- 1 cup canned applesauce
- 1 cup non-dairy milk
- 6 tbsp maple syrup + for sprinkling
- ¼ cup spelt flour
- ½ tsp apple pie spice
- A pinch of salt

Directions:

1. In a bowl, combine the applesauce, milk, maple syrup, flour, apple pie spice, and salt. Scoop into 4 heat-proof ramekins. Drizzle with more syrup.

2. Pour 1 cup of water into the pressure cooker and fit in a trivet. Place the ramekins on the trivet. Lock lid in place; set the time to 6 minutes on High. Once ready, perform a quick pressure release. Unlock the lid and let cool for a few minutes; take out the ramekins. Allow cooling for 10 minutes and serve.

Vanilla Berry Tarts

Servings:4
Cooking Time:35 Minutes + Cooling Time
Ingredients:

- 4 tbsp flaxseed powder
- 1/3 cup whole-wheat flour
- ½ tsp salt
- ¼ cup plant butter, crumbled
- 3 tbsp pure malt syrup
- 6 oz cashew cream
- 6 tbsp pure date sugar
- ¾ tsp vanilla extract
- 1 cup mixed frozen berries

Directions:

1. Preheat oven to 350 F and grease mini pie pans with cooking spray. In a bowl, mix flaxseed powder with 12 tbsp water and allow soaking for 5 minutes. In a large bowl, combine flour and salt. Add in butter and whisk until crumbly. Pour in the vegan "flax egg" and malt syrup and mix until smooth dough forms. Flatten the dough on a flat surface, cover with plastic wrap, and refrigerate for 1 hour.

2. Dust a working surface with some flour, remove the dough onto the surface, and using a rolling pin, flatten the dough into a 1-inch diameter circle. Use a large cookie cutter, cut out rounds of the dough and fit into the pie pans. Use a knife to trim the edges of the pan. Lay a parchment paper on the dough cups, pour on some baking beans, and bake in the oven until golden brown, 15-20 minutes. Remove the pans from the oven, pour out the baking beans, and allow cooling. In a bowl, mix cashew cream, date sugar, and vanilla extract. Divide the mixture into the tart cups and top with berries. Serve.

Chapter 8. Other Favorites

Homemade Almond Butter

Servings: 20
Cooking Time: 20 Minutes
Ingredients:
- 1 pound almonds
- A pinch of sea salt
- A pinch of grated nutmeg

Directions:
1. Roast the almonds in the preheated oven at 350 degrees F for approximately 9 minutes until your nuts are fragrant and lightly browned.
2. In your food processor or a high-speed blender, pulse the almonds until ground. Then, process the mixture for 5 minutes more, scraping down the sides and bottom of the bowl.
3. Add in the salt and nutmeg.
4. Run your machine for another 10 minutes or until your butter is completely creamy and smooth. Enjoy!

Delicious Lemon Butter

Servings: 8
Cooking Time: 10 Minutes
Ingredients:
- 1/2 cup granulated sugar
- 2 tablespoons cornstarch
- 1/2 teaspoon lemon zest, grated
- 1 cup water
- 2 tablespoons fresh lemon juice
- 2 tablespoons coconut oil

Directions:
1. In a saucepan, combine the sugar, cornstarch and lemon zest over a moderate heat.
2. Stir in the water and lemon juice and continue to cook until the mixture has thickened. Heat off.
3. Stir in the coconut oil. Bon appétit!

Crunchy Peanut Butter

Servings: 20
Cooking Time: 10 Minutes
Ingredients:
- 2 ½ cups peanuts
- 1/2 teaspoon coarse sea salt
- 1/2 teaspoon cinnamon powder
- 10 dates, pitted

Directions:
1. Roast the peanuts in the preheated oven at 350 degrees F for approximately 7 minutes until the peanuts are fragrant and lightly browned.
2. In your food processor or a high-speed blender, pulse the peanuts until ground. Reserve for about 1/2 cup of the mixture.
3. Then, process the mixture for 2 minutes more, scraping down the sides and bottom of the bowl.
4. Add in the salt, cinnamon and dates.

5. Run your machine for another 2 minutes or until your butter is smooth. Add in the reserved peanuts and stir with a spoon. Enjoy!

10-minute Basic Caramel

Servings: 10
Cooking Time: 10 Minutes
Ingredients:
- 1/4 cup coconut oil
- 1 ½ cups granulated sugar
- 1/3 teaspoon coarse sea salt
- 1/3 cup water
- 2 tablespoons almond butter

Directions:
1. Melt the coconut oil and sugar in a saucepan for 1 minute.
2. Whisk in the remaining ingredients and continue to cook until everything is fully incorporated and your caramel is deeply golden.
3. Bon appétit!

Mediterranean Tomato Gravy

Servings: 6
Cooking Time: 20 Minutes
Ingredients:
- 3 tablespoons olive oil
- 1 red onion, chopped
- 3 cloves garlic, crushed
- 4 tablespoons cornstarch
- 1 can tomatoes, crushed
- 1/2 teaspoon dried basil
- 1/2 teaspoon dried oregano
- 1/2 teaspoon dried thyme
- 1 teaspoon dried parsley flakes
- Sea salt and black pepper, to taste

Directions:
1. Heat the olive oil in a large saucepan over medium-high heat. Once hot, sauté the onion and garlic until tender and fragrant.
2. Add in the cornstarch and continue to cook for 1 minute more.
3. Add in the canned tomatoes and bring to a boil over medium-high heat; stir in the spices and turn the heat to a simmer.
4. Let it simmer for about 10 minutes until everything is cooked through.
5. Serve with vegetables of choice. Bon appétit!

Homemade Apple Butter

Servings: 16
Cooking Time: 35 Minutes
Ingredients:
- 5 pounds apples, peeled, cored and diced
- 1 cup water
- 2/3 cup granulated brown sugar

- 1 tablespoon ground cinnamon
- 1 teaspoon ground cloves
- 1 tablespoon vanilla essence
- A pinch of freshly grated nutmeg
- A pinch of salt

Directions:

1. Add the apples and water to a heavy-bottomed pot and cook for about 20 minutes.

2. Then, mash the cooked apples with a potato masher; stir the sugar, cinnamon, cloves, vanilla, nutmeg and salt into the mashed apples; stir to combine well.

3. Continue to simmer until the butter has thickened to your desired consistency.

4. Bon appétit!

Indian-style Mango Chutney

Servings: 7
Cooking Time: 1 Hour
Ingredients:

- 5 mangoes, peeled and diced
- 1 yellow onion, chopped
- 2 red chilies, chopped
- 3/4 cup balsamic vinegar
- 1 ½ cups granulated sugar
- 1 teaspoon coriander seeds
- 1 tablespoon chana dal
- 1/2 teaspoon jeera
- 1/4 teaspoon turmeric powder
- 1/4 teaspoon Himalayan salt
- 1/2 cup currants

Directions:

1. In a saucepan, place the mangoes, onion, red chilies, vinegar, granulated sugar, coriander seeds, chana dal, jeera, turmeric powder and salt. Bring the mixture to a boil.

2. Immediately turn the heat to simmer; continue to simmer, stirring occasionally, for approximately 55 minutes, until most of the liquid has absorbed.

3. Set aside to cool and add in the currants. Store in your refrigerator for up to 2 weeks.

4. Bon appétit!

Homemade Vegan Yogurt

Servings: 6
Cooking Time: 10 Minutes
Ingredients:

- 1 ½ cups full-fat coconut milk
- 1 teaspoon maple syrup
- A pinch of coarse sea salt
- 2 capsules vegan probiotic

Directions:

1. Spoon the coconut milk into a sterilized glass jar. Add in the maple syrup and salt.

2. Empty your probiotic capsules and stir with a wooden spoon (not metal!)

3. Cover the jar with a clean kitchen towel and let it stand on the kitchen counter to ferment for 24-48 hours.

4. Keep in your refrigerator for up to a week. Bon appétit!

Swiss-style Potato Cake (rösti)

Servings: 5
Cooking Time: 25 Minutes
Ingredients:

- 1 ½ pounds russets potatoes, peeled, grated and squeezed
- 1 teaspoon coarse sea salt
- 1/2 teaspoon red pepper flakes, crushed
- 1/2 teaspoon freshly ground black pepper
- 4 tablespoons olive oil

Directions:

1. Mix the grated potatoes, salt, red pepper and ground black pepper.

2. Heat the oil in a cast-iron skillet.

3. Drop handfuls of the potato mixture into the skillet.

4. Cook your potato cake over medium for about 10 minutes. Cover the potatoes and cook for another 10 minutes until the bottom of the potato cake is golden brown. Bon appétit!

Classic Pear Butter

Servings: 10
Cooking Time: 30 Minutes
Ingredients:

- 2 pounds ripe pears, peeled, cored and diced
- 1/4 cup water
- 1 tablespoon fresh lemon juice
- 2 tablespoons maple syrup
- 1 teaspoon ground cinnamon
- 1/4 teaspoon nutmeg
- 4-5 whole cloves
- 1/2 teaspoon vanilla beans
- A pinch of coarse salt

Directions:

1. Add the pears and water to a heavy-bottomed pot and cook for about 20 minutes.

2. Then, mash the cooked pears with a potato masher; stir in the remaining ingredients; stir to combine well.

3. Continue to simmer until the pear butter has thickened to your desired consistency.

4. Bon appétit!

Mediterranean-style Zucchini Pancakes

Servings: 4
Cooking Time: 20 Minutes
Ingredients:

- 1 cup all-purpose flour
- 1/2 teaspoon baking powder
- 1/2 teaspoon dried oregano
- 1/2 teaspoon dried basil
- 1/2 teaspoon dried rosemary
- Sea salt and ground black pepper, to taste
- 1 ½ cups zucchini, grated
- 1 chia egg
- 1/2 cup rice milk
- 1 teaspoon garlic, minced
- 2 tablespoons scallions, sliced

- 4 tablespoons olive oil

Directions:
1. Thoroughly combine the flour, baking powder and spices. In a separate bowl, combine the zucchini, chia egg, milk, garlic and scallions.
2. Add the zucchini mixture to the dry flour mixture; stir to combine well.
3. Then, heat the olive oil in a frying pan over a moderate flame. Cook your pancakes for 2 to 3 minutes per side until golden brown.
4. Bon appétit!

South Asian Masala Paratha

Servings: 5
Cooking Time: 20 Minutes
Ingredients:
- 2 cups all-purpose flour
- 1 teaspoon Kala namak salt
- 1/2 teaspoon garam masala
- 1/2 cup warm water
- 1 tablespoon canola oil
- 10 tablespoons coconut oil, softened

Directions:
1. In a mixing bowl, thoroughly combine the flour, salt and garam masala. Make a well in the flour mixture and gradually add in the water and canola oil; mix to combine.
2. Knead the dough until it forms a sticky ball. Let it rest in your refrigerator overnight.
3. Divide the dough into 5 equal balls and roll them out on a clean surface. Spread the coconut oil all over the paratha and fold it in half. Spread the coconut oil over it and fold it again.
4. Roll each paratha into a circle approximately 8 inches in diameter.
5. Heat a griddle until hot. Cook each paratha for about 3 minutes or until bubbles form on the surface. Turn over and cook on the other side for 3 minutes longer. Serve warm.

Cinnamon Plum Preserves

Servings: 20
Cooking Time: 40 Minutes
Ingredients:
- 5 pounds ripe plums rinsed
- 2 pounds granulated sugar
- 2 tablespoons lemon juice
- 3 cinnamon sticks

Directions:
1. Mix all the ingredients in a saucepan.
2. Continue to cook over medium heat, stirring constantly, until the sauce has reduced and thickened for about 30 minutes.
3. Remove from the heat. Leave your jam to sit for 10 minutes. Ladle into sterilized jars and cover with the lids. Let it cool completely.
4. Bon appétit!

Easy Orange Butter

Servings: 7
Cooking Time: 10 Minutes

Ingredients:
- 2 tablespoons granulated sugar
- 2 tablespoons cornstarch
- 1 teaspoon orange zest
- 1 teaspoon fresh ginger, peeled and minced
- 2 tablespoons orange juice
- 1/2 cup water
- A pinch of grated nutmeg
- A pinch of grated kosher salt
- 7 tablespoons coconut oil, softened

Directions:
1. In a saucepan, combine the sugar, cornstarch, orange zest and ginger over a moderate heat.
2. Stir in the orange juice, water, nutmeg and salt; continue to cook until the mixture has thickened. Heat off.
3. Stir in the coconut oil. Bon appétit!

Traditional Korean Buchimgae

Servings: 4
Cooking Time: 20 Minutes
Ingredients:
- 1/2 cup all-purpose flour
- 1/2 cup chickpea flour
- 1/2 teaspoon baking powder
- 1 teaspoon garlic powder
- 1/4 teaspoon ground cumin
- 1/2 teaspoon sea salt
- 1 carrot, trimmed and grated
- 1 small onion, finely chopped
- 1 cup Kimchi
- 1 green chili, minced
- 1 flax egg
- 1 tablespoon bean paste
- 1 cup rice milk
- 4 tablespoons canola oil

Directions:
1. Thoroughly combine the flour, baking powder and spices. In a separate bowl, combine the carrot, onion, Kimchi, green chili, flax egg, bean paste and rice milk.
2. Add the vegetable mixture to the dry flour mixture; stir to combine well.
3. Then, heat the oil in a frying pan over a moderate flame. Cook the Korean pancakes for 2 to 3 minutes per side until crispy.
4. Bon appétit!

Basic Cashew Butter

Servings: 12
Cooking Time: 20 Minutes
Ingredients:
- 3 cups raw cashew nuts
- 1 tablespoon coconut oil

Directions:
1. In your food processor or a high-speed blender, pulse the cashew nuts until ground. Then, process them for 5 minutes more, scraping down the sides and bottom of the bowl.
2. Add in the coconut oil.

3. Run your machine for another 10 minutes or until your butter is completely creamy and smooth. Enjoy!

Healthy Chocolate Peanut Butter

Servings: 20
Cooking Time: 15 Minutes
Ingredients:
- 2 ½ cups peanuts
- 1/2 teaspoon coarse sea salt
- 1/2 teaspoon cinnamon powder
- 1/2 cup cocoa powder
- 10 dates, pitted

Directions:
1. Roast the peanuts in the preheated oven at 350 degrees F for approximately 7 minutes until the peanuts are fragrant and lightly browned.
2. In your food processor or a high-speed blender, pulse the peanuts until ground. Then, process the mixture for 2 minutes more, scraping down the sides and bottom of the bowl.
3. Add in the salt, cinnamon, cocoa powder and dates.
4. Run your machine for another 2 minutes or until your butter is completely creamy and smooth. Enjoy!

Sweet Cinnamon Walnut Spread

Servings: 16
Cooking Time: 20 Minutes
Ingredients:
- 1 ½ cups raw walnuts
- 2 ounces dark chocolate, broken into chunks
- 1 teaspoon ground cinnamon
- A pinch of sea salt
- A pinch of grated nutmeg
- 1/3 cup agave syrup

Directions:
1. Roast the walnuts in the preheated oven at 350 degrees F for approximately 10 minutes until they are fragrant and lightly browned.
2. In your food processor or a high-speed blender, pulse the walnuts until ground. Then, process the mixture for 5 minutes more, scraping down the sides and bottom of the bowl.
3. Add in the remaining ingredients.
4. Run your machine for a further 5 minutes or until the mixture is completely creamy and smooth. Enjoy!

Classic Vegan Butter

Servings: 16
Cooking Time: 10 Minutes
Ingredients:
- 2/3 cup refined coconut oil, melted
- 1 tablespoon sunflower oil
- 1/4 cup soy milk
- 1/2 teaspoon malt vinegar
- 1/3 teaspoon coarse sea salt

Directions:
1. Add the coconut oil, sunflower oil, milk and vinegar to the bowl of your blender. Blitz to combine well.

2. Add in the sea salt and continue to blend until creamy and smooth; refrigerate until set.
3. Bon appétit!

Traditional Belarusian Draniki

Servings: 4
Cooking Time: 30 Minutes
Ingredients:
- 4 waxy potatoes, peeled, grated and squeezed
- 4 tablespoons scallions, chopped
- 1 green chili pepper, chopped
- 1 red chili pepper, chopped
- 1/3 cup besan
- 1/2 teaspoon baking powder
- 1 teaspoon paprika
- Sea salt and red pepper, to taste
- 1/4 cup canola oil
- 2 tablespoons fresh cilantro, chopped

Directions:
1. Thoroughly combine the grated potatoes, scallions, pepper, besan, baking powder, paprika, salt and red pepper.
2. Preheat the oil in a frying pan over a moderate heat.
3. Spoon 1/4 cup of potato mixture into the pan and cook your draniki until golden brown on both sides. Repeat with the remaining batter.
4. Serve with fresh cilantro. Bon appétit!

Mediterranean-style Tahini Spread

Servings: 16
Cooking Time: 10 Minutes
Ingredients:
- 10 ounces sesame seeds
- A pinch of sea salt
- 1/4 teaspoon ground black pepper, or more to taste
- 1 tablespoon fresh parsley leaves
- 1 tablespoon fresh basil
- 1 tablespoon fresh chives
- 1 tablespoon lime juice
- 2 garlic cloves
- 2 tablespoons grapeseed oil

Directions:
1. Toast the sesame seeds in a nonstick skillet for about 4 minutes, stirring continuously. Cool the sesame seeds completely.
2. Transfer the sesame seeds to the bowl of your food processor. Process for about 1 minute.
3. Add in the remaining ingredients and process for a further 4 minutes, scraping down the bottom and sides of the bowl.
4. Store your spread in the refrigerator for up to 1 month. Bon appétit!

Pecan And Apricot Butter

Servings: 16
Cooking Time: 15 Minutes
Ingredients:
- 2 ½ cups pecans
- 1/2 cup dried apricots, chopped
- 1/2 cup sunflower oil
- 1 teaspoon bourbon vanilla
- 1/4 teaspoon ground anise
- 1/2 teaspoon cinnamon
- 1/8 teaspoon grated nutmeg
- 1/8 teaspoon salt

Directions:
1. In your food processor or a high-speed blender, pulse the pecans until ground. Then, process the pecans for 5 minutes more, scraping down the sides and bottom of the bowl.
2. Add in the remaining ingredients.
3. Run your machine for a further 5 minutes or until the mixture is completely creamy and smooth. Enjoy!

Old-fashioned Sweet Potato Cakes

Servings: 5
Cooking Time: 30 Minutes
Ingredients:
- 1 ½ pounds sweet potatoes, peeled, grated and squeezed
- 1 Vidalia onion, chopped
- 2 cloves garlic, minced
- 1 cup all-purpose flour
- 1/4 cup cornstarch
- 1 teaspoon baking powder
- 2 flax eggs
- Sea salt and freshly ground black pepper, to taste
- 1 teaspoon Za'atar spice
- 1/3 cup olive oil

Directions:
1. In a mixing bowl, thoroughly combine the sweet potatoes, Vidalia onion, garlic, flour, cornstarch, baking powder, flax eggs, salt, black pepper and Za'atar spice.
2. Preheat the oil in a frying pan over a moderate heat.
3. Spoon 1/4 cup of the potato mixture into the pan and cook the potato cakes until golden brown on both sides or about 10 minutes. Repeat with the remaining batter.
4. Serve with toppings of choice. Bon appétit!

Traditional Norwegian Flatbread (lefse)

Servings: 7
Cooking Time: 20 Minutes
Ingredients:
- 3 medium-sized potatoes
- 1/2 cup all-purpose flour
- 1/2 cup besan
- Sea salt, to taste
- 1/4 teaspoon ground black pepper
- 1/2 teaspoon cayenne pepper
- 2 tablespoons olive oil

Directions:

1. Boil the potatoes in a lightly salted water until they've softened.
2. Peel and mash the potatoes and then, add in the flour, besan and spices.
3. Divide the dough into 7 equal balls. Roll out each ball on a little floured work surface.
4. Heat the olive oil in a frying pan over medium-low heat and cook each flatbread for 2 to 3 minutes. Serve immediately.
5. Bon appétit!

Middle-eastern Tahini Spread

Servings: 16
Cooking Time: 10 Minutes
Ingredients:
- 10 ounces sesame seeds
- 3 tablespoons cocoa powder
- 1 teaspoon vanilla seeds
- 1/4 teaspoon kosher salt
- 1/2 cup fresh dates, pitted
- 3 tablespoons coconut oil

Directions:
1. Toast the sesame seeds in a nonstick skillet for about 4 minutes, stirring continuously. Cool the sesame seeds completely.
2. Transfer the sesame seeds to the bowl of your food processor. Process for about 1 minute.
3. Add in the remaining ingredients and process for a further 4 minutes, scraping down the bottom and sides of the bowl.
4. Store your tahini spread in the refrigerator for up to 1 month. Bon appétit!

Pepper And Cucumber Relish

Servings: 10
Cooking Time: 20 Minutes
Ingredients:
- 6 cucumbers, chopped
- 1 red bell pepper, seeded and chopped
- 1 green bell pepper, seeded and chopped
- 2 tablespoons coarse sea salt
- 1/2 cup wine vinegar
- 2/3 cup granulated sugar
- 1/2 teaspoon fennel seeds
- 1/4 teaspoon mustard seeds
- 1/4 teaspoon ground turmeric
- 1/2 teaspoon ground allspice
- 1 tablespoon mixed peppercorns
- 4 teaspoons cornstarch

Directions:
1. Place the cucumber, bell pepper and salt in a sieve set over a bowl; drain for a few hours. Squeeze out as much liquid as possible.
2. Bring the vinegar and sugar to a boil; add in the 1/3 teaspoon of the sea salt and let it boil until the sugar has dissolved.
3. Add in the cucumber-pepper mixture and continue to simmer for 2 to 3 minutes more. Stir in the spices and cornstarch; continue to simmer for 1 to 2 minutes more.

4. Transfer the relish to a bowl and place, uncovered, in your refrigerator for about 2 hours. Bon appétit!

Authentic Spanish Tortilla

Servings: 4
Cooking Time: 30 Minutes
Ingredients:
- 2 tablespoons olive oil
- 1 ½ pounds russet potatoes, peeled and sliced
- 1 onion, chopped
- Sea salt and ground black pepper, to taste
- 1/4 cup rice milk
- 8 ounces tofu, pressed and drained
- 1/2 cup besan
- 2 tablespoons cornstarch
- 1/2 teaspoon ground cumin
- 1/4 teaspoon ground allspice

Directions:
1. Heat 1 tablespoon of the olive oil in a frying pan. Then, add the potatoes, onion, salt and black pepper to the frying pan.
2. Cook for about 20 minutes or until the potatoes have softened.
3. In a mixing bowl, thoroughly combine the remaining ingredients. Add in the potato mixture and stir to combine.
4. Heat the remaining 1 tablespoon of the olive oil in a frying pan over medium-low heat. Cook your tortilla for 5 minutes per side. Serve warm.
5. Bon appétit!

Easy Vegetable Pajeon

Servings: 4
Cooking Time: 20 Minutes
Ingredients:
- 1/2 cup all-purpose flour
- 1/2 cup potato starch
- 1 teaspoon baking powder
- 1/3 teaspoon Himalayan salt
- 1/2 cup kimchi, finely chopped
- 4 scallions, chopped
- 1 carrot, trimmed and chopped
- 2 bell peppers, chopped
- 1 green chili pepper, chopped
- 1 cup kimchi liquid
- 2 tablespoons olive oil
- Dipping sauce:
- 2 tablespoons soy sauce
- 2 teaspoons rice vinegar
- 1 teaspoon fresh ginger, finely grated

Directions:
1. Thoroughly combine the flour, potato starch, baking powder and salt. In a separate bowl, combine the vegetables and kimchi liquid.
2. Add the vegetable mixture to the dry flour mixture; stir to combine well.
3. Then, heat the oil in a frying pan over a moderate flame. Cook the Pajeon for 2 to 3 minutes per side until crispy.

4. Meanwhile, mix the sauce ingredients. Serve your Pajeon with the sauce for dipping. Bon appétit!

Spiced Cauliflower Bites

Servings: 4
Cooking Time: 25 Minutes
Ingredients:
- 1 pound cauliflower florets
- 1 cup all-purpose flour
- 1 tablespoon olive oil
- 1 tablespoon tomato paste
- 1 teaspoon onion powder
- 1 teaspoon garlic powder
- 1 teaspoon smoked paprika
- 1/2 teaspoon dried oregano
- 1/2 teaspoon dried basil
- 1/4 cup hot sauce

Directions:
1. Begin by preheating your oven to 450 degrees F. Pat the cauliflower florets dry using a kitchen towel.
2. Mix the remaining ingredients until well combined. Dip the cauliflower florets in the batter until well coated on all sides.
3. Place the cauliflower florets in a parchment-lined baking pan.
4. Roast for about 25 minutes or until cooked through. Bon appétit!

Apple And Cranberry Chutney

Servings: 7
Cooking Time: 1 Hour
Ingredients:
- 1 ½ pounds cooking apples, peeled, cored and diced
- 1/2 cup sweet onion, chopped
- 1/2 cup apple cider vinegar
- 1 large orange, freshly squeezed
- 1 cup brown sugar
- 1 teaspoon fennel seeds
- 1 tablespoon fresh ginger, peeled and grated
- 1 teaspoon sea salt
- 1/2 cup dried cranberries

Directions:
1. In a saucepan, place the apples, sweet onion, vinegar, orange juice, brown sugar, fennel seeds, ginger and salt. Bring the mixture to a boil.
2. Immediately turn the heat to simmer; continue to simmer, stirring occasionally, for approximately 55 minutes, until most of the liquid has absorbed.
3. Set aside to cool and add in the dried cranberries. Store in your refrigerator for up to 2 weeks.
4. Bon appétit!

Roasted Pepper Spread

Servings: 10
Cooking Time: 10 Minutes
Ingredients:
- 2 red bell peppers, roasted and seeded
- 1 jalapeno pepper, roasted and seeded
- 4 ounces sun-dried tomatoes in oil, drained
- 2/3 cup sunflower seeds
- 2 tablespoons onion, chopped
- 1 garlic clove
- 1 tablespoon Mediterranean herb mix
- Sea salt and ground black pepper, to taste
- 1/2 teaspoon turmeric powder
- 1 teaspoon ground cumin
- 2 tablespoons tahini

Directions:
1. Place all the ingredients in the bowl of your blender or food processor.
2. Process until creamy, uniform and smooth.
3. Store in an airtight container in your refrigerator for up to 2 weeks. Bon appétit!

Raw Mixed Berry Jam

Servings: 10
Cooking Time: 1 Hour 5 Minutes
Ingredients:
- 1/4 pound fresh raspberries
- 1/4 pound fresh strawberries, hulled
- 1/4 pound fresh blackberries
- 2 tablespoons lemon juice, freshly squeezed
- 10 dates, pitted
- 3 tablespoons chia seeds

Directions:
1. Puree all the ingredients in your blender or food processor.
2. Let it sit for about 1 hour, stirring periodically.
3. Store your jam in sterilized jars in your refrigerator for up to 4 days. Bon appétit!

Cashew Cream Cheese

Servings: 6
Cooking Time: 10 Minutes
Ingredients:
- 1 ½ cups cashews, soaked overnight and drained
- 1/3 cup water
- 1/4 teaspoon coarse sea salt
- 1/4 teaspoon dried dill weed
- 1/4 teaspoon garlic powder
- 2 tablespoons nutritional yeast
- 2 probiotic capsules

Directions:
1. Process the cashews and water in your blender until creamy and uniform.
2. Add in the salt, dill, garlic powder and nutritional yeast; continue to blend until everything is well incorporated.
3. Spoon the mixture into a sterilized glass jar. Add in the probiotic powder and combine with a wooden spoon (not metal!)

4. Cover the jar with a clean kitchen towel and let it stand on the kitchen counter to ferment for 24-48 hours.
5. Keep in your refrigerator for up to a week. Bon appétit!

Easy Ukrainian Deruny

Servings: 4
Cooking Time: 30 Minutes
Ingredients:
- 4 medium-sized potatoes, peeled and diced
- 1/2 cup all-purpose flour
- 1/2 cup besan flour
- 1/2 teaspoon baking powder
- 1 sweet onion, peeled and chopped
- 1 flax egg
- Sea salt and ground black pepper, to taste
- 1 teaspoon paprika
- 1/4 cup olive oil, or as needed

Directions:
1. Boil the potatoes in a lightly salted water until they've softened.
2. Peel and mash the potatoes in a mixing bowl.
3. Then, add in the flour, besan, baking powder, sweet onion, flax egg, salt, black pepper and paprika.
4. Then, heat the oil in a frying pan over a moderate flame. Cook the potato cakes for about 3 minutes per side until crispy and golden brown.
5. Bon appétit!

Coconut "feta" Cheese

Servings: 12
Cooking Time: 30 Minutes
Ingredients:
- 1 ½ cups full-fat coconut milk
- 1/2 cup hot water
- 1 teaspoon Himalayan salt
- 1/2 teaspoon garlic powder
- 1/4 teaspoon dried dill weed
- 1 tablespoon coconut oil
- 2 tablespoons nutritional yeast
- 4 teaspoons agar agar powder
- 1 tablespoon white vinegar

Directions:
1. In a saucepan, place the milk and water.
2. Add in the salt, garlic powder, dill, coconut oil, nutritional yeast and agar agar powder and whisk to combine well.
3. Heat the mixture over medium heat, stirring continuously; bring to a rapid boil. Add in the vinegar and stir to combine well.
4. Turn the heat to a simmer and continue to whisk for 6 to 7 minutes more or until the mixture is uniform and smooth.
5. Spoon the mixture into lightly greased molds. Let it stand for 20 minutes at room temperature. Place in your refrigerator for at least 2 hours or until set.
6. Store in your refrigerator for up to a week. Enjoy!

Traditional Hanukkah Latkes

Servings: 6
Cooking Time: 30 Minutes
Ingredients:
- 1 ½ pounds potatoes, peeled, grated and drained
- 3 tablespoons green onions, sliced
- 1/3 cup all-purpose flour
- 1/2 teaspoon baking powder
- 1/2 teaspoon sea salt, preferably kala namak
- 1/4 teaspoon ground black pepper
- 1/2 olive oil
- 5 tablespoons applesauce
- 1 tablespoon fresh dill, roughly chopped

Directions:
1. Thoroughly combine the grated potato, green onion, flour, baking powder, salt and black pepper.
2. Preheat the olive oil in a frying pan over a moderate heat.
3. Spoon 1/4 cup of potato mixture into the pan and cook your latkes until golden brown on both sides. Repeat with the remaining batter.
4. Serve with applesauce and fresh dill. Bon appétit!

Vegan Ricotta Cheese

Servings: 12
Cooking Time: 10 Minutes
Ingredients:
- 1/2 cup raw cashew nuts, soaked overnight and drained
- 1/2 cup raw sunflower seeds, soaked overnight and drained
- 1/4 cup water
- 1 heaping tablespoon coconut oil, melted
- 1 tablespoon lime juice, freshly squeezed
- 1 tablespoon white vinegar
- 1/4 teaspoon Dijon mustard
- 2 tablespoons nutritional yeast
- 1/2 teaspoon garlic powder
- 1/2 teaspoon turmeric powder
- 1/2 teaspoon salt

Directions:
1. Process the cashews, sunflower seeds and water in your blender until creamy and uniform.
2. Add in the remaining ingredients; continue to blend until everything is well incorporated.
3. Keep in your refrigerator for up to a week. Bon appétit!

Apple And Almond Butter Balls

Servings: 12
Cooking Time: 15 Minutes
Ingredients:
- 1/2 cup almond butter
- 1 cup apple butter
- 1/3 cup almonds
- 1 cup fresh dates, pitted
- 1/2 teaspoon ground cinnamon
- 1/4 teaspoon ground cardamom
- 1/2 teaspoon almond extract

- 1/2 teaspoon rum extract
- 2 ½ cups old-fashioned oats

Directions:
1. Place the almond butter, apple butter, almonds, dates and spices in the bowl of your blender or food processor.
2. Process the mixture until you get a thick paste.
3. Stir in the oats and pulse a few more times to blend well. Roll the mixture into balls and serve well-chilled.

Homemade Chocolate Milk

Servings: 4
Cooking Time: 10 Minutes
Ingredients:
- 4 teaspoons cashew butter
- 4 cups water
- 1/2 teaspoon vanilla paste
- 4 teaspoons cocoa powder
- 8 dates, pitted

Directions:
1. Place all the ingredients in the bowl of your high-speed blender.
2. Process until creamy, uniform and smooth.
3. Keep in a glass bottle in your refrigerator for up to 4 days. Enjoy!

Chocolate Walnut Spread

Servings: 15
Cooking Time: 20 Minutes
Ingredients:
- 1 cup walnuts
- 1 teaspoon pure vanilla extract
- 1/2 cup agave nectar
- 4 tablespoons cocoa powder
- A pinch of ground cinnamon
- A pinch of grated nutmeg
- A pinch of sea salt
- 4 tablespoons almond milk

Directions:
1. Roast the walnuts in the preheated oven at 350 degrees F for approximately 10 minutes until they are fragrant and lightly browned.
2. In your food processor or a high-speed blender, pulse the walnuts until ground. Then, process the mixture for 5 minutes more, scraping down the sides and bottom of the bowl.
3. Add in the remaining ingredients.
4. Run your machine for a further 5 minutes or until the mixture is completely creamy and smooth. Enjoy!

Raspberry Star Anise Jelly

Servings: 20
Cooking Time: 35 Minutes
Ingredients:
- 2 pounds fresh raspberries
- 2 pounds granulated sugar
- 1 heaping teaspoon anise star
- 1 vanilla bean, split lengthwise

Directions:
1. Mix all the ingredients in a saucepan.

2. Continue to cook over medium heat, stirring constantly, until the sauce has reduced and thickened for about 25 minutes.
3. Remove from the heat. Leave your jam to sit for 10 minutes. Ladle into sterilized jars and cover with the lids. Let it cool completely.
4. Store in the cupboard for a few months. Bon appétit!

Old-fashioned Pecan Spread

Servings: 16
Cooking Time: 10 Minutes
Ingredients:
- 2 cups pecan, soaked and drained
- 5 tablespoons coconut oil
- 4 tablespoons orange juice
- 1 cup dates, pitted

Directions:
1. In your food processor or a high-speed blender, pulse the pecans until ground.
2. Then, process the nuts for 2 minutes more, scraping down the sides and bottom of the bowl.
3. Add in the coconut oil, orange juice and dates. Continue to blend until your desired consistency is achieved.
4. Bon appétit!

Traditional Swedish Raggmunk

Servings: 5
Cooking Time: 30 Minutes
Ingredients:
- 1 ½ pounds waxy potatoes, peeled, grated and squeezed
- 3 tablespoons shallots, chopped
- 2 chia eggs
- 1/2 cup all-purpose flour
- 1 teaspoon baking powder
- Sea salt and ground black, to season
- 1 teaspoon cayenne pepper
- 1/2 cup canola oil
- 6 tablespoons applesauce

Directions:
1. Thoroughly combine the grated potatoes, shallots, chia eggs, flour, baking powder, salt, black pepper and cayenne pepper.
2. Preheat the oil in a frying pan over a moderate heat.
3. Spoon 1/4 cup of the potato mixture into the pan and cook the potato cakes for about 5 minutes per side. Repeat with the remaining batter.
4. Serve with applesauce and enjoy!

Creamed Vegan "tuna" Salad

Servings: 8
Cooking Time: 10 Minutes
Ingredients:
- 2 cans chickpeas, rinsed
- 3/4 cup vegan mayonnaise
- 1 teaspoon brown mustard
- 1 small red onion, chopped
- 2 pickles, chopped
- 1 teaspoon capers, drained

- 1 tablespoon fresh parsley, chopped
- 1 tablespoon fresh coriander, chopped
- Sea salt and ground black pepper, to taste
- 2 tablespoons sunflower seeds, roasted

Directions:
1. Mix all the ingredients until everything is well incorporated.
2. Place your salad in the refrigerator until ready to serve.
3. Bon appétit!

Grandma's Cornichon Relish

Servings: 9
Cooking Time: 15 Minutes
Ingredients:
- 3 cups cornichon, finely chopped
- 1 cup white onion, finely chopped
- 1 teaspoon sea salt
- 1/3 cup distilled white vinegar
- 1/4 teaspoon mustard seeds
- 1/3 cup sugar
- 1 tablespoon arrowroot powder, dissolved in 1 tablespoon water

Directions:
1. Place the cornichon, onion and salt in a sieve set over a bowl; drain for a few hours. Squeeze out as much liquid as possible.
2. Bring the vinegar, mustard seeds and sugar to a boil; add in the 1/3 teaspoon of the sea salt and let it boil until the sugar has dissolved.
3. Add in the cornichon-onion mixture and continue to simmer for 2 to 3 minutes more. Stir in the arrowroot powder mixture and continue to simmer for 1 to 2 minutes more.
4. Transfer the relish to a bowl and place, uncovered, in your refrigerator for about 2 hours. Bon appétit!

Spicy Cilantro And Mint Chutney

Servings: 9
Cooking Time: 10 Minutes
Ingredients:
- 1 ½ bunches fresh cilantro
- 6 tablespoons scallions, sliced
- 3 tablespoons fresh mint leaves
- 2 jalapeno peppers, seeded
- 1/2 teaspoon kosher salt
- 2 tablespoons fresh lime juice
- 1/3 cup water

Directions:
1. Place all the ingredients in the bowl of your blender or food processor.
2. Then, combine the ingredients until your desired consistency has been reached.
3. Bon appétit!

Cinnamon Cashew Butter

Servings: 9
Cooking Time: 15 Minutes
Ingredients:

- 2 cups raw cashew nuts
- A pinch of sea salt
- A pinch of grated nutmeg
- 1 teaspoon ground cinnamon
- 4 tablespoons agave syrup
- 2 tablespoons peanut oil

Directions:

1. Roast the cashew nuts in the preheated oven at 350 degrees F for approximately 8 minutes until the peanuts are fragrant and lightly browned.
2. In your food processor or a high-speed blender, pulse the cashew nuts until ground. Then, process the nuts for 2 minutes more, scraping down the sides and bottom of the bowl.
3. Add in the salt, nutmeg, cinnamon, agave syrup and oil.
4. Run your machine for another 2 minutes or until your butter is completely creamy and smooth. Enjoy!

Classic Onion Relish

Servings: 6
Cooking Time: 35 Minutes
Ingredients:

- 4 tablespoons vegan butter
- 1 pound red onions, peeled and sliced
- 4 tablespoons granulated sugar
- 4 tablespoons white vinegar
- 1 ½ cups boiling water
- 1 teaspoon sea salt
- 1 teaspoon mustard seeds
- 1 teaspoon celery seeds

Directions:

1. In a frying pan, melt the butter over medium-high heat. Then, sauté the onions for about 8 minutes, stirring frequently to ensure even cooking.
2. Add in the sugar and continue sautéing for 5 to 6 minutes more. Add in the vinegar, boiling water, salt, mustard seeds and celery seeds.
3. Turn the heat to a simmer and continue to cook, covered, for about 20 minutes.
4. Remove the lid and continue to simmer until all the liquid has evaporated. Bon appétit!

Easy Homemade Nutella

Servings: 20

Cooking Time: 25 Minutes
Ingredients:

- 3 ½ cups hazelnuts
- 1 teaspoon vanilla seeds
- A pinch of coarse sea salt
- A pinch of grated nutmeg
- 1/2 teaspoon ground cinnamon
- 1/2 teaspoon ground cardamom
- 1 cup dark chocolate chips

Directions:

1. Roast the hazelnuts in the preheated oven at 350 degrees F for approximately 13 minutes until your hazelnuts are fragrant and lightly browned.
2. In your food processor or a high-speed blender, pulse the hazelnuts until ground. Then, process the mixture for 5 minutes more, scraping down the sides and bottom of the bowl.
3. Add in the remaining ingredients.
4. Run your machine for a further 4 to 5 minutes or until the mixture is completely creamy and smooth. Enjoy!

Nutty Chocolate Fudge Spread

Servings: 16
Cooking Time: 25 Minutes
Ingredients:

- 1 pound walnuts
- 1 ounce coconut oil, melted
- 2 tablespoons corn flour
- 4 tablespoons cocoa powder
- A pinch of grated nutmeg
- 1/3 teaspoon ground cinnamon
- A pinch of salt

Directions:

1. Roast the walnuts in the preheated oven at 350 degrees F for approximately 10 minutes until your walnuts are fragrant and lightly browned.
2. In your food processor or a high-speed blender, pulse the walnuts until ground. Then, process them for 5 minutes more, scraping down the sides and bottom of the bowl; reserve.
3. Melt the coconut oil over medium heat. Add in the corn flour and continue to cook until the mixture starts to boil.
4. Turn the heat to a simmer, add in the cocoa powder, nutmeg, cinnamon and salt; continue to cook, stirring occasionally, for about 10 minutes.
5. Fold in the ground walnuts, stir to combine and store in a glass jar. Enjoy!

21 day meal plan

Day 1

Breakfast: Crunch Cereal With Almonds

Lunch: Basic Amaranth Porridge

Dinner: Mediterranean Vegetable Stew

Day 2

Breakfast: Frybread With Peanut Butter And Jam

Lunch: Barley Pilaf With Wild Mushrooms

Dinner:

Day 3

Breakfast: Mexican-style Omelet

Lunch: Mexican Chickpea Taco Bowls

Dinner: Lime Lentil Soup

Day 4

Breakfast: Almond & Raisin Granola

Lunch: Spiced Roasted Chickpeas

Dinner: Rotini & Tomato Soup

Day 5

Breakfast: Oatmeal With Banana And Figs

Lunch: Lentil Salad With Pine Nuts

Dinner: Spicy Winter Farro Soup

Day 6

Breakfast: Tropical Smoothie Bowl

Lunch: Bulgur Pancakes With A Twist

Dinner: Creamy Golden Veggie Soup

Day 7

Breakfast: Breakfast Banana Muffins With Pecans

Lunch: Authentic African Mielie-meal

Dinner: Basil Coconut Soup

Day 8

Breakfast: Cinnamon-banana French Toast

Lunch: Indian Chaat Bean Salad

Dinner: Vegetable Chili

Day 9

Breakfast: Mixed Seeds Bread

Lunch: Cremini Mushroom Risotto

Dinner: Pumpkin Soup With Apples

Day 10

Breakfast: Almond & Coconut Granola With Cherries

Lunch: Classic Chickpea Curry

Dinner: Asparagus And Chickpea Salad

Day 11

Breakfast: Old-fashioned Cornbread

Lunch: Middle Eastern Chickpea Stew

Dinner: Indian Chana Chaat Salad

Day 12

Breakfast: Mushroom & Spinach Chickpea Omelet

Lunch: Amarant Grits With Walnuts

Dinner: Pumpkin & Garbanzo Chili With Kale

Day 13

Breakfast: Tropical French Toasts

Lunch: Old-fashioned Pilaf

Dinner: Greek-style Roasted Pepper Salad

Day 14

Breakfast: Spring Onion Flat Bread

Lunch: Easy Barley Risotto

Dinner: Traditional French Onion Soup

Day 15

Breakfast: Scallion And Pepper Omelet

Lunch: Brown Lentil Bowl

Dinner: Mexican-style Chili Soup

Day 16

Breakfast: Sweet Orange Crepes

Lunch: Pea Dip With Herbs

Dinner: Potato Soup With Kale

Day 17

Breakfast: Orange-carrot Muffins With Cherries

Lunch: Sweet Oatmeal "grits"

Dinner: Spinach, Rice & Bean Soup

Day 18

Breakfast: Spicy Apple Pancakes

Lunch: Rice Pudding With Currants

Dinner: Chicago-style Vegetable Stew

Day 19
Breakfast: Almond Flour English Muffins
Lunch: Creamed Chickpea Salad With Pine Nuts
Dinner: Carrot & Mushroom Broth
Day 20
Breakfast: Delicious Matcha Smoothie

Lunch: Freekeh Pilaf With Chickpeas
Dinner: Traditional Ukrainian Borscht
Day 21
Breakfast: Raspberry Almond Smoothie
Lunch: Potage Au Quinoa
Dinner: Fennel & Parsnip Bisque

INDEX

Made in the USA
Coppell, TX
07 January 2022

71156468R10083